Exploring Dance Forms and Styles

A GUIDE TO CONCERT, WORLD, SOCIAL, AND HISTORICAL DANCE

Helene Scheff, RDE

Marty Sprague, MA

Susan McGreevy-Nichols

Human Kinetics

Library of Congress Cataloging-in-Publication Data

Scheff, Helene, 1939-
  Exploring dance forms and styles : a guide to concert, world, social, and historical dance /
Helene Scheff, Marty Sprague, Susan McGreevy-Nichols.
    p. cm.
  Includes bibliographical references.
  ISBN-13: 978-0-7360-8023-1 (soft cover)
  ISBN-10: 0-7360-8023-6 (soft cover)
  1. Dance. I. Sprague, Marty, 1950- II. McGreevy-Nichols, Susan, 1952- III. Title.
  GV1594.S38 2010
  793.3--dc22

                                   2009036947
  ISBN-10: 0-7360-8023-6
  ISBN-13: 978-0-7360-8023-1

The Web addresses cited in this text were current as of September 2009, unless otherwise noted.

Acquisitions Editor: Judy Patterson Wright, PhD; **Developmental Editor:** Amy Stahl; **Assistant Editors:** Anne Rumery, Lauren B. Morenz, and Derek Campbell; **Copyeditor:** Joanna Hatzopoulos Portman; **Permission Manager:** Dalene Reeder; **Graphic Designer:** Nancy Rasmus; **Graphic Artist:** Kathleen Boudreau-Fuoss; **Cover Designer:** Keith Blomberg; **Photographer (cover):** © Human Kinetics/Neil Bernstein; **Photographer (interior):** © Human Kinetics, unless otherwise noted; **Art Manager:** Kelly Hendren; **Associate Art Manager:** Alan L. Wilborn; **Illustrators:** Figure on page 230 by Tim Offenstein. All other illustrations by Mike Meyer; **Printer:** Versa Press

Printed in the United States of America   10   9   8   7   6   5   4   3   2   1

The paper in this book is certified under a sustainable forestry program.

Human Kinetics
Web site: www.HumanKinetics.com

United States: Human Kinetics
P.O. Box 5076, Champaign, IL 61825-5076
800-747-4457
e-mail: humank@hkusa.com

Canada: Human Kinetics
475 Devonshire Road Unit 100,
Windsor, ON N8Y 2L5
800-465-7301 (in Canada only)
e-mail: info@hkcanada.com

Europe: Human Kinetics
107 Bradford Road, Stanningley,
Leeds LS28 6AT, United Kingdom
+44 (0) 113 255 5665
e-mail: hk@hkeurope.com

Australia: Human Kinetics
57A Price Avenue, Lower Mitcham,
South Australia 5062
08 8372 0999
e-mail: info@hkaustralia.com

New Zealand: Human Kinetics
P.O. Box 80
Torrens Park, South Australia 5062
0800 222 062
e-mail: info@hknewzealand.com

We dedicate this book to Judy Patterson Wright.
We have seen many editors in various stages
in the development of our books,
but she has been with us from the beginning
as we began to *Build Dances.*

CONTENTS

Dance Finder   vii   •   Preface   xi   •   Acknowledgments   xv
How to Use This Book and DVD Package   xvii

PART I   Building Critical Thinking Skills in Dance

CHAPTER 1   Viewing: What Did You See?   5

CHAPTER 2   Connecting: What Do You Know?   13

CHAPTER 3   Responding: What Do You Think?
What Do You Wonder?   17

CHAPTER 4   Performing: What Can You Do?   21

PART II   Sorting Dances Into Categories and Subcategories

CHAPTER 5   Concert or Theatrical Dance   27

CHAPTER 6   World Dance   95

CHAPTER 7   Social Dance   193

CHAPTER 8   Historical Dance   229

PART III   Using Dance Forms: Looking at Dance Through Different Lenses

CHAPTER 9   Helping Students Develop Aesthetic Values   259

CHAPTER 10   Comparing Dance Forms and Dances   265

CHAPTER 11   Focusing on Universal Themes
and Sociopolitical Issues   273

CHAPTER 12   Reflecting on Diversity and Blending
of Cultural Aspects   283

Appendix   291   •   Glossary   303   •   References & Resources   309
About the Authors   311   •   DVD-ROM User Instructions   314

DANCE FINDER

(•DVD) = Video clip of dance appears on bound-in DVD

M = Main dance category (dance category the KQ form will be found under in the book)

A = Alternate dance category

		DANCE STYLES			
Dance title	Page number	Concert or theatrical dance	World dance	Social dance	Historical dance
Barong dance (Asia)	160	A	M		
Bharatanatyam (Asia) (•DVD)	163	A	M		
Bollywood dance (Crossover style)	91	M	A		
La Bomba (North America) (•DVD)	118		M	A	A
Brahms Waltz (Modern dance) (•DVD)	45	M			A
Break dancing (Alone in a group) (•DVD)	197	A	A	M	
Cakewalk (18th and 19th centuries)	253	A		A	M
Cancan (Europe)	145	A	M		
Capoeira (South America)	105		M		A
Cha-cha (Partner) (•DVD)	216			M	
Conflict (Modern dance) (•DVD)	65	M			
Consent to Gravity (Contemporary ballet) (•DVD)	42	M			
Contemporary dance (Crossover style)	87	M			
Contra dance (Dances done in a line)	225		A	M	
Cossack dance (Europe)	133	A	M		
Dabkee (Asia and Middle East) (•DVD)	166		M	A	
East Coast Swing (Partner) (•DVD)	204			M	
Farandole (Middle Ages) (•DVD)	232			A	M
Flamenco (Europe)	129	A	M		
El Fon de la Negra (North America) (•DVD)	112	A	M		
Fox-trot (Partner) (•DVD)	210			M	A
Freilach (Europe) (•DVD)	141		M	A	
Gavotte (14th century through Renaissance and Baroque)	241			A	M
Gumboot dance (South Africa)	170		M	A	
Hip-hop (Crossover style)	83	M	A	A	

> *continued*

> *continued*

Dance title	Page number	DANCE STYLES			
		Concert or theatrical dance	World dance	Social dance	Historical dance
Hmong dance (Asia) ⊙DVD	152		M		
Hula (Oceania) ⊙DVD	181		M		
Hustle (Partner) ⊙DVD	213			M	
Irish dancing (Europe)	137	A	M	A	
Kathak (Asia) ⊙DVD	148		M		
"Mambo in the Gym" (Musical theater)	74	M			
Maori Haka dance (Oceania)	189		M		
Minuet (Baroque)	245			A	M
Native American dances (North America) ⊙DVD	99		M	A	
Paquita Variation (Romantic ballet) ⊙DVD	36	M			
"Parsons Repertory Etude" (Modern dance) ⊙DVD	61	M			
Pavane (Renaissance)	238				M
Perico Ripiao (North America) ⊙DVD	109		M	A	
Polka (Partner) ⊙DVD	219		A	M	A
Quadrille (18th and 19th centuries)	249			A	M
"Rainbow Repertory Etude" (Modern dance) ⊙DVD	57	M			
Raks Assaya (North Africa) ⊙DVD	174	A	M		A
Raqs al Balas (North Africa and Middle East) ⊙DVD	156		M		
Salsa (Partner) ⊙DVD	207		A	M	
Shim Sham (Tap) ⊙DVD	80	M			
Soft shoe (Tap) ⊙DVD	77	M			
Ta-Da! (Jazz or musical theater) ⊙DVD	68	M			
Tahitian dance (Oceania) ⊙DVD	185		M		
Technically Difficult (Jazz dance after Jack Cole and Matt Mattox styles) ⊙DVD	71	M			
El Tilingo Lingo (North America) ⊙DVD	115	A	M		
Tinku (South America)	121		M		
Tiriba (West Africa) ⊙DVD	177		M	A	
The Traitor (Modern dance)	53	M			
Two-step (Partner) ⊙DVD	222			M	

Dance title	Page number	DANCE STYLES			
		Concert or theatrical dance	World dance	Social dance	Historical dance
Der Unterwestner (Europe) ⊙DVD	125		M	A	
Virginia Reel (North America) ⊙DVD	102		M	A	A
Waltz (Partner) ⊙DVD	201			M	A
"Waltz of the Flowers" (Classical ballet) ⊙DVD	39	M			
Washerwoman's Branle (Middle Ages)	235			A	M
Water Study (Modern dance) ⊙DVD	49	M			

PREFACE

Welcome to the diverse world of dance, presented uniquely through text and DVD technology. To help familiarize students with the world of dance, the dance forms in this book have been divided into four categories: concert, world, social, and historical dance. The book includes a bound-in DVD with 60 examples of dance forms and styles, including 39 video clips recorded especially for this book and 21 dances found through Internet searches. How you incorporate these videos into your curriculum can be as varied as the dances.

This book was written as a response to the increased awareness of dance as a learning tool in both the educational and the lay community. Dance is being integrated into K-12 education as a means to explore other subjects through interdisciplinary learning. We first explored interdisciplinary learning at Roger Williams Middle School and then at Providence Academy of International Studies, both in Providence, RI. In California, where Sue is a national arts education consultant, many times classroom teachers are required to address dance standards with little or no training and with lack of financial resources. To expose students to a variety of dance forms, schools are limited in bringing dance groups into schools to perform or sending students out to view live performances because of lack of funds and time. Thus, we were approached about developing a resource that would fill this need and the idea to write this book was born.

Exploring Dance Forms and Styles provides students and teachers the opportunity to view a wide range of dances representing the many ways people experience dance in their lives. Through analyzing and understanding dance as an art form—seeing it through a historical and cultural context and understanding its social function—students are able to meet dance content standards and practice critical and creative thinking skills. Teachers will no longer have to own a vast number of dance videos in order to expose their students to multiple dance forms; all that they need is in this book and DVD package. In addition to the wide variety of dance experiences in four dance categories, teachers are also given the tools and processes to help students dig deeply into dance content, saving hours of class preparation time.

This book is written for a wide variety of educators. For dance specialists, music teachers, media specialists, and classroom teachers who would like to teach other subject matter through dance, *Exploring Dance Forms and Styles* will add historical, cultural, and social influences to the curriculum. These motivated teachers are not required to have prior knowledge about dance specifics. However, it is helpful for them to have an element of play in how they teach their students, no matter their ages.

The goal of this book is to familiarize the audience with a basic knowledge of a variety of dance forms and styles. Because of the many definitions and multiple uses of the term *genre,* the word *form* in this book means type of dance. For the purpose of this book, the word *style* means characteristic movement and expression of the choreographer or dancer. The text and the student worksheets (Student

Knowledge Quest Worksheet) cover materials that you can use whether you are a dance expert or you have no dance experience or expertise at all.

Features and Benefits of This Book

This book is a significant addition to any dance library. The most unique feature among many in this book is clearly the DVD, which includes video clips of 39 dances. Presently no other single resource explores 60 dances. Also there is appropriate background information on the dances and student worksheets. These Knowledge Quest worksheets can be altered to fit the particular needs of educators and students. The more familiar you become with the process of working with the worksheets, the more capable and comfortable you and your students will be with researching even more dances that are not included on the DVD, further broadening your knowledge base. Students of all ages can enhance their research skills using traditional or newer methods. Most important, they will see the practicality and the fun of learning about the dances in the context of historical, social, and world cultures and how the field of concert dance can bring them to life.

This book includes the following benefits:

- This is a resource for one-stop shopping to find dances from historical, to world, to social, and to stage (concert). This makes using the book and the resources in it very practical and an efficient and user-friendly way to pass along knowledge.

- All in compact form, the reader can view these dances, get the background information, and learn about additional resources available to them which expand their knowledge even more.

- The reader can find commonalities among many dances.

- The reader can take time and really see how traditions travel from one area of the world to others.

Structure of This Book

In part I, Building Critical Thinking Skills in Dance, we prepare students to explore the dances and respond to the Knowledge Quest worksheets that follow in part II. We explain the four parts of the Knowledge Quest worksheets: viewing, connecting, responding, and performing. Within each worksheet students are asked these four related questions: What did you see? (chapter 1), What do you know? (chapter 2), What do you think? What do you wonder? (chapter 3), and What can you do? (chapter 4).

Part II, Sorting Dances Into Categories and Subcategories, then shows the organization of dance forms into four categories of dance: concert or theatrical dance, world dance, social dance, and historical dance. Chapters 5 through 8 discuss each of these categories more specifically. This organization allows for broad looks into dance forms and deep investigation into specific dances. Each set of Knowledge Quest worksheets gives teachers the information that is needed to delve into the individual dances.

In part III, Using Dance Forms: Looking at Dance Through Different Lenses, chapters 9 through 12 extend the student work into lessons, themes, and a unit.

The teachers then share this information with students who will be able to answer the questions on the worksheets. Teachers may find themselves involved in direct teaching and facilitating observations, discussions, and movement activities.

Get Ready, On Your Mark, Get Set, Go!

Exploring Dance Forms and Styles is an essential tool for both dance and nondance educators and their students. It can be a companion and resource for educators who are integrating dance into the curriculum as well as those teaching other subjects through dance.

It enables you to adopt and adapt research methods and information for your unique circumstances. No matter your level or your venue, with this book and DVD you can easily travel through the world of dance through the process of research.

Now that you have been introduced to *Exploring Dance Forms and Styles* you are ready to take part in an adventure in viewing, connecting, responding, and performing. The following section, How to Use this Book and DVD Package, is your guide for exploring all the dance forms and styles in this book and DVD package and in other resources. It will take you places you may have never been or experienced. The tools given to you in this resource will take you beyond this book and into your future in appreciating the field of dance and all it has to offer. So, *get ready* (DVD, monitors, and computers), *on your mark* (excitement is building; make sure you get your students in that mode), *get set* (look at and print out any forms you will need from the easily-accessible DVD), and *go!*

ACKNOWLEDGMENTS

A project of this magnitude could not be completed without the help of many people. We were gratified by the cooperation of the Isadora Duncan Archives; Doris Humphrey Films, housed at Goucher College; the José Limón Foundation; the American Dance Legacy Institute; and the Island Moving Company in Newport, RI. We are grateful to Bill Wilson from Rhode Island College. The theatre department staff was instrumental in making the filming of the video clips possible by providing space and technical expertise.

All of the dancers and musicians who signed on to this project and shared their talents have our gratitude. Through their performances, they show the DVD audience what the dances are all about. We also thank our dedicated readers for supporting us in our work; we couldn't be where we are without your reading, buying, and talking up our publications.

We continue to be indebted to Human Kinetics for their trust in us throughout our many-year history together. From acquisitions through final printing, we always count on them for their concern and mentoring.

HOW TO USE THIS BOOK AND DVD PACKAGE

This book and DVD package supports learning through viewing, observing, connecting, responding, and performing. It includes ways to involve students in the performing process by using the video clips on the DVD as a starting point to create and re-create. All of the forms found in this book, including those found in part II, can also be found in full-size format on the DVD for easy printing. Use the dance finder to locate specific Knowledge Quest materials. The bound-in DVD includes the following resources:

- 39 video clips of dances from four categories: concert or theatrical dance, world dance, social dance, and historical dance

- 21 additional recommended video clip Web searches

- 60 Student Knowledge Quest (KQ) worksheets, teacher resource pages (Information and Teaching Tips), and answer sheets for KQ worksheets (one for each dance video clip and video clip Web search suggestion that appears in part II and on the DVD)

- A blank KQ video clip search template that can be adapted to fit your own needs

- Two blank versions (levels 1 and 2) of a 4-Square form, a tool that will help students of all levels observe and analyze dances

- A video viewing guide that can be used as an alternative tool that students can use to analyze any dance

All of the forms in part II of the book appear on the DVD. Some forms from other parts of the book appear on the DVD as well. To help you identify which of these forms are included, a DVD icon ⓄⒹⓋⒹ is placed on those forms not appearing in part II of the book.

In addition, references are listed on the teacher resource pages, called Knowledge Quest: Information and Teaching Tips. Web explorations provide a great way for students to engage in Web-based research and technology. At the end of the book is a glossary that defines words that appear in boldface throughout the book.

You will find that some of the KQ worksheets are more rigorous than others. You can approach the viewing of video clips from different levels of experience, and thus the activity is less about grade level and more about exploration tailored to student experience level.

The video clips on the DVD may not always be of professional dancers or dance companies, but they do show how many different types of people with various body shapes, ages, and skill levels can dance and are familiar with so many dance forms and styles. Anyone can dance if given the proper tools and settings.

Understanding and Working With Student KQ Worksheets

Based on your students' grade level and especially their experience level with dance, decide whether you will use the student KQ worksheet as it is formatted in the book (recommended for early grades) or add to the basic form by copying and pasting additional questions from the Teaching Strategies section of the Knowledge Quest: Information and Teaching Tips page to the adaptable student KQ worksheet found on the DVD for that specific dance. Specifically you need to decide whether to do the following:

1. Have students write or share their observations for each section.
2. Use the discussion starters and suggested questions listed in the Knowledge Quest: Information and Teaching Tips for question 1. Remember that if you decide to add these more detailed questions to the student KQ worksheet, you will need to copy these questions from their page found on the DVD and paste them into the adaptable student KQ worksheet, also found on the DVD.
3. Use the 4-Square forms in addition to the Viewing: What did you see? section on the student KQ worksheet to help students identify the elements of movement. Choose to have students complete the 4-Square Level 1 form or the 4-Square Level 2 form. See the following section for more information on what you will find in each of the 4-Square forms.

Viewing: What Did You See?— Using the 4-Square Forms

Use the 4-Square Level 1 form in addition to the first question on the student KQ worksheet (Viewing: What did you see?). It uses everyday language to help younger students or those with little or no dance experience to break down the movement of the dancers using everyday language. The following table explains the sections of the 4-Square Level 1 form in more detail.

This category breaks down what body part is used, the shape the body makes, if movement is isolated to a specific body part, and whether the body moves only in place or travels. In dance the category is defined as body, shape, motion.

In dance language this category is about the quality of movement or what degree or type of energy or force the dancer used; intention; and time which relates to the duration (how long) of the movement and relationship to tempo (speed) and rhythms (patterns).

4-SQUARE LEVEL 1

How do the dancers use their bodies?

Body parts most often in use
torso (chest, hips)   legs   feet
arms   shoulders   hands   head

Shape of body
angles   curves   straight   twisted
same on both sides
different on both sides

Moving one body part at a time

Moving in place
bending   stretching   twisting

Movement that travels
walk   hop   jump   slide   leap

other (describe): _____

How do the dancers move?

Movement elements
with power
with little power
surprisingly
continuously
looking and moving in one direction
looking and moving in more than one direction
controlled
uncontrolled

Speed of movement
fast   medium   slow

Are any movements accented or emphasized?
yes   no

How long do the movements last?
long   medium   short

Are there repeated rhythmic patterns?
yes   no

Types of movements include
suspended   shaking   swinging
percussive   collapsing   vibratory

other: _____

In dance language this category is defined as space. It defines where the body is located in the performance space and the pathways in which it moves.

How do the dancers use the space around them?

Size of movement
large   medium   small

Body levels
low   middle   high

Movement done close to the body

Movement done far from the body

Dancers stand
in circles   in squares   in lines
scattered (spread out)

Foot patterns traced on the floor
curved   straight   circular

Directions in which dancers travel
forward   sideways
backward   diagonal

What are the dancers' relationships to each other?

Dancers dance
alone   in partners
in groups (trio, quartet, etc.)

Dancers relate to
other dancer(s)   object   audience

Dancers' relationships to each other are mostly
over   under   around   through
in front   behind   beside
near each other   far from each other

Contact between and among dancers
touching   holding
supporting each other's weight
lifting each other

other: _____

This category identifies how the dancer worked with other dancers.

Use the 4-Square Level 2 form for the Viewing: What did you see? question on the Student KQ Worksheet. It helps the students to break down the movement of the dancers using specific dance terminology for older students or those with dance experience. The following table explains the sections of the 4-Square Level 2 form in more detail.

Laban is a system and language for observing, describing, and notating all movement. Invented by Rudolf Laban, this system uses his theories of effort and shape to describe, interpret, and document human movement.

Both sides of the body being the same (symmetrical) versus both sides of the body not being the same (asymmetrical).

Parts of the body moving independently.

The extremes of space are direct (channeled singular focused awareness) to indirect (flexible all-encompassing attention).

Movement created by a combination of weight, time, and space movement elements.

The time/force/energy reference below uses the method of categorizing movement coined by dance education pioneer Margaret H'Doubler.

The extremes of weight from light to heavy sensation.

The extremes of time are sustained (prolonging, lingering, decelerating) and quick (sense of urgency and rapidity).

Space + Weight + Time = Flow

dab: direct (s), light (w), sudden (t)

punch: direct (s), strong (w), sudden (t)

float: indirect (s), light (w), sustained (t

glide: direct (s), light (w), sustained (t

wring: indirect (s), strong (w), sustained (t)

press: direct (s), stron (w), sustained (t)

flick: indirect (s), light (w), sudden (t)

slash: indirect (s), strong (w), sudden (

4-SQUARE LEVEL 2

How do the dancers use their bodies?

Body parts most often in use
torso (chest, hips)   legs   feet
arms   shoulders   hands   head

Shape of body
angles   curves   straight   twisted
symmetrical   asymmetrical

Isolations

Nonlocomotor
(axial):
bending   stretching   twisting
(peripheral):
spoke   arc   carve

Locomotor
walk   hop   jump   slide   leap
sissonne (2 feet to 1 foot)
assemblé (1 foot to 2 feet)

other (describe): _____

How do the dancers move?

Movement elements (Laban efforts)

Weight: with strength (powerfully)
with lightness (delicately)

Time: suddenly (surprisingly)
sustained (continuously)

Space: direct (one focus)
indirect (multifocal)

Flow: bound (controlled)
free (uncontrolled)

Effort elements (Laban effort actions)
dab   punch   float   glide
wring   press   flick   slash

Time
Tempo: fast   medium   slow

Are movements organized into distinct phrases?
yes   no

Are any movements accented or emphasized?
yes   no

Duration of movements
long   medium   short

Are there repeated rhythmic patterns?
yes   no

Movement qualities (force or energy)
suspended   shaking   swinging
percussive   collapsing   vibratory

other: _____

How do the dancers use the space around them?

Size of movement
large   medium   small

Levels
low   middle   high

Near space (movement done close to the body)

Far space (movement done far from the body)

Formations
circles   squares   lines   scattered

Pathways (floor patterns)
curved   straight   circular

Air patterns (trace patterns in the air left by dancers' movements, e.g., figure 8)
curved   straight   circular

Directions in which dancers travel
forward   sideways
backward   diagonal

What are the dancers' relationships to each other?

Dancers dance
alone   in partners
in groups (trio, quartet, etc.)

Dancers relate to
other dancer(s)   object   audience

Dancers' relationships to each other are mostly
over   under   around   through
in front   behind   beside
near each other   far from each other

Contact between and among dancers
touching   holding
supporting each other's weight
lifting each other

other: _____

For both levels of the form, be sure to impress on students that they only need to record what they see, regardless of the form that they are using.

Begin to teach dance vocabulary by having students compare the level 1 and level 2 forms to each other. They are aligned so students can compare what they circled in level 1 to its technical term in level 2.

For differentiating instruction, appropriate adjustments can be made for students with limited English, special needs, or reading difficulties by doing the following:

- Having students collaborate in pairs or groups to draw on each other's strengths
- Having a class discussion instead of reading and writing on worksheets
- For younger students, using the thinking routine I See, I Think, I Wonder (see page 294) and charting out student responses as a class.

Using the Teacher and Student Knowledge Quest Worksheets

Each dance included in the book and on the DVD has a series of forms: two of the forms are for the teacher and one is for the student. The Knowledge Quest: Information and Teaching Tips form on pages xxii-xxiii provides basic information for the teacher about the dance and teaching tips with a menu of suggested questions specific to each dance. These questions can be discussed as a class or answered in writing.

KNOWLEDGE QUEST:

INFORMATION AND TEACHING TIPS

Category M: Social Dance (Alone in a group)
Category A: Concert
Cateogry A: World (North America)
Name of Dance: Break Dancing

*"The winner was the one who could bust out moves
that hadn't been witnessed before;
who could do something the other guy couldn't match."*

Mandalit del Barco
(www.npr.org/programs/morning/features/patc/breakdancing)

BACKGROUND INFORMATION

Before students view the video clip, share the following information with them.

- *Translation:* Break dancing was introduced and promoted by superstar James Brown, with his big hit "Get on the Good Foot." The dance called good foot was soon called B-boy; shortly afterward it was called break dancing, or breaking.

- *Timeline:* Break dancing first came about in the late 1960s.

- *Function or reason:* What began as a way for rival street gangs to solve turf disputes, soon became a dance phenomenon. "As the 70's evolved, much emphasis was placed on groundwork involving stylized leg movements (so-called Floor Rock or Down Rock)." Soon spectacular moves were invented and were added to the mix. "Still, the basic form of both rocking and breakdance 'cutting' contests remained the same until the 'Rock Steady Crew' and the 'Electronic Boogaloo Lockers' (later renamed the 'Electric Boogaloos') literally hit the streets of New York with the spectacular hand-gliding, back-spinning, windmilling, and head-spinning ground moves that have since become synonymous with the word breakdance. The dance gained in worldwide popularity during the '80s and '90s with break-dance moves being incorporated into movies and musical theater productions and European and Asian aficionados adding their own exuberant spins and whirls to the mix" (www.centralhome.com/breakdance.htm). Today breakdancing is as popular and exciting as ever and combines with other street dance such as locking, popping, and krumping.

- *Who does this dance:* Boys, girls, men, and women do this dance.

- *Music and rhythms:* Break dancing is usually done to hip-hop music.

- *Traditional clothing or costume:* Hip-hop fashion is a must. Hooded sweatshirts, ball caps, headbands, bandanas, baggy pants, and big brand-name basketball shoes are favorites.

- *Other information:* Four types of movements that make up break dancing:

  - *Toprock* refers to any series of steps performed from a standing position. It is usually the first display of style and it serves as a warm-up for transitions into more athletic maneuvers.

  - *Downrock* includes all footwork performed on the floor such as a six step. Normally performed with the hands and feet on the floor, downrock displays the break dancer's foot speed and control and transitions into power moves.

  - *Power moves* are actions that require momentum and physical power to execute. In power moves, the break dancer relies more on upper body strength and is usually on his or her hands during moves. Power moves include the windmill, swipe, and flare.

  - *Freezes* usually end the routine and halt all motion in a stylish pose. The more difficult freezes require the breakdancer to suspend himself or herself off the ground, using upper body strength, in poses such as the handstand or pike.

REFERENCES

http://en.wikipedia.org/wiki/Breakdance
www.globaldarkness.com/articles/history%20of%20breaking.htm
www.centralhome.com/breakdance.htm

Margin annotations:

Although some dances list more than one category, the first category listed on the KQ worksheet describes its most natural fit.

An interesting quote or comment on the dance

The function or reason for why people do this dance

Age- or gender-specific information on who performs the dance

The style, type, or tempo of music

Any special clothing required to enhance or embellish performance

Specific Web sites used to create the Background Information section. KQs for other dances may include other types of resources.

Specific type or style of dance

This section contains interesting information about the dance that is not addressed in the other sections. Sometimes this information can be used to inform KQ section 3, Responding: What do you think? What do you wonder?, and section 4, Performing: What can you do?.

Information on the teaching process

Specific details on what the student observes. Choose to use the Viewing: What did you see? question, the 4-Square form (either level 1 or 2), the viewing guide, or just have a class discussion using the suggested discussion starters and questions. See more information on this section in chapter 1.

This section enables students to apply knowledge from the other sections or discover new information to create a new dance, re-create a dance, or both. See more information on this section in chapter 4.

Questions used to access prior student knowledge and connect to new student knowledge. Select any of the following questions to ask the students, or simply ask students about what they already know. See more information on this section in chapter 2.

Questions used to get students to make observations about, compare and contrast, or analyze the dance. Select any of the following questions or simply ask students about what they think about the dance and what questions they may have that could be researched. See more information on this section in chapter 3.

TEACHING STRATEGIES

The video clip should be viewed at least three times (see chapter 1). After students record and discuss their observations and before the third viewing, use the discussion starters listed next to facilitate class discussion. Feel free to paraphrase and choose the questions that work best with your students.

Viewing: What Did You See?.

Suggested discussion starters and questions: What is the first thing that strikes you about this dance? How would you describe this dance in three words? What body parts are used the most?

Connecting: What Do You Know?

Suggested discussion starters and questions: When have you ever seen a dance like this performed? How was it like this dance? How was it different?

Responding: What Do You Think? What Do You Wonder?

Suggested discussion starters and questions: Some experts think that break dancing is linked to Capoeira, a Brazilian dance invented by African slaves. Do a Web search for a video of Capoeira. Compare and contrast it to break dancing.

What questions do you have about this dance? Write them down and continue your research. Some of these questions can be answered through movement.

Performing: What Can You Do?

Choose both Re-create and Create, one of these two activities, or make your own performing work that you think is most appropriate for your students.

Re-create

Choose three movements that you can perform safely from the video to re-create.
Note: Use ideas from recorded observations from question 1 (What did you see?).

Create

There are four basic elements that form the foundation of break dance. They are toprock, downrock, power moves, and freezes. Create one movement that represents the big idea of each element and perform your routine.

*If you need music and don't have it among your resources, use the video.

FUN FACTS

A break dancer, breaker, or B-boy or B-girl refers to a person who practices break dancing. Groups of break dancers are called crews.

WEB EXPLORATIONS

Key terms to search for include break dancing, hip-hop, vernacular dance, and street dance.

The second form, the Student KQ Worksheet, is a basic student worksheet that can be used as is for younger and less experienced dance students or modified by copying and pasting questions from the list of discussion starters and suggested questions that are contained in the Teaching Strategies section on the Knowledge Quest: Information and Teaching Tips form located on the DVD for each dance. The second teacher form is the Answer Sheet for the KQ worksheet and lists several possible answers for each section of the student worksheet. Following are explanations of all three forms.

The student worksheet can be used just as it is for all grades, or you can choose some or all of the specific discussion questions from the Knowledge Quest: Information and Teaching Tips to copy and paste from the DVD. Have students record answers directly in worksheets or chart out answers as part of a class discussion.

Name: _____ Class: _____ Date: _____

STUDENT KNOWLEDGE QUEST WORKSHEET

Name of Dance: Break Dancing

1. Viewing: What did you see?
   Record your observations. Describe what you see. Be specific.

   _____

   _____

   _____

   _____

2. Connecting: What do you know?

   _____

   _____

   _____

   _____

3. Responding: What do you think? What do you wonder?

   _____

   _____

   _____

   _____

4. Performing: What can you do?

   _____

   _____

   _____

   _____

ANSWER SHEET FOR STUDENT KNOWLEDGE QUEST WORKSHEET

Name of Dance: Break Dancing

1. **Viewing: What did you see?**
   Record your observations. Describe what you see. Be specific.
   Rhythmic footwork, spin, twist, poses, holds, flipping, tricks, walking on hands,
   swinging, rhythmic turning foot movements, strength movements, hopping,
   skip-like movement, spin on back, helicopter. Dancing at all levels. Dancer
   does not look at audience, however body is facing almost all positions at some
   point. Generally involves fast movement except when doing holds or freezes.

The answer sheet contains some of the answers to look for on student worksheets, including what to look for should you decide to have students use the 4-Square, levels 1 or 2.

4-SQUARE LEVEL 1

How do the dancers use their bodies?

Body parts most often in use
torso (chest, hips)   legs   feet
arms   shoulders   hands   head

Shape of body
angles   curves   straight   twisted
same on both sides
different on both sides

Moving one body part at a time

Moving in place
bending   stretching   twisting

Movement that travels
walk   hop   jump   slide   leap

other (describe): _____

How do the dancers move?

Movement elements
with power
with little power
surprisingly
continuously
looking and moving in one direction
looking and moving in more than one direction
controlled
uncontrolled

Speed of movement
fast   medium   slow

Are any movements accented or emphasized?
yes   no

How long do the movements last?
long   medium   short

Are there repeated rhythmic patterns?
yes   no

Types of movements include
suspended   shaking   swinging
percussive   collapsing   vibratory

other: _____

How do the dancers use the space around them?

Size of movement
large   medium   small

Body levels
low   middle   high

Movement done close to the body

Movement done far from the body

Dancers stand
in circles   in squares   in lines
scattered (spread out)

Foot patterns traced on the floor
curved   straight   circular

Directions in which dancers travel
forward   sideways
backward   diagonal

What are the dancers' relationships to each other?

Dancers dance
alone   in partners
in groups (trio, quartet, etc.)

Dancers relate to
other dancer(s)   object   audience

Dancers' relationships to each other are mostly
over   under   around   through
in front   behind   beside
near each other   far from each other

Contact between and among dancers
touching   holding
supporting each other's weight
lifting each other

other: _____

4-SQUARE LEVEL 2

How do the dancers use their bodies?

Body parts most often in use
torso (chest, hips)   legs   feet
arms   shoulders   hands   head

Shape of body
angles   curves   straight   twisted
symmetrical   asymmetrical

Isolations

Nonlocomotor

(axial):
bending   stretching   twisting

(peripheral):
spoke   arc   carve

Locomotor
walk   hop   jump   slide   leap
sissonne (2 feet to 1 foot)
assemblé (1 foot to 2 feet)

other (describe): _____

How do the dancers move?

Movement elements (Laban efforts)

Weight: with strength (powerfully)
with lightness (delicately)

Time: suddenly (surprisingly)
sustained (continuously)

Space: direct (one focus)
indirect (multifocal)

Flow: bound (controlled)
free (uncontrolled)

Effort elements (Laban effort actions)
dab   punch   float   glide
wring   press   flick   slash

Time

Tempo: fast   medium   slow

Are movements organized into distinct phrases?
yes   no

Are any movements accented or emphasized?
yes   no

Duration of movements
long   medium   short

Are there repeated rhythmic patterns?
yes   no

Movement qualities (force or energy)
suspended   shaking   swinging
percussive   collapsing   vibratory

other: _____

How do the dancers use the space around them?

Size of movement
large   medium   small

Levels
low   middle   high

Near space (movement done close to the body)

Far space (movement done far from the body)

Formations
circles   squares   lines   scattered

Pathways (floor patterns)
curved   straight   circular

Air patterns (trace patterns in the air left by dancers' movements, e.g., figure 8)
curved   straight   circular

Directions in which dancers travel
forward   sideways
backward   diagonal

What are the dancers' relationships to each other?

Dancers dance
alone   in partners
in groups (trio, quartet, etc.)

Dancers relate to
other dancer(s)   object   audience

Dancers' relationships to each other are mostly
over   under   around   through
in front   behind   beside
near each other   far from each other

Contact between and among dancers
touching   holding
supporting each other's weight
lifting each other

other: _____

Answers will appear directly after each question, which is boldfaced.

2. **Connecting: What do you know?**

   Possible answers: When have you ever seen a dance like this performed? TV shows like *So You Think You Can Dance?* and *America'a Best Dance Crews.* **How was it like this dance?** This dance had the basic elements of breaking. **How was it different?** The dances on TV are really exciting and have extreme moves.

3. **Responding: What do you think? What do you wonder?**

   Note: At this level of thinking, there is seldom one right answer.

   Possible answers: Some experts think that break dancing is linked to Capoeira, a Brazilian dance invented by African slaves. Do a Web search for a video of Capoeira. Compare and contrast it to break dancing. Break dancing and Capoeira are alike in that they both have footwork at standing and ground levels, the dancers are competing with each other, the dances both involve poses and power moves. Capoeira is slightly different. Because it uses more tumbling moves, the dancers are closer to each other and appear to be fighting with each other.

   Chart questions that students wonder about. Have them do more research on these questions and solve problems through movement.

4. Performing: What can you do?

Re-create

When re-creating the dance, the students should do the following:

- Identify three movements from the video.
- Be able to re-create some of the movements.

Create

The dance should contain one movement that expresses the big idea (in parentheses) for each of the four basic elements that form the foundation of break dance. These elements are as follows:

- Toprock (a series of movements on your feet)
- Downrock (a series of movements with hands and feet on the floor)
- Power moves (as appropriate, stunts or movements that require strength and flexibility)
- Freezes (dramatic pose that end the routine)

Dancers perform their routine.

*If you need music and don't have it among your resources, use the video.

Using Video Search KQ Forms and Creating Your Own KQ Forms for Dances Not Highlighted in This Book

In each category in part II of this book, some KQs do not have a video clip included on the DVD, but they do have a video search KQ form included in the book and on the DVD. These KQs are provided as a way to encourage both you and your students to use the Internet (more specifically YouTube) as a way to find many dance resources. Whether you are searching for instructional or performance videos, the Internet is a vast source of usable video clips for dance.

We also provide a blank video search KQ template, so you can create your own KQ forms for any dance or type of dance that you and your students want to learn more about or that is not highlighted in this book and DVD package. Searching YouTube is quick and easy. Simply go to the Web site at www.youtube.com and type in key words such as the country, type, and name of the dance. Up pops any number of dances! The quality is not always the best and the authenticity in some cases may be questionable, but enough is available to make the search worth your while. There are, however, some problems involved. For instance, many schools block the use of YouTube. In this case, have your students do searches as homework either on their home computers or at the local library. You can give them an actual site address such as www.youtube.com/watch?v=bTvG_8QLZwM or tell them what key search words to use, such as *Flamenco dance*.

Note: For dances that include video search KQs, if students have to do this video search at home or at the local library, you should consider copying the background information from the Knowledge Quest: Information and Teaching Tips page and also providing them with the appropriate 4-Square and Student Knowledge Quest worksheet with the selected questions cut and pasted into it.

Sometimes videos are removed from YouTube after you locate them. This can be a problem if you have relied on a specific clip. A way to get around this and in fact solve the YouTube blocking problem is by converting YouTube clips at home into QuickTime or MP4 files. Some Web sites and programs are available for this conversion and they are certainly worth exploring. Once converted, you can access the video clip from your computer without logging on to the Internet. We have used the Web site www.videodownloadx.com to convert videos. Once the videos are copied to the desktop we convert them using a program called iSquint (available online), which converts the downloaded file to a QuickTime file. There are a variety of sites available; just do a little search using words such as *converting YouTube files to play on your PC or Mac.*

To get the most out of *Exploring Dance Forms and Styles,* be sure to read through all of the various chapters in this book. They contain a wealth of ideas that not only will help with sharing this book's information with your students, it will inform your teaching practice. So get ready! On your mark. Get set. Go!

PART I

Building Critical Thinking Skills in Dance

Dance education provides many opportunities for students to use critical-thinking skills within the processes of creating, performing, and responding. This book uses two commonly used levels or hierarchies of thinking and research-based learning: Bloom's taxonomy and depth of knowledge (DOK) (Webb 2006). These thinking skills help scaffold the teaching and learning, challenge and deepen student knowledge, and broaden their experience. In addition, studio habits of mind (Hetland 2007) helps to better design research-based instruction. Studio habits of mind describes behaviors used when one participates in the artistic process. You can read more details about these three theories by reading the documents referenced in the Recommended Resources section of this book.

The overall framework for the teaching and learning suggested in this book was designed using the thinking routine *I see, I think, I wonder*. This routine was developed through the Artful Thinking program, a research project of Harvard University's Project Zero. See the form on page 2 that shows how the student Knowledge Quest worksheets in this book integrate this thinking routine.

This framework—combined with suggested questions that are aligned with the three theories of thinking and learning noted earlier—build on each other and deepen students' knowledge as they work through each step. The Knowledge Quest (KQ) worksheets found at the end of chapters 5, 6, 7, and 8 will lead students through the learning process, using the DVD video clips and the suggested video searches. Answer sheets for KQ worksheets and Information and Teaching Tips pages are offered for more effective teaching. Student work is centered on what students see (viewing; chapter 1), what students know (connecting; chapter 2), what students think and wonder (responding; chapter 3), and what students can do (performing; chapter 4). This book provides tools for different levels of dance experience as opposed to different

> "The goals of education are to teach for understanding; to help students learn to use knowledge to solve unexpected problems rather than simply recite back facts; and to develop a culture of thinking in the classroom so that students think critically and creatively thereby gaining intellectual empowerment. The primary skill worth learning is deep thinking which involves the flexible and active use of knowledge."
>
> —David Perkins (www.newfoundations .com/GALLERY/Perkins.html)

Kathak

Name: _____ Class: _____ Date: _____

STUDENT KNOWLEDGE QUEST WORKSHEET

Name of Dance: Kathak

1. Viewing: What did you see?
   Record your observations. Describe what you see. Be specific.

   _____

   _____

   _____

   _____

   _____

2. Connecting: What do you know?

   _____

   _____

   _____

   _____

   _____

3. Responding: What do you think? What do you wonder?

   _____

   _____

   _____

   _____

   _____

4. Performing: What can you do?

   _____

   _____

   _____

   _____

   _____

ages or grade levels so teachers can adapt lessons according to individual and class needs.

States and school districts have identified particular standards that inform all teaching and learning. For this reason, specific key words are listed in the standards charts included in this book so that each teacher can more easily identify the appropriate standard(s) for their students. The standards chart is divided into different sections that parallel the four tasks (viewing, connecting, responding, performing) of the KQ worksheets. Appropriate key words are listed in one column and the other column is a blank space where the teacher can record the corresponding state or local standards. Once that task is done, the teacher can use this completed standards chart to align all the student work.

Viewing: What Did You See?

Key words to look for in standards	Insert state and local standards
name, select, repeat, observe, identify, discuss	

Connecting: What Do You Know?

Key words to look for in standards	Insert state and local standards
name, select, repeat, observe, identify, describe, compare, differentiate, understand, learn, relate, connect, discuss, summarize	

Responding: What Do You Think? What Do You Wonder?

Key words to look for in standards	Insert state and local standards
relate, discuss, connect, synthesize, evaluate, observe, respond, identify, describe, interpret, select, analyze, compare, communicate	

Performing: What Can You Do?

Key words to look for in standards	Insert state and local standards
express, communicate, imagine, improvise, re-create, explore, discover, create, develop, plan, prepare, choreograph, analyze, reflect, demonstrate, refine, perform, present	

FIGURE I.1
Standards chart.

The following words can be used to search for specific dance content in district, state, and national standards that deal with viewing, analyzing, and responding to dance in a variety of categories.

- Aesthetics
- Ceremonial
- Culture
- Dance terminology or vocabulary
- Diversity
- Ethnic dance

- Folk dance
- Function of dance
- Genres or forms
- Historical cultural context
- Historical dance
- Movement skills and elements
- Musicality
- Rhythm
- Ritual
- Social dance

- Socioeconomic
- Sociopolitical
- Styles
- Theatrical dance
- Time period/era/historical periods
- Traditional dances
- Universal themes
- Values and beliefs
- World dance

CHAPTER 1

Viewing: What Did You See?

Viewing, also called observation, is an important skill that can be taught and improved upon. For this book, viewing is the gateway into the dance content. According to Larry Lavender in his book, *Dancers Talking Dance,* "During observation, one carefully and consciously sees, or attends to, the work of art" (1996, p. 2). Often people think they are observing when they are only looking at the surface. True observation requires paying careful attention to detail and deconstructing the event. The viewer must be careful to use a clean slate, not clouding the observation with personal bias. In other words, the viewer must ask, "What do I see?" not "What do I think I should see?"

One purpose of section 1, Viewing: What Did You See?, of the Knowledge Quest (KQ) worksheet is to familiarize students with the dance they are studying. It is simply an exercise on what the student notices while watching the dance; there are no right or wrong answers. It also helps to engage students by presenting an opportunity for some initial conversations about the dance.

4-Square Forms

Students can record what they observe directly in the Viewing: What Did You See? section of the Student KQ worksheet, or use a version of the 4-Square worksheets to focus the viewing process. The 4-Square worksheets are also on the DVD. The 4-Square worksheets provide an organized way to view the dance and, at the same time, provide four categories that describe types of movement. The categories focus on four questions, which are listed in table 1.1.

Table 1.1   4-Square Categories

Category	Description
How do the dancers use their bodies?	This category helps define locomotor and non-locomotor/axial movement, body shape, use of body parts, and isolation of body movement.
How do the dancers use the space around them?	This category describes size of movement, amount of space used, body levels, formations, pathways, and directions traveled.
How do the dancers move?	This category involves the elements of dance, including both the Laban version (weight, time, space, and flow) and the D'Houbler version (time space, energy/force).
What are the dancers' relationships to each other?	This category involves how the dancers work together (solo, duet, trio, groups); what spatial relationships the dancers mostly have towards each other (over, under, around, through, in front, behind, beside, near, far); and what type of contact the dancers have between or among themselves (touching, holding, supporting each other's weight, lifting each other).

There are two versions of the 4-Square form:

1. Level 1 (see table 1.2), which is geared to students with limited dance knowledge and uses simple, generic terms
2. Level 2 (see table 1.3), which is geared to students with dance experience and uses specific dance terminology

Table 1.2   4-SQUARE LEVEL 1

How do the dancers use their bodies?	How do the dancers move?

Body parts most often in use
    torso (chest, hips)   legs   feet
    arms   shoulders   hands   head
 	
Shape of body
    angles   curves   straight   twisted
        same on both sides
        different on both sides
 	
Moving one body part at a time
 	
Moving in place
    bending   stretching   twisting
 	
Movement that travels
    walk   hop   jump   slide   leap
 	
other (describe): _____
	Movement elements
	                with power
	            with little power
	
	                surprisingly
	                continuously
	        looking and moving in one direction
	    looking and moving in more than one direction
	                controlled
	                uncontrolled
	
	Speed of movement
	            fast medium slow
	
	Are any movements accented or emphasized?
	                yes no
	
	How long do the movements last?
	            long medium short
	
	Are there repeated rhythmic patterns?
	                yes no
	
	Types of movements include
	        suspended shaking swinging
	        percussive collapsing vibratory
	
	other: _____

How do the dancers use the space around them?	What are the dancers' relationships to each other?
Size of movement large medium small *Body levels* low middle high *Movement done close to the body* *Movement done far from the body* *Dancers stand* in circles in squares in lines scattered (spread out) *Foot patterns traced on the floor* curved straight circular *Directions in which dancers travel* forward sideways backward diagonal	*Dancers dance* alone in partners in groups (trio, quartet, etc.) *Dancers relate to* other dancer(s) object audience *Dancers' relationships to each other are mostly* over under around through in front behind beside near each other far from each other *Contact between and among dancers* touching holding supporting each other's weight lifting each other other: _____

Table 1.3   4-SQUARE LEVEL 2

How do the dancers use their bodies?	How do the dancers move?
Body parts most often in use torso (chest, hips) legs feet arms shoulders hands head *Shape of body* angles curves straight twisted symmetrical asymmetrical *Isolations* *Nonlocomotor* *(axial):* bending stretching twisting *(peripheral):* spoke arc carve *Locomotor* walk hop jump slide leap sissonne (2 feet to 1 foot) assemblé (1 foot to 2 feet) other (describe): _____	*Movement elements (Laban efforts)* *Weight:* with strength (powerfully) with lightness (delicately) *Time:* suddenly (surprisingly) sustained (continuously) *Space:* direct (one focus) indirect (multifocal) *Flow:* bound (controlled) free (uncontrolled) *Effort elements (Laban effort actions)* dab punch float glide wring press flick slash
	Time *Tempo:* fast medium slow *Are movements organized into distinct phrases?* yes no *Are any movements accented or emphasized?* yes no *Duration of movements* long medium short *Are there repeated rhythmic patterns?* yes no *Movement qualities (force or energy)* suspended shaking swinging percussive collapsing vibratory other: _____

> continued

> continued

How do the dancers use the space around them?	What are the dancers' relationships to each other?
Size of movement large medium small *Levels* low middle high *Near space (movement done close to the body)* *Far space (movement done far from the body)* *Formations* circles squares lines scattered *Pathways (floor patterns)* curved straight circular *Air patterns (trace patterns in the air left by dancers' movements, e.g., figure 8)* curved straight circular *Directions in which dancers travel* forward sideways backward diagona	*Dancers dance* alone in partners in groups (trio, quartet, etc.) *Dancers relate to* other dancer(s) object audience *Dancers' relationships to each other are mostly* over under around through in front behind beside near each other far from each other *Contact between and among dancers* touching holding supporting each other's weight lifting each other other: _____

Use these two versions to differentiate between novice and experienced classes or even within classes of mixed experience levels. The following process is recommended:

1. Select the appropriate 4-Square viewing form for the level of your class, or use more than one worksheet for a class that requires differentiated instruction.

2. Have students view the dance video clip at least three times. The first time the students should just watch the clip. After this initial viewing you can open a discussion using the following questions:

   • What was your first impression of this dance and how did it impact you?

   • What part or movement of the dance stands out in your mind?

   • With what personal memory or experience does this dance connect?

   • Write any other thoughts that come to your mind.

   In addition to these general questions, included on each dance-specific KQ are more specific questions that relate to that particular dance. Teachers may choose to continue the conversation along these lines or keep the discussion more general, depending on individual or class goals. Each question is simply about what the student is seeing, so the answer is specific to each student.

3. Have students look at the 4-Square viewing forms you have chosen for them to work with so that they can familiarize themselves with what they have to observe during the second viewing. At the second viewing, students should watch the video clip, looking for movements and qualities that are prevalent or emphasized in the dance.

4. Ask students to fill out their viewing worksheets (alone, with partners, or in small groups). The third viewing of the clip is to be used for the students to have another look and add any additional observations to their 4-Square viewing forms.

5. You might also use the questions from the four categories on the 4-Square as general prompts to begin discussions on what the students observed. (See table 1.1 for a reminder of these four questions.)

This section of the student KQ worksheet will look like figure 1.1. Notice the additional questions listed that are specific to that dance. You can copy and paste these questions from the list of discussion starters and suggested questions on the Knowledge Quest: Information and Teaching Tips page that is located on the DVD for each specific dance highlighted in the book.

Name of Dance: Kathak

1. Viewing: What did you see?

   Record your observations. Describe what you see. Be specific.

   Suggested discussion starters and questions: What are the main body parts used? What are some key movements used? How is sound used in this dance? What do you notice about the way the feet are used? What do you notice about the way the hands are used in this dance? What do you notice about the facial expressions?

FIGURE 1.1
Example of the Viewing section from a student KQ worksheet.

Figure 1.2 illustrates how possible answers for the 4-Square forms for both levels will be displayed in the answer section of the KQ.

1. **Viewing: What did you see?**

   Record your observations. Describe what you see. Be specific.

   Repeating rhythmic footwork; various sounds produced by bells on ankles; stamping; spinning; graceful hand movements; traveling side to side and diagonally backward; arms reach down, side, and up; twirl around in front and end at chest height; repeat to other side; speed of dance begins slow and then gradually gets faster.

FIGURE 1.2
Example of the answer section of the KQ.

> continued

> *figure 1.2 continued*
4-SQUARE LEVEL 1

How do the dancers use their bodies?

Body parts most often in use
torso (chest, hips) **legs** **feet**
arms shoulders **hands** **head**

Shape of body
angles **curves** **straight** twisted
same on both sides
different on both sides

Moving one body part at a time

Moving in place
bending **stretching** **twisting**

Movement that travels
walk hop jump **slide** leap

other (describe): _____

How do the dancers move?

Movement elements
with power
with little power
surprisingly
continuously
looking and moving in one direction
looking and moving in more than one direction
controlled
uncontrolled

Speed of movement
fast **medium** slow

Are any movements accented or emphasized?
yes no

How long do the movements last?
long **medium** short

Are there repeated rhythmic patterns?
yes no

Types of movements include
suspended shaking swinging
percussive collapsing vibratory

other: _____

How do the dancers use the space around them?

Size of movement
large **medium** small

Body levels
low **middle** **high**

Movement done close to the body

Movement done far from the body

Dancers stand
in circles in squares in lines
scattered (spread out)

Foot patterns traced on the floor
curved straight circular

Directions in which dancers travel
forward **sideways**
backward diagonal

What are the dancers' relationships to each other?

Dancers dance
alone in partners
in groups (trio, quartet, etc.)

Dancers relate to
other dancer(s) object **audience**

Dancers' relationships to each other are mostly
over under around through
in front behind beside
near each other far from each other

Contact between and among dancers
touching holding
supporting each other's weight
lifting each other

other: _____

4-SQUARE LEVEL 2

How do the dancers use their bodies?

Body parts most often in use
torso (chest, hips)   legs   feet
arms   shoulders   hands   head

Shape of body
angles   curves   straight   twisted
symmetrical   asymmetrical

Isolations

Nonlocomotor

(*axial*):
bending   stretching   twisting

(*peripheral*):
spoke   arc   carve

Locomotor
walk   hop   jump   slide   leap
sissonne (2 feet to 1 foot)
assemblé (1 foot to 2 feet)

other (describe): *step side to side, traveling turns, step cross while maintaining rhythmic pattern with feet*

How do the dancers move?

Movement elements (Laban efforts)

Weight: with strength (powerfully)
with lightness (delicately)

Time: suddenly (surprisingly)
sustained (continuously)

Space: direct (one focus)
indirect (multifocal)

Flow: bound (controlled)
free (uncontrolled)

Effort elements (Laban effort actions)
dab   punch   float   glide
wring   press   flick   slash

Time

Tempo: fast   medium   slow

Are movements organized into distinct phrases?
yes   no

Are any movements accented or emphasized?
yes   no

Duration of movements
long   medium   short

Are there repeated rhythmic patterns?
yes   no

Movement qualities (force or energy)
suspended   shaking   swinging
percussive   collapsing   vibratory

other: _____

How do the dancers use the space around them?

Size of movement
large   medium   small

Levels
low   middle   high

Near space (movement done close to the body)

Far space (movement done far from the body)

Formations
circles   squares   lines   scattered

Pathways (floor patterns)
curved   straight   circular

Air patterns (trace patterns in the air left by dancers' movements, e.g., figure 8)
curved   straight   circular

Directions in which dancers travel
forward   sideways
backward   diagonal

What are the dancers' relationships to each other?

Dancers dance
alone   in partners
in groups (trio, quartet, etc.)

Dancers relate to
other dancer(s)   object   audience

Dancers' relationships to each other are mostly
over   under   around   through
in front   behind   beside
near each other   far from each other

Contact between and among dancers
touching   holding
supporting each other's weight
lifting each other

other: _____

Section 1 Levels of Thinking

Answers from the 4-Square worksheets and section 1 of the KQ (Viewing: What Did You See?) inform KQ sections 2, 3, and 4. Table 1.4 shows the level of thinking involved for the various thinking frameworks being used in this book. Refer to the part I introduction and the Recommended Resources section in the back of the book for a more in-depth explanation of the various thinking frameworks.

Table 1.4   Levels of Thinking for Viewing: What Did You See?

Research base	Thinking skills
Depth of knowledge (DOK)	**Level 1:** identify, list, draw, label, name, recall
Bloom's taxonomy	**Knowledge:** describe, identify, list, record, name, select
Studio habits of mind	**Observe:** unpacking what they see in the video clip and in their own work

Section 1 in State and Local Standards

Use figure 1.3 to help identify key words in state and local standards as they relate to the Viewing: What Did You See? section of the KQ form.

Viewing: What Did You See?

FIGURE 1.3
Key words for state and local standards.

Key words to look for in standards	Insert state and local standards
name, select, repeat, observe, identify, discuss	

CHAPTER 2

Connecting: What Do You Know?

Before presenting students with new information, educators usually assess students' prior knowledge on the topic they are studying. This assessment serves the following purposes:

1. To connect to what students already know about the topic
2. To create an opportunity for all students to contribute equally without judgment
3. To provide a hook, or point of entry, for engaging student interest
4. To give the teacher a more accurate perspective on students' reactions, responses, and thinking processes
5. To help the teacher decide how to approach the teaching and learning process

According to general pedagogical theory, tapping into prior knowledge helps students to sort, connect, and blend the new learning in a more efficient way and it enables students to attach and store new knowledge. Less is written about students' use of emotion and imagination to make links to new information. In dance, people's personal reactions to or thoughts about what they see are as important as information learned through traditional pedagogical methods. Students in the same class observing the same dance are likely to come from various backgrounds with various degrees of knowledge and experience. Their reactions to the work are equally unique and equally informative. Even if students are totally unfamiliar with a particular type of dance, they still can access their imagination and emotions and react.

One strategy that classroom teachers use to activate prior knowledge in literacy is called making text-to-self connections. Research clearly shows that prior knowledge, including experiences and emotions, or *schema,* is a major factor in students' ability to comprehend what they read (Harvy and Goudvis 2000). When students read they make one or more of the following connections: text-to-self, text-to-text, and text-to-world. This book applies the same concept to viewing (the dance student's way of reading) dance. Following are ways that students can use these connections to view and understand dance more deeply.

• When students make text-to-self connections they link the reading to personal experiences. When making dance-to-self connections, students can relate clips of dances to past experiences. Teachers can ask students specific questions to prompt them to remember past experiences and then relate these experiences to the culture, background, and content of the dance.

• Text-to-text connections occur when one book reminds you of something that you read in another. In a dance-to-dance connection, students' knowledge of one dance can help them to understand another dance. Specifically students can compare two dances by the same or different choreographers, of the same or different form, or of the same theme or topic.

• Text-to-world connections enable students to connect text to the world around them. Teachers use literature to connect to themes, ideas, and perspectives. Teachers can connect with history and social studies subject areas, too. Dance-to-world connections can also provide this important link.

Students make these connections before, during, and after viewing. Thus, it is important to use strategic questioning to build student learning. For example, in section 1 of the KQ worksheet (Viewing: What did you see?), students describe exactly what they observe without reaction or judgment. In section 2 (Connecting: What do you know?), students comment on what they know, think about, imagine, and feel about the dance. This question is designed to access and assess prior knowledge and connect to new learning. This section of the KQ also provides an opportunity for students to compare and contrast, classify information, make observations, identify patterns, and organize information. Figure 2.1 shows an example of how this works for the Kathak dance. Notice the additional questions listed that are specific to that dance. You can copy and paste these questions from the list of suggested discussion starters and questions on the KQ: Information and Teaching Tips page located on the DVD for each specific dance highlighted in the book.

Students generally should refer to their responses in section 1 of the KQ worksheet (Viewing: What did you see?) or on their 4-Square forms to help them answer the suggested questions under section 2 of the KQ (Connecting: What

Name of Dance: Kathak

Connecting: What Do You Know?

FIGURE 2.1

An example of Connecting: What Do You Know? from the Kathak dance.

Suggested discussion starters and questions: What other dances do you know that tell a story? What are some of the ways the dancer moves to create different sounds with the bells? How is speed represented in this dance? Look at a clip of Flamenco dance (do a Web search for one). What similarities and differences can you see between these two world dance forms?

do you know?). These combined answers will then inform and help students address KQ sections 3 (Responding) and 4 (Performing).

Section 2 Levels of Thinking

Table 2.1 shows the levels of thinking involved for the various thinking frameworks being used in this book, specific to the thinking used for section 2 of the KQ (Connecting: What do you know?).

Table 2.1 Levels of Thinking for Connecting: What Do You Know?

Research base	Thinking skills
DOK (depth of knowledge)	**Level 2:** observe, classify, interpret, compare, identify patterns, organize
Bloom's taxonomy	**Comprehension:** interpret, paraphrase, predict, rewrite, summarize, translate
Studio habits of mind	**Observation:** learning to attend to visual and aural contexts more closely than ordinary looking or hearing requires, and thereby to see or hear things that otherwise might not be seen or heard. **Understanding the art world:** domain (learning about art history and current practice).

Section 2 in State and Local Standards

Use figure 2.2 to help identify key words in state and local standards as they relate to this section of the KQ form.

Connecting: What Do You Know?

Key words to look for in standards	Insert state and local standards
name, select, repeat, observe, identify, describe, compare, differentiate, understand, learn, relate, connect, discuss, summarize	

FIGURE 2.2
Key words for state and local standards.

CHAPTER 3

Responding: What Do You Think? What Do You Wonder?

One of the primary goals of classroom teaching is to help students develop their thinking skills. Teachers can do this through thought-provoking questions, discussions, and assignments. Such activities contribute to a thoughtful classroom and need to be modeled and developed through intentional instruction. This concept applies equally to helping students observe, think more deeply about, and discuss dance. Asking students what they think about a dance and why they believe it to be true is an important first step in this process.

Another method to help students deepen their thinking involves having them deduce the meaning, intent, or purpose of a dance. Students can make logical conclusions based on information from a video clip of a dance and from their prior knowledge. You can ask students to find evidence, form hunches, recall facts, draw conclusions, and ultimately comprehend the art form more fully. Encourage analytical skills by asking probing questions, such as the following:

- What do you think this dance might be about?
- Why? What evidence do you see in the dance?

- What does this dance remind you of?
- What do you already know about this dance?

Questions play an important role in many classrooms. Section 2 of the KQ (Connecting: What do you know?) encourages students to share their prior knowledge while section 3 (Responding: What do you think? What do you wonder?) guides students to connect their prior knowledge to new learning and to ask questions. When preparing your own questions, focus on using Bloom's taxonomy or DOK to scaffold layers of questions to lead your students to a higher level of thinking and responding. For example, you can use questions that require students to use analysis to see patterns, recognize hidden meanings, and identify key components. At the synthesis level, or connecting, students use old ideas to create new ones, generalize from given facts, relate knowledge from several areas, predict, and draw conclusions. Questions that involve the evaluation level, or responding, allow students to compare and discriminate between ideas, assess value of theories, make choices based on reasoned argument, and verify value of evidence. Following are some strategies for facilitating the questioning process and ways to challenge student thinking:

- Ask for a summary (to promote active listening): "Could you please summarize John's point?"
- Survey the class: "How many people agree with . . ?"
- Allow students to call on other students: "Richard, will you please call on someone else to respond?"
- Play devil's advocate: Require students to defend their reasoning against different points of view.
- Ask students to think about their thinking: "Describe how you arrived at your answer." Have students think aloud, sharing their thinking process with peers to help them understand how they came to their conclusions.
- Cue student responses: "There is no single correct answer for this question. I want you to consider alternatives."
- Call on students randomly: Don't just call on those with raised hands.
- Use think-pair-share: Give students 2 minutes of think time, 2 minutes discussion with a partner, then open class discussion.
- Remember wait time: Wait 10 to 20 seconds following a higher-level question.
- Ask follow-up questions: "Why? Do you agree? Can you elaborate? Tell me more. Can you give an example?"
- Withhold judgment: Respond to students in a nonevaluative fashion.
- Encourage questioning: Encourage students to develop their own questions.

Maryland State Department of Education, www.bcps.org/offices/lis/office/inst/think.html

Section 3 of the KQ (Responding: What do you think? What do you wonder?) gives students an opportunity to consider and pose questions that they may have about a dance. This triggers student curiosity and encourages an independent quest for knowledge. Students can try to find answers to their questions using traditional research methods or, in some cases, they can solve questions through movement. For example, students might ask, "How might wearing a tight corset limit one from doing certain movements?" They then could wrap fabric tightly around their middle and explore ways they can and cannot move. When facilitating students' discussions around the questions What do you think? and What do you wonder?, consider charting out student wonderings and use them as ongoing research questions. Post them and refer back to them as students explore and learn more about various dance forms and eventually discover answers to their questions. See figure 3.1 for an example of how this works. Notice the additional questions listed that are specific to that dance. You can copy and paste these questions from the list of suggested discussion starters and questions on the Knowledge Quest: Information and Teaching Tips page located on the DVD for each specific dance highlighted in the book.

Name of Dance: Kathak

Responding: What Do You Think? What Do You Wonder?

Suggested discussion starters and questions: What idea or emotion do you think this dance is expressing? What is the role of facial expressions in this dance? Why do you think that Kathak dance might sometimes be referred to as a whirling dance? Why do you think such a strong similarity exists between Flamenco and Kathak dance?

What questions do you have about this dance? Write them down and continue your research. Some of these questions can be solved through movement.

FIGURE 3.1
Section 3 of the KQ, Responding: What Do You Think? What Do You Wonder?.

Section 3 Levels of Thinking

Answers to the questions offered in section 3 (Responding: What do you think? What do you wonder?) will inform and help students address the KQ section 4 (Performing: What can you do?). Table 3.1 shows the level of thinking involved for the various thinking frameworks used in this book and specific to the thinking used for section 3 of the KQ (Responding: What do you think? What do you wonder?).

Table 3.1   Levels of Thinking for Responding: What Do You Think? What Do You Wonder?

Research base	Thinking skills
DOK (depth of knowledge)	**Level 3:** inferring, analyzing, reacting emotionally, hypothesizing
Bloom's taxonomy	**Application:** apply, change, compute, construct, demonstrate, discover, manipulate, modify, operate, predict, prepare, produce, relate, show, solve, use **Analysis:** analyze, arrange, break down, classify, compare, connect, contrast, deconstruct, diagram, divide, differentiate, discriminate, distinguish, explain, identify, illustrate, infer, order, outline, relate, select, separate **Synthesis:** combine, integrate, modify, rearrange, substitute, plan, create, design, invent, ask What if?, compose, formulate, prepare, generalize, rewrite **Evaluation:** assess, decide, rank, grade, test, measure, recommend, convince, select, judge, explain, discriminate, support, conclude, compare, summarize
Studio habits of mind	**Envision:** Encourage students to imagine what the choreographer was thinking when the piece was created. What steps would they take to create a similar piece? Encourage them to picture that dance in their minds. **Observe:** unpacking what they see in the clip and their own work **Reflect:** questioning, explaining, and evaluating their own work and the work of others; responding to feedback; revising

Section 3 in State and Local Standards

Use figure 3.2 to identify state and local standards as they relate to this section of the KQ worksheet.

Responding: What Do You Think? What Do You Wonder?

FIGURE 3.2
Key words for state and local standards.

Key words to look for in standards	Insert state and local standards
relate, discuss, connect, synthesize, evaluate, observe, respond, identify, describe, interpret, select, analyze, compare, communicate	

CHAPTER 4

Performing: What Can You Do?

"Education in theatre, dance and the visual arts is one of the most creative ways we have to find the gold that is buried just beneath the surface. They (children) have an enthusiasm for life, a spark of creativity and vivid imagination that need training, training that prepares them to become confident young men and women."

Former secretary of education, Richard Riley (Interview for AMC News 1998)

Providing students of the arts with opportunities to create, perform, and respond offers life-transforming experiences. The need to support student critical thinking and creativity is highlighted in the 2006 report *Are They Really Ready to Work? Employers' Perspectives on the Basic Knowledge and Applied Skills of New Entrants to the 21st Century U.S. Workforce* (Casner-Lotto and Benner 2006). This report concludes that "*Creativity/Innovation* is projected to 'increase in importance' for future workforce entrants, according to more than 70 percent (73.6 percent) of employer respondents" (p. 10). The report, which was initiated by the Conference Board and used information from surveys of 431 human resources officials, also comments that "while the 'three Rs' are still fundamental to any new workforce entrant's ability to do the job, employers emphasize that applied skills like *Teamwork/Collaboration* and *Critical Thinking* are 'very important' to success at work" (p. 9). The National Center on Education and the Economy (NCEE) report, *Tough Choices or Tough Times* (NCEE 2007), recommends that the new 21st-century workforce needs to "be comfortable with ideas and abstractions, good at both analysis and synthesis, creative and innovative . . ." (page 10).

To further support the importance of involving students in the process of creating, during the 1990s, a new group of cognitive psychologists, led by Lorin Anderson (a former student of Benjamin Bloom), updated Bloom's taxonomy, originally developed in 1956, to reflect relevance to 21st-century work. Table 4.1 compares the original and updated versions.

Table 4.1   A Comparison of Bloom's Original Taxonomy and Anderson's Revised Taxonomy

Bloom's original taxonomy	Anderson's revised taxonomy*
Knowledge	Remembering
Comprehension	Understanding
Application	Applying
Analysis	Analyzing
Synthesis	Evaluating
Evaluation	Creating

ANDERSON, L.W., A TAXONOMY FOR LEARNING, TEACHING AND ASSESSING: A REVISION OF BLOOM'S TAXONOMY OF EDUCATIONAL OBJECTIVES, © 2001, p. 310. Adapted by permission of Pearson Education, Inc., Upper Saddle River, NJ.

Section 4 of the KQ (Performing: What can you do?) provides students with opportunities to re-create and create. When students re-create a dance, the goal is to replicate a dance or a section of a dance exactly as it was performed in the video clip that they observed. When students create, they use the dance in the video clip as an inspiration for an original piece. Students use the information from KQ sections 1, 2, and 3 to guide this process, identifying key movements and patterns in the dance. (They have to go back to the clips to do this.) Through re-creating a dance students can do the following:

- Hone observation skills
- Extend movement vocabulary and expressive qualities (students' abilities to express themselves physically)
- Better understand a culture or time by learning movement and origins of movement
- Be ultimately inspired to learn more
- Learn to solve spatial and movement problems

See figure 4.1 for an example of how this works. Notice the directions listed that are specific to that dance. You can copy and paste these directions from section 4, Performing: What can you do? on the Knowledge Quest: Information and Teaching Tips page located on the DVD for each specific dance highlighted in the book.

Name of Dance: Kathak

4. Performing: What Can You Do?

Choose both Re-create and Create, one of these two activities, or make your own performing work that you think is most appropriate for your students.

Re-create

1. In small groups, students re-create the basic 16-count rhythmic pattern of the feet demonstrated in the first video clip.

- Count 1: Stamp right
- Count 2: Stamp left
- Count 3: Stamp right
- Count 4: Stamp left
- Count 5: Stamp left
- Count 6: Stamp right
- Count 7: Stamp left
- Count 8: Stamp right
- Count 9: Stamp right
- Count 10: Stamp left
- Count 11: Stamp right
- Count 12: Stamp left
- Count 13: Stamp right
- Count 14: Stamp right
- Count 15: Stamp left
- Count 16: Stamp right

2. Try to speed up the tempo of the movement.
3. Replicate some of the arm and hand movements.

Create

Create an original dance using repeating patterns of gestures, facial movements, and body movements that express one of the following themes expressed through traditional Kathak dance:

- Beauty and attraction
- Compassion and sadness
- Pride and confidence
- Anger and ferocity
- Disgust and aversion
- Laughter and joy
- Fear and fright
- Surprise and wonder
- Peace

*If you need music and don't have it among your resources, use the video.

FIGURE 4.1
Section 4 of the KQ, Performing: What can you do?.

Section 4 Levels of Thinking

Table 4.2 shows the level of thinking involved for the various thinking frameworks being used in this book and specific to the thinking used for section 4 of the KQ (Performing: What can you do?)

Table 4.2 Levels of Thinking for Performing: What Can You Do?

Research base	Thinking skills
DOK (depth of knowledge)	**Level 4:** design, create, apply concepts, connect
Bloom's taxonomy (revised)	**Creating:** assemble, construct, create, design, develop, formulate, write
Studio habits of mind	**Envision:** Encourage students to imagine what the choreographer was thinking when the piece was created. What steps would they take to create a similar piece? Encourage them to picture that dance in their minds.
	Express: idea, personal meaning, feeling (the basis for the physical product); the way you show what is in your head
	Observe: unpacking what they see in the clip and their own work
	Develop craft: technical suggestions; safe movement habits
	Engage and persist: improving their movement in their dance
	Stretch and explore: pushing students beyond their comfort zone and encouraging them to learn from the revision process; "Have you ever done this before?" "Is this the best solution?" "Can you think of another way?"
	Reflect: questioning, explaining, and evaluating their own work and the work of others; responding to feedback; revising
	Understanding the art world: creating in groups; working as an artist with other artists

Section 4 in State and Local Standards

Use figure 4.2 to identify state and local standards as they relate to this section of the KQ worksheet.

Responding: What Can You Do?

Key words to look for in standards	Insert state and local standards
express, communicate, imagine, improvise, recreate, explore, discover, create, develop, plan, prepare, choreograph, analyze, reflect, demonstrate, refine, perform, present	

FIGURE 4.2
Key words for state and local standards.

PART II

Sorting Dances Into Categories and Subcategories

As stated in the preface, the dance forms in this book have been divided into four categories. Included in each category are subcategories. Within the subcategories are styles and techniques. One goal is to have students become aware of and exposed to the depth and breadth of dance.

The selections chosen for the video clips on the DVD represent four basic categories:

1. Concert or theatrical dance
2. World dance
3. Social dance
4. Historical dance

These categories provide a way of sorting dances using like criteria (e.g., purpose and intent of a dance.) Concert or theatrical dance represents a broad spectrum of dance that appears on the stages of the world for the benefit, enjoyment, and education of an audience. World dance represents dances of the many cultures of the world. These are dances of the people; they capture the spirit of community and express the traditions, beliefs, and values of the people who dance them. Social dance represents recreational dances that are being done by the populace and sometimes reflect social issues. Historical dance represents dances from past eras that are not currently danced by the general populace.

Under the category of concert dance (noted in this book with this icon 🖼) this book provides information on the subcategories of ballet, modern dance, jazz dance, musical theater, musical comedy dance, tap dance, and crossover styles. Under the category of world dance (noted in this book with this icon 🌐) are the common geographic subcategories: North America, South and Central America, Europe, Asia, Africa, and Oceania. Under

> "Wherever dancing prospers and whatever bodily movements different cultures favor, there are at least two basic kinds of dance. One exists primarily for the benefit, edification, or amusement of the dancers who perform it. The other basic kind of dance assumes that its movements can be watched with pleasure; in fact, it exists to be watched."
>
> —Jack Anderson, Dance
> (1974, p. 8)

the category of social dance (noted in this book with this icon 🕸) the subcategories are divided into alone in a group, partners, dances done in a line, and dances done in a circle. Under the category of historical dance (noted in this book with this icon ⌛) the subcategories in this book are Middle Ages, Renaissance, Baroque, and 18th and 19th centuries.

The dances chosen and the categories into which they have been placed were not easy choices. Sorting dances is not an exact science. Many of the dances fit into more than one category. They blend, they borrow, and they can be seen through different eyes. World dance can be staged for an audience in a theatrical setting as well as at community gatherings. At times, world dances are also social in nature. Sometimes a historical dance that is carried from one country to another can be construed to be in the world category; if it is practiced recreationally, it is also social. Shim Sham is an example that covers more than one category. It comes from a background of social dance, becomes a concert dance, and fits neatly into world dance. The Freilach is another example of a social dance that is part of the world dance category. The categories and subcategories provide a basic format to begin the study of dance forms and styles.

Shim Sham 🕸 🖼 🌎

Freilach 🕸 🌎

CHAPTER 5

Concert or Theatrical Dance

For the purposes of this book, **concert dance** or **theatrical dance** covers a broad spectrum of dance that appears on the stages of the world for the benefit, enjoyment, and education of an audience. The subcategories discussed in this chapter are ballet, modern dance, jazz dance, musical theater or musical comedy dance, tap dance, and crossover styles. Again, for the purposes of this book, *style* is defined as characteristic movement and expression of the choreographer or dancer. **Techniques** are the skills a dancer needs to achieve a particular style. Styles are usually ascribed to a person. The same could be said for a **codified** technique, which is a formalized or systematized course of study.

Ballet

Ballet has three major styles: romantic, classical, and contemporary. Before ballet dance became formalized, European dance masters trained nobles in dance skills so that they could participate in court dances. Gradually, ambitious dance masters required more rigorous training which resulted in codified (formalized) movement vocabulary. This led to the development of the dance form called *ballet*.

Romantic Ballet

The **Romantic ballet** period started in 1832 with the ballet *La Sylphide*. *La Sylphide* served to launch ballet as a distinct art form with established male and female dancers. This ballet contained most of the characteristics of the romantic ballet style: Romantic ballets told stories. Magic and unrequited love were part of the stories. The women were ethereal and sylphlike. They began to wear the early **pointe shoes** that were the prototypes of the ones seen and used today.

Another such dance piece of the Romantic ballet period is *Pas de Quatre*. Mr. Lumley, the manager of Her Majesty's Theatre in London, was inspired to create this ballet. He wanted to bring the four greatest ballerinas of the world together. These four ladies all had their strengths, but they were terribly jealous of each other and each prided herself as being the best. With careful diplomacy, Mr. Lumley managed to get them all to London. Their on-stage squabbling is currently reproduced and performed with humor.

Classical Ballet

The **classical ballet** style is over 300 years old. It is based on precise positions and movements which require trained dancers. It is one of the first codified dance forms. Classical ballet includes various techniques, listed and described here:

- Vaganova (Russian): The Vaganova technique is a method of teaching classical ballet that was founded by Agrippina Vaganova. Her method fuses elements of French, Italian, and other methods including influences from other Russian dancers and teachers. It also includes the development of lower back strength; arm plasticity; and the requisite strength, flexibility, and endurance for ballet, especially in **pas de deux.**

- Royal Academy of Dance (RAD, English): The RAD technique is very precise as is the training. RAD instructors and examiners look for long lines and clean steps, not necessarily more difficult steps and tricks. They depend on quality of technique as well as performance.

- Cecchetti (Italian): Named for its founder, Enrico Cecchetti, this method reduces the dancer's training to an exact science. It imposes a fixed regimen in which various types of steps are practiced in a planned sequence; each part of the body is worked evenly. The Cecchetti method teaches the student to think of the movement of the foot, leg, arm, and head, not as something apart, but in relation to the whole body. Cecchetti espoused that it is more important to execute an exercise correctly once than to do it a dozen times carelessly. Quality rather than quantity is the guiding rule. The Cecchetti technique is classic in its focus on line without extravagance or fussiness of movement.

- Balanchine (United States, but in the early days based on Vaganova): George Balanchine brought academic excellence and quality performance to the American ballet, which up until his presence had been merely a weak copy of the great European companies. He emphasized the body as a work of art and held the standards of his dancers to high marks, building strength, flexibility, and familiarity with a modern style.

- Bournonville (Danish): Named for the choreographer of the Royal Danish Ballet, August Bournonville, this style of ballet is characterized by bravura dancing and expressive mime. It is also known to use great jumps and leaps.

Many choreographers of the classical period spent hours setting the ballets that told of fairy tales or legends. However, Francis Mason (Balanchine and Mason 1954, p. 137) tells about the time when noted ballerina Anna Pavlova asked choreographer Michel Fokine to set a variation for her: "It was almost an improvisation. I danced in front of her, she directly behind me. Then she danced and I walked along side her. . . " This was the birth of *The Dying Swan* (1905). "Prior to this ballet I was accused of barefoot tendencies and of rejecting toe dancing in general. *The Dying Swan* was my answer to such criticism."

Contemporary Ballet

Contemporary ballet is a relatively new dance form. Early in the 20th century, when Vaslav Nijinski was performing in Europe, he had different ideas about what ballet could be. He started what was thought to be the newest of dance forms by turning the feet in, making angular shapes with the arms, and bending the knees slightly. One of his most revolutionary ballets was *Le Sacre du Printemps,* translated as *The Rite of Spring.* At the premier performance in 1913, the audience took offense and rioted. They shouted, threw things, and jeered. The dancers kept going with Nijinski counting the music off stage for them, since they could no longer hear the orchestra over the din of the audience. Fortunately, after a respite of a few years, another choreographer, Leonide Massine, rechoreographed *Le Sacre du Printemps* and tamed it down for a newer audience.

George Balanchine is one of the first to choreograph contemporary ballet in the United States. Like Nijinski, he rejected the usual turned-out feet and legs of classical ballet technique and made his dancers turn in and work in parallel for certain works. Balanchine also enjoyed using modern dance movement and often asked modern dance choreographers to set pieces on his company (New York City Ballet). He did not abandon pointe shoes or pointe work. In Romantic and classical ballet the dancer used the floor for kneeling or to portray a death scene. Contemporary ballet began to make greater use of the floor as part of choreography. Contemporary ballet choreographers took chances. They were risk takers. For example, Balanchine was the first to put an African American dancer, Arthur Mitchell, in a lead role in a traditional ballet. Later, Mitchell started the now-famous Dance Theatre of Harlem. This company prides itself on the diversity of its members and for casting dancers of color in traditional ballet roles. Other contemporary ballet choreographers include Robert Joffrey, Gerald Arpino, Alonzo King, Lar Lubovitch, and Jiří Kylián. As in modern dance, contemporary ballet has as many choreographic styles as it has choreographers.

Modern Dance

Modern dance is an all-encompassing phrase that has come to mean a dance form where self-expression is at the very core. In the 1890s and the early 20th century, the term meant taking the opposing view to ballet. Modern dances dealt with feelings and abstract ideas as much as stories and were centered on dancers' interpretations. Also, the dancers often wore no shoes. As the form grew and matured, the will and creativity of the choreographers guided the dancers. As in ballet, the field now encompasses a variety of techniques and styles. Today the varying dance techniques show the exacting demands of the choreographer. The list of choreographers and dancers is endless.

In modern dance, the styles and techniques are based on the lineage from the seminal forerunners through the first and second generations to the current generation. This lineage is as follows:

- *The forerunners:* Isadora Duncan and the combination of Ruth St. Denis and her husband, Ted Shawn (Denishawn Dance Company), were the forerunners of modern dance. Isadora's inspirations were rebellion against repressive industrialized society and the confining structure of ballet. She wanted to return to nature and natural movements, including the use of Greek-like costumes.

  The main inspirations for Ruth St. Denis and Ted Shawn were Oriental and other ethnic dance forms. Ted Shawn advocated for and embodied the essence of the virile male. He formed an all-male dance troupe called Ted Shawn and His Men Dancers. Another choreographer who can be considered a forerunner was Mary Wigman (Germany). Her inspirations were conflict of powers, low-level movement, and the use of masks.

  - *The first generation:*
    - Doris Humphrey, in partnership with Charles Weidman, is known for the first-generation concept of **fall and recovery**.
    - Martha Graham, a disciple of the Denishawn school, is known for the concept of **contract–release.**
    - Hanya Holm developed her own style and technique based on Mary Wigman's work.

  - *The second generation:*
    - Dancer and choreographer Merce Cunningham, who was in the Graham Company, experimented with **chance dance** and collaborated with composer John Cage.
    - Another ex-Graham dancer is Paul Taylor. In his choreography he uses pedestrian gestures to contrast technical virtuosity and is not afraid to deal with controversial issues. Technical virtuosity is the dancer's ability to extend the body and techniques beyond what is usually required for this brand of dance.
    - José Limón, a Mexican-born choreographer and dancer, fought in World War II. His original training was with Humphrey and Weidman.
    - Alvin Ailey is best known for his signature work, *Revelations,* that celebrates the African American experience.
    - Lester Horton, who trained with Ailey, developed his own dance style and teaching technique.
    - Other second-generation choreographers include Bella Lewitsky, Erick Hawkins, Alwin Nikolais, Anna Sokolow, Donald McKayle, Katherine Dunham, Pearl Primus, Jean Erdman, and Sophie Maslow.

- *The current generation:* The current generation, some of whom started in the 1960s, seems to have taken off in an explosive barrage of a new collection of young dancers who are also choreographers. One reason for this influx of large and small dance companies might have been a higher level of government funding. One thing that can be said about this generation of choreographers is that they are free to be individuals and to follow their own styles and techniques.

  - Twyla Tharp's work is eclectic and she is comfortable using movements from both ballet and modern dance.
  - Elizabeth Streb is known for her use of unusual equipment (trampolines, free-standing walls covered in hook-and-loop fasteners, and suspended wooden boxes) in designing her dances.

- David Parsons is known for the ways he combines gymnastics, modern dance, and ballet with music, lighting, and sound. His signature piece, "Caught" (1982), uses a strobe light to make the dancer appear suspended in the air.
- Mikhail Baryshnikov formed the White Oak Dance Project, a modern dance company. This was unusual for a leading ballet star.
- Bill T. Jones is inspired by social issues. His work often takes the form of performance art and he uses film, dialogue, and written material with his choreography.
- Liz Lerman works with people in the community. Her dance company (Dance Exchange) includes people of all ages and abilities.

The video clips provided on the DVD do not include works by all of these choreographers. It is beneficial, however, to share works by these choreographers with your students in order to help them understand how these artists use a variety of inspirations in their work.

Jazz Dance

Jazz dance is characterized by the use of improvisation and influenced by rhythms and techniques of American jazz music. Characteristics of jazz dance include bent knees, low center of gravity, body isolations, syncopation, pirouettes and high kicks, movement emanating from the torso and pelvis, and percussive movements. Some other criteria for identifying this dance form are as follows: parallel and turned-out feet, high energy, quick movement, accented beats, contractions, and exuberant delivery and performance.

From its African American roots in the South, jazz dance and music traveled up the Mississippi River together. The uniqueness of the two art forms grew up parallel to each other. In fact, jazz bands usually traveled with a tap or jazz dancer. There has always been a strong connection between the jazz and the vernacular dance. Following is an example of the ongoing effect of vernacular dance on jazz styles: The African American slave dance called "Ring Shout" is the foundation for jazz dance improvisation done in an open circle; a solo dancer comes to the center to improvise a dance to the rhythm of the surrounding dancers' singing, clapping, and stomping.

Many styles of jazz appear in film, on the theatrical stage, on television, in music videos, and even in commercials. Vaudeville had tap and early jazz performers. Busbee Berkeley was one of the most prominent choreographers in Vaudeville and early films. He created the overhead shots where the camera looked down on the dancers. He choreographed especially for those shots.

Jazz dance also has African and Cuban influences. Katherine Dunham and Pearl Primus, who both choreographed for Broadway, used earthiness and groundedness in their dance works. Choreographers of jazz dance have their own styles and techniques. The dance vocabulary is similar to ballet in that the foot positions are the same except that at times the feet can be turned out, parallel, or turned in. There is great use of leaps, turns, and low levels.

Jack Cole, a choreographer who was said to be the father of jazz dance, was influenced by Ted Shawn and East Indian dancing. He was followed in the 1950s and 1960s by Matt Mattox, a teacher who is best known for using isolations as the basis of his technique. Mattox further codified jazz technique. Luigi was told he would never walk again after a near-fatal car accident. He developed a series of exercises to help him move. These exercises became the basis for his technique and style. Bob Fosse also created his style because of his physical disabilities. Hunched shoulders, turned-in feet, and wearing a hat to cover his baldness became his signature. His choreography shows these influences. Gus Giordano, Frank Hatchett, and other jazz choreographers each had their own style of moving and supported that style by developing a technique of their own.

Musical Theater or Musical Comedy Dance

Musical theater or musical comedy dance is sometimes known as Broadway dance. This form uses many dance styles and techniques, so at the very least Broadway dancers need training in ballet, modern, and jazz. They have to be ready for whatever the choreographer asks them to do. Dance was originally put in a production as a break in the action. The dances became truly integrated when they were used to move the storyline forward. A good example of this integration is when Agnes De Mille choreographed the "Dream Ballet" in *Oklahoma*. The now-famous dance piece foreshadows the plot and shows tensions between the heroine and villain. The same can be said for Jerome Robbins, who was comfortable in both ballet and musical productions. His choreography of the fight scene in *West Side Story* also foreshadows the outcome of the play.

Musicals are performed around the world. American musicals have been translated into many languages. British musicals such as *Cats* and *Starlight Express* have come to the United States and they also have been translated into many languages. The musical has a place in pop culture. *Grease* and *Bye Bye Birdie* are still being produced by and for young and old. *High School Musical* and its sequels are making this form accessible to today's youth. Some shows, such as *The Lion King* (Garth Fagan, choreographer), *A Chorus Line* (Michael Bennett, choreographer), and *Bring in 'Da Noise, Bring in 'Da Funk* (Savion Glover, choreographer) are mainly dance shows with story line and song.

Tap Dance

Tap dance is dance in which the rhythm is sounded out by the clicking taps (metal pieces screwed into the soles and heels of a dancer's shoes). It often uses **syncopation** which emphasizes the weak beats (see figure 5.1).

Tap dance can be done with or without music because the tapping rhythms actually are the music. Another characteristic of the form is that the movement usually starts on the last count of the **pick-up beat,** which can be translated as the eighth count of the preceding musical measure. As with other concert or theatrical forms, many tap dance styles and techniques have been developed

FIGURE 5.1

(a) The numbers are strong beats and the ampersands are weak beats. *(b)* Syncopation emphasizes weak beats.

a **1** & **2** & **3** & **4** &

b 1 **&** 2 **&** 3 **&** 4 **&**

32

over the years. Tap dance is said to have been developed in the United States during the 19th century. Influences on American tap dance include traditional clog dance of northern England, jigs and reels of Ireland and Scotland, and rhythmic foot stamping and groundedness of African dances. Tap dance was part of **minstrel shows** in America.

Early films included tap dancing. One of the characteristics of tap is that it has specific combinations of steps that are each given a name. Shirley Temple's partner, Bill "Bojangles" Robinson made the waltz clog popular. As the title of the dance indicates, the music is counted in 3/4 time instead of the traditional 4/4 time. Buck-and-wing dance gets its name from the two steps called buck and wing. The Nicholas Brothers (Fayard and Harold) used to execute the buck and wing steps and added their own style. Fred Astaire, Ginger Rogers, and Donald O'Connor did the soft shoe in many films. It is a tap dance form done with or without taps on the shoes. In soft-shoe dances sometimes sand was applied to the floors and the dancers would slide their feet to make yet another percussive sound like the scraping of brushes across the drum heads or cymbals on the drum set.

Tap dance is also a street dance. Tap dancers would hold impromptu contests and use a type of **call and response**, where one dancer does a step and the others try to repeat it. The next part of the occasion was the challenge, where dancers played one-upmanship and tried to outdo each other.

Tap dance was popular in Vaudeville and early Broadway shows. As with jazz dance it traveled on to films, stage, and later to television, both as part of review shows and commercials. Memorable tap dancers and what they are known for include the following:

- Fred Astaire and Ginger Rogers: partner dancing
- Charles "Honi" Coles and Jimmy Slyde: being in a hoofer dance group called The Copasetics
- Ann Miller: fast turns
- Tommy Tune and Ray Bolger: their long, lanky styles
- Gene Kelly: a very physical style
- Eleanor Powell: her exuberant solo dancing and fast feet
- Sammy Davis, Jr., Gregory Hines, and young Savion Glover: their almost classical tap styles

Crossover Styles

Lyrical dance blends several styles. You can recognize lyrical dance style from the flowing moves that connect throughout the dance. The upper body movements are different from traditional ballet styles and the use of the torso resembles modern dance.

Another crossover style is the street dancing called hip-hop. Related dance styles are:

- *Break dance, breaking,* or *b-boying* is a street dance style that evolved as part of the hip-hop movement among African American and Puerto Rican youths in Manhattan and the South Bronx of New York City during the early 1970s.
- *Popping* is a funk dance and street dance style based on the technique of quickly contracting and relaxing muscles to cause a jerk in the dancer's body.

- *Locking* (originally campbellocking) is a style of funk dance and street dance that is today also associated with hip-hop. It relies on fast and distinct arm and hand movements combined with more relaxed hips and legs.

- *Krumping* is an urban street dance form that began in the San Francisco Bay Area and is characterized by free, expressive, and highly energetic moves involving the arms, head, legs, chest, and feet. It has become a major part of hip-hop dance culture.

Contemporary dance also crosses and blends. Though it is not bound by a specific technique, it does employ elements such as the use of gravity (groundedness), contract–release, fall and recovery, balance and off-balance, emotion, opposition and tension–relaxation. Many contemporary dancers are trained in the techniques of other dance forms.

Summary

Definite forms go along with the categorizations of concert or theatrical dance. In many instances the forms cross from one category to another. *Borrow,* **adapt,** **adopt,** and *refine* are all words that can describe what a choreographer can use as a basis for the creative process. In the next three chapters you will be presented with more dance forms that can fit into the field of concert or theatrical dance.

The following pages contain the Knowledge Quest worksheets for the following dances, unless otherwise noted. Those with a DVD icon next to them have video clips that appear on the DVD.

Ballet

- *DVD* *Paquita* Variation (Romantic ballet)
- *DVD* "Waltz of the Flowers" (classical ballet)
- *DVD* *Consent to Gravity* (contemporary ballet)

Modern Dance

- *DVD* Brahms Waltz (forerunner)
- *DVD* *Water Study* (first generation)
- *The Traitor* (second generation)
- *DVD* "Rainbow Repertory Etude" (second generation)
- *DVD* "Parsons Repertory Etude" (current generation)
- *DVD* *Conflict* (current generation)

Jazz Dance

- *DVD* *Ta-Da!* (based on Fosse's style)
- *DVD* *Technically Difficult* (based on Cole's and Mattox's styles)

Musical Theater or Musical Comedy Dance

- "Mambo in the Gym" (*West Side Story*)

Tap Dance

- *DVD* Soft shoe
- *DVD* Shim Sham

Crossover Styles
- Hip-hop
- Break dancing (see KQ worksheet in chapter 7)
- Contemporary or lyrical dance
- Bollywood dance

Paquita Variation

KNOWLEDGE QUEST

INFORMATION AND TEACHING TIPS

Category M: Concert Dance (Subcategory: Romantic Ballet)
Name of Dance: *Paquita* Variation

A twist of the wrist and olé we go!

BACKGROUND INFORMATION   Before students view the video clip, share the following information with them.

- **Country or culture of origin:** The ballet was first choreographed and performed in France. Originally the idea for the whole ballet was conceived as a Romantic period ballet by Marius Petipa (the producer). He asked Joseph Mazillier to do the choreography to music commissioned by Ernest Deldevez.

- **Timeline:** The ballet premiered at the Paris Opera in 1846. One year later it premiered in Russia. Currently many ballet repertory companies still perform it.

- **Function or reason:** This variation, or **divertissement,** was made to be a **tour de force** for the ballerina, one that the audience would remember.

- **Who does this dance:** In the United States, the American Ballet Theatre performs this piece as part of their repertoire. Other ballet companies around the world also have this ballet in their repertoire; they sometimes use this variation as a part of an evening of entertainment of variations. Often young people in training for the ballet profession use this piece for auditions.

- **Music and rhythms:** The traditional ballet music was composed by Ernest Deldevez especially for the variation.

- **Traditional clothing or costume:** A short, Romantic style tutu, with trim to add to the Spanish influence.

- **Other information:** It is considered a story ballet. Most story ballets are based on fairy tales, legends, or fantasy. *Sleeping Beauty, Nutcracker, A Midsummer Night's Dream,* and *Rodeo* are but a few ballets that fit this category. Through the years the original variation has been rechoreographed by different choreographers to fit the needs of the ballet companies for whom they worked.

REFERENCES

Lawson, J. 1978. *Ballet stories*. New York: Mayflower Books.

http://en.wikipedia.org/wiki/Paquita

TEACHING STRATEGIES   The video clip should be viewed at least three times (see chapter 1). After students record and discuss their observations and before the third viewing, use the suggested discussion starters listed next to facilitate class discussion. Feel free to paraphrase and choose the questions that work best with your students.

From H. Scheff, M. Sprague, and S. McGreevy-Nichols, 2010, *Exploring dance forms and styles: A guide to concert, world, social, and historical dance* (Champaign, IL: Human Kinetics).

Paquita Variation

Viewing: What Did You See?

Suggested discussion starters and questions: What kind of shoe is the dancer wearing? Look at some of the arm positions and how they are used. The dancer makes definite floor patterns during the dance. How would you describe them?

Connecting: What Do You Know?

Suggested discussion starters and questions: Look at the Fun Facts. How would you compare this story to another story told in a ballet, fairytale, or legend?

Responding: What Do You Think? What Do You Wonder?

Suggested discussion starters and questions: Female ballet dancers tend to look light on their feet. How would the kind of shoes they wear impact how they danced? This dance was created with a Spanish dance influence. How does the choreography show the Spanish influence?

What questions do you have about this dance? Write them down and continue your research. Some of these questions can be answered through movement.

Performing: What Can You Do?

Choose both Re-create and Create, choose one of these two activities, or make your own performing work that you think is most appropriate for your students.

Re-create   Although untrained dancers cannot replicate the movements from the video clip, they certainly can re-create the floor patterns they see. *Note:* Use ideas from recorded observations from question 1 (What do you see?). These paths or patterns can be made by running and then by gallops (**chassés**). They can be done at low, medium, or high levels.

Create   Create a dance movement phrase based on the arm movements seen in the video clip. Walk forward for eight counts, raising the arms (with elbows out and wrists turned in) to a point above the head. Turn the body to the right and glide with alternating feet on the diagonal while bringing the arms down behind the back. Take eight counts (two counts for each glide).

Repeat the sequence four times.

*If you need music and don't have it among your resources, use the video.

FUN FACTS   The original story had a Spanish theme. A young woman (the ballerina) is kidnapped by Gypsies. She then saves a young and handsome military officer from certain death. She is the heroine.

WEB EXPLORATIONS   Key terms to search for include story ballets, romantic ballets, schools of ballet, and Bolshoi ballet.

From H. Scheff, M. Sprague, and S. McGreevy-Nichols, 2010, *Exploring dance forms and styles: A guide to concert, world, social, and historical dance* (Champaign, IL: Human Kinetics).

Paquita Variation

Name: _____ Class: _____ Date: _____

STUDENT KNOWLEDGE QUEST WORKSHEET

Name of Dance: *Paquita* Variation

1. Viewing: What did you see?
   Record your observations. Describe what you see. Be specific.

   _____

   _____

   _____

   _____

   _____

   _____

2. Connecting: What do you know?

   _____

   _____

   _____

   _____

   _____

   _____

3. Responding: What do you think? What do you wonder?

   _____

   _____

   _____

   _____

   _____

4. Performing: What can you do?

   _____

   _____

   _____

   _____

   _____

From H. Scheff, M. Sprague, and S. McGreevy-Nichols, 2010, *Exploring dance forms and styles: A guide to concert, world, social, and historical dance* (Champaign, IL: Human Kinetics).

KNOWLEDGE QUEST

INFORMATION AND TEACHING TIPS
Category M: Concert Dance (Subcategory: Classical Ballet)
Name of Dance: "Waltz of the Flowers" (From *Nutcracker Suite*)

"Everything is Beautiful at the Ballet"

A Chorus Line

"Waltz of the Flowers"

BACKGROUND INFORMATION   Before students view the video clip, share the following information with them.

- **Country or culture of origin:** This variation (dance from a larger group of dances) comes from the ballet called the *Nutcracker Suite*. The origin of this classical ballet stems from Russia, where the art form goes back to the 17th century.

- **Timeline:** The *Nutcracker Suite* was first presented on December 18, 1892. From the beginning of the *Nutcracker Suite's* history in the United States, it was seen as a money maker. It provided income that helped to support all dance companies that included it in their repertoire.

- **Function or reason:** The Russian czar did much to encourage and support the practice of the ballet but at that time it was mostly for the rich. This piece, which has become a rich tradition of entertainment at Christmas time, was looked at as a means to attract an audience for ballet.

- **Who does this dance:** Adult male and female dancers perform in this piece. In most productions a young girl dances the part of Clara.

- **Music and rhythms:** This is a Waltz done in 3/4 time. The composer is Pyotr Ilyich Tchaikovsky. The score for "Waltz of the Flowers" can be found under the title the *Nutcracker Suite*.

- **Traditional clothing or costume:** As each ballet company produces the ballet they use different costuming for their version. They go from modifications of the dress of the time to more modern dance dress. "Waltz of the Flowers" has been done in both romantic and classical tutus. The romantic tutu is the short, stiff skirt that stands out from the dancer. The classical tutu is the long, soft skirt.

- **Other information:** Marius Petipa created the original choreography. He presented the ballet's detailed scenario to Tchaikovsky, even specifying the rhythm, tempo, and number of measures for each dance. The Russian Ballet of Monte-Carlo was first to bring it to the United States in 1940, in a version that just had all the variations from the second act. In 1954, George Balanchine choreographed for the NYC Ballet, and it became the version that inspired several ballet companies throughout the world. Versions of the ballet are performed by young children, by minimum level dancers, and by professional ballet companies.

REFERENCES

www.pbs.org/wnet/gperf/episodes/the-nutcracker-from-the-royal-ballet/introduction/107

www.musiccenter.org/events/dance_0809_kirov.html

http://en.wikipedia.org/wiki/The_Nutcracker

TEACHING STRATEGIES   The video clip should be viewed at least three times (see chapter 1). After students record and discuss their observations and before the third viewing, use the discussion starters listed next to facilitate class discussion. Feel free to paraphrase and choose the questions that work best with your students.

From H. Scheff, M. Sprague, and S. McGreevy-Nichols, 2010, *Exploring dance forms and styles: A guide to concert, world, social, and historical dance* (Champaign, IL: Human Kinetics).

"Waltz of the Flowers"

Viewing: What Did You See?

Suggested discussion starters and questions: What did you notice about the patterns the dancers made as they progressed through the dance? Where was their focus?

Connecting: What Do You Know?

Suggested discussion starters and questions: How did the adult dancers relate to one another? How did they relate to Clara?

Responding: What Do You Think? What Do You Wonder?

Suggested discussion starters and questions: Why do you think that *Nutcracker Suite* has become one of the most performed ballets? Viewing this clip shows you only one small section of the ballet. Do you think you would like to see the whole thing? Explain.

What questions do you have about this dance? Write them down and continue your research. Some of these questions can be answered or solved through movement.

Performing: What Can You Do?

Choose both Re-create and Create, choose one of these two activities, or make your own performing work that you feel is most appropriate for your students.

Re-create After viewing the video clip, re-create three of the arm movements with other students.

Note: Use ideas from recorded observations from question 1 (What did you see?).

Create Using a Waltz step, create a dance phrase with other people where your lines intersect.

Waltz Step

1. Step out with the right foot at a low level (demi-plié).
2. Step out with the left foot on the ball of the foot.
3. Step out with the right foot on the ball of the foot.

To continue, alternate the above movement like this:

1. Step out with the left foot at a low level (demi-plié).
2. Step out with the right foot on the ball of the foot.
3. Step out with the left foot on the ball of the foot.

This makes up two Waltz steps traveling in a forward direction.

*If you need music and don't have it among your resources, use the video.

FUN FACTS There is a collection of letters between the choreographer and the composer detailing how they saw the final product. Tchaikovsky told Petipa that the music he wrote for the growing of the Christmas tree was the "biggest" music and the Christmas tree was the true prima ballerina (the lead) of the ballet. Since the training of ballet dancers was limited in the early stages, the landowners had their serfs perform their version of the ballet.

WEB EXPLORATIONS Key terms to search for include Nutcracker, classical ballet, Tchaikovsky, and Marius Petipa.

From H. Scheff, M. Sprague, and S. McGreevy-Nichols, 2010, *Exploring dance forms and styles: A guide to concert, world, social, and historical dance* (Champaign, IL: Human Kinetics).

Name: _____ Class: _____ Date: _____

STUDENT KNOWLEDGE QUEST WORKSHEET

Name of Dance: "Waltz of the Flowers" (From *Nutcracker Suite*)

1. Viewing: What did you see?
   Record your observations. Describe what you see. Be specific.

   _____

   _____

   _____

   _____

   _____

2. Connecting: What do you know?

   _____

   _____

   _____

   _____

   _____

3. Responding: What do you think? What do you wonder?

   _____

   _____

   _____

   _____

   _____

4. Performing: What can you do?

   _____

   _____

   _____

   _____

   _____

From H. Scheff, M. Sprague, and S. McGreevy-Nichols, 2010, *Exploring dance forms and styles: A guide to concert, world, social, and historical dance* (Champaign, IL: Human Kinetics).

**Consent
to Gravity**

KNOWLEDGE QUEST

INFORMATION AND TEACHING TIPS
Category M: Concert Dance (Subcategory: Contemporary Ballet)
Name of Dance: *Consent to Gravity*

Agree or not agree—That is the question.

BACKGROUND INFORMATION Before students view the video clip, share the following information with them.

- **Country or culture of origin:** This dance was created in the United States.
- **Timeline:** It was choreographed in the early 2000s on the Island Moving Company of Rhode Island.
- **Function or reason:** This dance adds to the repertoire of the dance company and a different form and style beyond classical ballet.
- **Who does this dance:** In this piece we see men and women. Contemporary ballet has a proven place in the evolution of the ballet form in many professional and regional dance companies.
- **Music and rhythms:** The dancers respond to the musicians, who are off to the side of the stage yet visible to the audience.
- **Traditional clothing or costume:** They are wearing traditional ballet costumes for modern or contemporary pieces. See the DVD clip for a clearer understanding of the look of the costume.
- **Other information:** Contemporary ballet is dedicated to being an integral part of the evolution of ballet. Innovative concepts are added to the classical form and style with the use of regular ballet vocabulary. The difference is that in the contemporary ballet form there are influences of modern dance and modification in the strict adherence to the classical form. It permits a greater range of movement that may not look like the strict body lines of the schools of ballet technique. Many of its concepts come from the ideas and innovations of 20th century modern dance, including floor work and turn-in of the legs.

George Balanchine is often considered one of the pioneers of this style of ballet. He used parallel legs and feet and pushing of the hips. He used nontraditional romantic and classical costume, exchanging leotards for tights and tunics that showed body lines. When his company, New York City Ballet, was young this also saved costs. It was also much easier to go on tour (travel) with the dance company.

Contemporary ballet choreographers keep the essence of traditional ballet, with some ballets danced on pointe while others dance in ballet shoes or with bare feet. (*Consent to Gravity* is done barefoot.) Names of choreographers that might be known for their work in the field of contemporary ballet are Robert Joffrey, Twyla Tharp, Mikhail Baryshnikov, Gerald Arpino, Alonzo King, and Paul Taylor. Often these people worked on Broadway along with the men and women who are known for their Broadway success.

REFERENCES
http://en.wikipedia.org/wiki/Contemporary_ballet

www.dancehere.com/contemporary-ballet

TEACHING STRATEGIES The video clip should be viewed at least three times (see chapter 1). After students record and discuss their observations and before the third viewing, use the suggested discussion starters listed next to facilitate class

From H. Scheff, M. Sprague, and S. McGreevy-Nichols, 2010, *Exploring dance forms and styles: A guide to concert, world, social, and historical dance* (Champaign, IL: Human Kinetics).

discussion. Feel free to paraphrase and choose the questions that work best with your students.

Viewing: What Did You See?

Suggested discussion starters and questions: What did you notice when you looked at the dancers? Describe the relationship of the dancers.

Connecting: What Do You Know?

Suggested discussion starters and questions: Female ballet dancers usually wear pointe shoes. What was different in this dance piece? What did you notice about the floor patterns and levels?

Responding: What Do You Think? What Do You Wonder?

Suggested discussion starters and questions: The musicians and singers were on stage. How do you think that makes a difference to the audience and the dancers? What would you think the difference is between working with live music and working with recorded music?

What questions do you have about this dance? Write them down and continue your research. Some of these questions can be answered through movement.

Performing: What Can You Do?

Choose both Re-create and Create, choose one of these two activities, or make your own performing work that you think is most appropriate for your students.

Re-create   Re-create some of the ways the dancers get from one level to another without a break in the action. Use a contained space.

Note: Use ideas from recorded observations from question 1 (What did you see?).

Create   Working in groups, create a small dance phrase using eight counts for each section. Vary sections by facings, levels, and strength.

*If you need music and don't have it among your resources, use the video.

FUN FACTS   In the early 1950s, as this dance form was evolving, the female dancers were sometimes called barefoot ballerinas.

WEB EXPLORATIONS   Key terms to search for include contemporary ballet, Mikhail Baryishnikov, Twyla Tharp, George Balanchine, and evolution of ballet.

From H. Scheff, M. Sprague, and S. McGreevy-Nichols, 2010, *Exploring dance forms and styles: A guide to concert, world, social, and historical dance* (Champaign, IL: Human Kinetics).

Consent to Gravity

Name: _____ Class: _____ Date: _____

STUDENT KNOWLEDGE QUEST WORKSHEET

Name of Dance: *Consent to Gravity*

1. Viewing: What did you see?
   Record your observations. Describe what you see. Be specific.

   _____

   _____

   _____

   _____

   _____

2. Connecting: What do you know?

   _____

   _____

   _____

   _____

   _____

3. Responding: What do you think? What do you wonder?

   _____

   _____

   _____

   _____

   _____

4. Performing: What can you do?

   _____

   _____

   _____

   _____

   _____

From H. Scheff, M. Sprague, and S. McGreevy-Nichols, 2010, *Exploring dance forms and styles: A guide to concert, world, social, and historical dance* (Champaign, IL: Human Kinetics).

KNOWLEDGE QUEST

INFORMATION AND TEACHING TIPS
Category M: Concert (Subcategory: Modern Dance)
Category A: Historical Dance (Subcategory: Early 20th Century)
Name of Dance: Brahms Waltz ("Rose Petals")

Brahms Waltz

Back to nature! Back to Greece!

BACKGROUND INFORMATION   Before students view the video clip, share the following information with them.

- **Translation:** Brahms Waltz is also called "Rose Petals" because the dancer releases rose petals from her hands throughout the dance.

- **Country or culture of origin:** Isadora Duncan was a U.S. citizen who for many years lived in Europe and Russia, where she produced most of her important work.

- **Timeline:** Isadora's career spanned the early 20th century. She lived from 1878 to 1927.

- **Function or reason:** Isadora danced to express emotion. She stressed that movement should come from within and not be for show or virtuosity. For this reason, many of her dances never looked exactly the same; she let her mood and the creativity of the moment influence each performance.

- **Who does this dance:** Isadora Duncan was, for the most part, a solo performer. The Isadorables were her adopted pupils. Three of these six children went on to bring her methods back to the United States. Today, there are dancers still carrying on her legacy.

- **Music and rhythms:** The music for this particular dance is Brahms' Waltz in A-Flat Major, op. 39, no. 3. Isadora most often danced to the music of the great composers. Her favorite composers, besides Johannes Brahms, were Frédéric Chopin, Johann Sebastian Bach, Ludwig Van Beethoven, Franz Schubert, Aleksandr Scriabin, and Pyotr Ilyich Tchaikovsky.

- **Traditional clothing or costume:** Isadora's trademark costuming was diaphanous, free-flowing gowns, often in Grecian styles that shocked much of polite and proper society of her time.

- **Other information:** Isadora's work could be thought of as a rebellion against the restrictions of Victorian clothing and ballet technique. She took much inspiration from Greek sculpture and other art styles such as Italian Renaissance and Art Nouveau style of the 1890s (especially its curving lines and swirls). She also valued natural movements such as walking, running, and skipping. Isadora did not develop a codified technique, but rather was able to devise a method for having each dancer discover a personal way to move to express the self from within. Isadora believed that the center of the body, the solar plexus, is energized by an emotion, which leads to movement. Isadora is noted for the use of an expressive, moveable torso, which was opposite to the ballet dancing of the time. For these two reasons, emotion creating motion and use of an expressive, moving torso, many consider Isadora as the mother of modern dance.

REFERENCES

Loewenthal, L. 1993. *The search for Isadora: The legend and legacy of Isadora Duncan.* Princeton Book Company, Publishers: Pennington, NJ.

www11.plala.or.jp/i-duncanslinks/thedanceofthefuture.html

From H. Scheff, M. Sprague, and S. McGreevy-Nichols, 2010, *Exploring dance forms and styles: A guide to concert, world, social, and historical dance* (Champaign, IL: Human Kinetics).

Brahms Waltz

Kuppers, P. 2002. *St. James encyclopedia of pop culture*. Gale Group. San Francisco, CA: CBS Interactive, Inc.

http://findarticles.com/p/articles/mi_g1epc/is_bio/ai_2419200339/

TEACHING STRATEGIES   The video clip should be viewed at least three times (see chapter 1). After students record and discuss their observations and before the third viewing, use the discussion starters listed next to facilitate class discussion. Feel free to paraphrase and choose the questions that work best with your students.

Viewing: What Did You See?

Suggested discussion starters and questions: What types of traveling (locomotor) movements did you see? How did the dancer use her arms? What was she dropping from her hands during the dance? How was she dressed? How would you describe the way the dancer used energy or force?

Connecting: What Do You Know?

Suggested discussion starters and questions: What did the shape of the last pose remind you of? Compare the types of traveling steps shown in this dance to the types of movements used by young children. Compare the clothing worn by the dancer (typical of what Isadora Duncan often wore) to the way other women usually dressed at the beginning of the 20th century and describe the possible reaction these clothes could have caused.

Responding: What Do You Think? What Do You Wonder?

Suggested discussion starters and questions: Why would the dancer drop rose petals? What do you think the rose petals represent? Please explain why you think this. If you were writing a story about this person, what would you imagine is the motivation or cause for this behavior?

   What questions do you have about this dance? Write them down and continue your research. Some of these questions can be answered through movement.

Performing: What Can You Do?

Choose both Re-create and Create, choose one of these two activities, or make your own performing work that you think is most appropriate for your students.

Re-create   Watch the video clip and copy the entrance step. Do the entrance step while dropping some construction paper just as the dancer dropped the rose petals. Reflect on how much practice it took for the performer to do this action just right without dropping too many petals at once. Remember that the petals were dropped throughout the dance, so the dancer could not drop too many petals at once.

Create   In small groups or alone, do the following:

1. Look at pictures of Greek vases, friezes, and statues, then choose three shapes to memorize.
2. Choose an order for the three shapes: one shape as the beginning shape, the second as a shape for the middle of the dance, and the third as an ending shape.
3. Choose at least two locomotor or traveling steps and decide which should go between the first and second shape and which should go between the second and last shape.

From H. Scheff, M. Sprague, and S. McGreevy-Nichols, 2010, *Exploring dance forms and styles: A guide to concert, world, social, and historical dance* (Champaign, IL: Human Kinetics).

Brahms Waltz

4. Practice your composition and share with the class.

***If you need music and don't have it among your resources, use the video.**

FUN FACTS   Isadora Duncan was also credited as being a symbol for the freedom of women's personal lives. Many people in her time considered her personal life to be scandalous because she had many male friends, danced during her pregnancies, and wore loose, filmy dance costumes. She thought women should have the same freedoms in society as men.

WEB EXPLORATIONS   Key terms to search for include Isadora Duncan, Isadorables, and dances of Isadora Duncan.

From H. Scheff, M. Sprague, and S. McGreevy-Nichols, 2010, *Exploring dance forms and styles: A guide to concert, world, social, and historical dance* (Champaign, IL: Human Kinetics).

Brahms Waltz

Name: _____ Class: _____ Date: _____

STUDENT KNOWLEDGE QUEST WORKSHEET

Name of Dance: Brahms Waltz ("Rose Petals")

1. Viewing: What did you see?
   Record your observations. Describe what you see. Be specific.

   _____

   _____

   _____

   _____

   _____

2. Connecting: What do you know?

   _____

   _____

   _____

   _____

   _____

   _____

3. Responding: What do you think? What do you wonder?

   _____

   _____

   _____

   _____

   _____

4. Performing: What can you do?

   _____

   _____

   _____

   _____

   _____

From H. Scheff, M. Sprague, and S. McGreevy-Nichols, 2010, *Exploring dance forms and styles: A guide to concert, world, social, and historical dance* (Champaign, IL: Human Kinetics).

KNOWLEDGE QUEST
INFORMATION AND TEACHING TIPS
Category M: Concert (Subcategory: Modern Dance)
Name of Dance: *Water Study* (Excerpt)

No music. Dance on its own terms.

Water Study

BACKGROUND INFORMATION   Before students view the video clip, share the following information with them.

- **Country or culture of origin:** Doris Humphrey was an important contributor to the development of the modern dance form in the United States, and for the purposes of this book, she is considered a first-generation choreographer.

- **Timeline:** *Water Study* was first performed in 1928, after Doris Humphrey left the Denishawn Company.

- **Function or reason:** In this dance, Doris Humphrey was exploring the energies of water movement. This dance shows the quiet hollow in the cresting wave, whirlpools, the seemingly suspended time at each side of an energy pull created by the ebb and flow of the water. Even the froth or foam left behind from a wave is represented by fluttering of fingers.

- **Who does this dance:** The original performers were sixteen students who performed in her company's first concert. Today, the Dance Notation Bureau has the dance written in **Labanotation** (a system of writing dance movement) and can restage this dance on any technically proficient group of dancers.

- **Music and rhythms:** *Water Study* was not choreographed to music. Humphrey wanted a dance that stood on its own without the support of music, rhythms, or even the drive of strong emotion. There is no measured timing or beat, but rather phrases based on breath. The dancers are able to synchronize their movement by listening for an aural (hearing) cue, breathing.

- **Other information.** At the time she choreographed this abstract dance, Doris Humphrey was experimenting with the physical laws that control movement. She wanted to make a dance that relied on movement alone and was not affected by traditional steps, current approved styles, or music. She was concerned with balance, unbalance, and all the movement that occurs because of these two opposing forces. Humphrey named this basic principle fall and recovery. This principle had to do with the giving in to the pull of gravity and the resistance of the pull of gravity. Doris Humphrey choreographed many dances by using "design, dynamics, rhythm and motivation" (Riley 1998, p. 243). In 1959, she wrote an important book called *The Art of Making Dances,* which outlined these ideas along with many other concepts of choreography.

REFERENCES

Chujoy, A., and P.W. Manchester. 1967. *The dance encyclopedia.* NY: Simon and Schuster.

Humphrey, D., and B. Pollack (ed.). 1991. *The art of making dances.* Hightstown, NJ: Princeton Book Company.

Riley, C. A. 1998. *The saints of modern art.* Hanover, NH: University Press of New England.

www.dorishumphrey.org

TEACHING STRATEGIES   The video clip should be viewed at least three times (see chapter 1). After students record and discuss their observations and before the third viewing, use the discussion starters listed next to facilitate class discussion. Feel free to paraphrase and choose the questions that work best with your students.

From H. Scheff, M. Sprague, and S. McGreevy-Nichols, 2010, *Exploring dance forms and styles: A guide to concert, world, social, and historical dance* (Champaign, IL: Human Kinetics).

Water Study

Viewing: What Did You See?

Suggested discussion starters and questions: What kind of locomotor or traveling steps did you see? How did the dancers create curves with their bodies? Describe the partnering. Which dance phrases were repeated? Describe them. Describe what you heard as you watched this dance.

Connecting: What Do You Know?

Suggested discussion starters and questions: Think about swinging on a swing and how it feels to swing down (like falling) and how it feels to be at the top of the arc (time feels like it has been suspended). Watch the video clip again to identify the moments in the dance that show fall and recovery. Compare the swinging movements, the falls to the floor, and how the dancers recovered to their feet to your experience of swinging on a swing. First, think about the seashore. Which movements and floor patterns (dancers' pathways on the floor as they move through space) reminded you of the movement of water?

Responding: What Do You Think? What Do You Wonder?

Suggested discussion starters and questions: Analyze and describe how the choreographer used low, middle, and high levels to create group shapes that remind the viewers of the shape of a wave. How did the dancers stay together (synchronized) without music?

What questions do you have about this dance? Write them down and continue your research. Some of these questions can be answered through movement.

Performing: What Can You Do?

Choose both Re-create and Create, choose one of these two activities, or make your own performing work that you think is most appropriate for your students.

Re-create   In the video clip, watch how the dancers did what is called a body wave. Sitting forward in your chair with your arms over your head, carve the fingertips down toward your knees until your back is rounded and you are in a forward curved shape. Then as your fingertips continue to carve behind your torso, shift your weight back behind your hips, keeping your abdominal muscles very tight. Turn your thumbs forward until your palms are away from your body. As your arms continue to circle up behind your torso, arch your back in this sequence: send your belly forward, your ribs forward, your upper chest forward, and your neck and your head forward until you are sitting upright again. You have just completed a body wave similar to the dancers in the video. Practice the movement until it is smooth. Practice the movement with classmates who will do the body wave in sequence after you.

Create   Use this quote and the directions to create a fall-and-recovery dance.

> "... natural movements of the human body are the visible evidence
> of man's ability to survive in a world dominated by gravity... gravita-
> tional force imposes itself upon every move he makes. All life fluctuates
> between resistance to and yielding to gravity."
>
> (Humphrey 1959, p. 106)

Sitting on the floor, experiment with balancing your body and falling. On your knees, experiment with giving in to gravity. Carefully, experiment from a standing position. Choose your favorite falling and balancing or resisting movement at each level. Add a transition movement that helps you to change levels between each of

From H. Scheff, M. Sprague, and S. McGreevy-Nichols, 2010, *Exploring dance forms and styles: A guide to concert, world, social, and historical dance* (Champaign, IL: Human Kinetics).

your selected falling and balancing or resisting movements. Practice your fall and recovery dance, then share it with your class.

*If you need music and don't have it among your resources, use the video.

FUN FACTS   Dancers performing *Water Study* use exhaled breath as cues to stay together. The dancers at Gallaudet University would not be able use this aural (hearing) cue because they are deaf. They use sight, memory, and many hours of practice to learn dances. When using music, they feel the sound vibrations through their feet.

WEB EXPLORATIONS   Key terms to search for include Doris Humphrey and Doris Humphrey's dance Water Study.

From H. Scheff, M. Sprague, and S. McGreevy-Nichols, 2010, *Exploring dance forms and styles: A guide to concert, world, social, and historical dance* (Champaign, IL: Human Kinetics).

Water Study

Name: _____   Class: _____   Date: _____

STUDENT KNOWLEDGE QUEST WORKSHEET

Name of Dance: *Water Study* (Excerpt)

1. Viewing: What did you see?
   Record your observations. Describe what you see. Be specific.

   _____

   _____

   _____

   _____

   _____

   _____

2. Connecting: What do you know?

   _____

   _____

   _____

   _____

   _____

   _____

3. Responding: What do you think? What do you wonder?

   _____

   _____

   _____

   _____

   _____

4. Performing: What can you do?

   _____

   _____

   _____

   _____

   _____

   _____

From H. Scheff, M. Sprague, and S. McGreevy-Nichols, 2010, *Exploring dance forms and styles: A guide to concert, world, social, and historical dance* (Champaign, IL: Human Kinetics).

KNOWLEDGE QUEST

INFORMATION AND TEACHING TIPS
Video Clip Search
Category M: Concert (Subcategory: Modern Dance)
Name of Dance: *The Traitor* (Choreographed by José Limón)

The Traitor

dance as a political statement

DIRECTIONS　Give the students the job of researching clips of and about this dance on the Internet. Many are available; have them choose one or two. They can do this in school if the Internet is available, at home, or at a library. Instruct them to take notes about the actual dancing so that they can complete the student worksheet.

BACKGROUND INFORMATION　Before students view the video clip, share the following information with them and give them the KQ worksheets to complete as a homework assignment.

- **Choreographer:** José Limón created this piece.
- **Country or culture of origin:** The work was created in the United States.
- **Timeline:** Limón's *The Traitor* was first performed August 19, 1954 in Palmer Auditorium at Connecticut College, New London, CT, by the José Limón Dance Company.
- **Function or reason:** *The Traitor* was Limón's response to a number of world events that were happening during the 1950s. These events include the McCarthy hearings and the climate of betrayal that haunted the arts and entertainment fields, the execution of two U.S. citizens for treason, and the wave of Russians who defected to the West. Limón was deeply troubled by these events and used Sholem Asch's novel *The Nazarene* as the basis for this retelling of the Christ and Judas story.
- **Who does this dance:** Eight men perform this dance.
- **Music and rhythms:** The musical score was composed by Gunther Schuller.
- **Traditional clothing or costume:** The men are wearing loose fitting clothing; a sheet is used to create a robe effect and identify the Christ figure.
- **Other information:** José Limón (1908-1972) expressed his need to make this piece as a way to express his observations of a 1950s world in *The Juilliard Review*. His experiences weren't new then, they aren't new today. He said the following about this piece:

> The tragedy of Judas Iscariot has been very close to me during the last few years, for the reason that there have been so many traitors around us, on both sides of the titanic antagonism. I have been affected by their accounts of treachery, and their confessions and self-justifications. I have great pity for these unhappy human beings, and for the anguish of spirit which they must experience and the torment in which they must live. And when I feel something very keenly, I have to make a dance about it.

Carla Maxwell, Artistic Director, Limón Dance Company.

Carla Maxwell, artistic director of the Limón Company since 1978, made the decision to reconstruct the piece and oversaw its rebirth. She says:

> This work is José at the pinnacle of his choreographic compositions. I believe that The Traitor *is among the greatest choreographic works of the twentieth century, and certainly ranks amongst Limón's best and*

From H. Scheff, M. Sprague, and S. McGreevy-Nichols, 2010, *Exploring dance forms and styles: A guide to concert, world, social, and historical dance* (Champaign, IL: Human Kinetics).

The Traitor

most important offerings. … [it is] one of the most complex pieces ever composed by José Limón. … Every aspect of the piece works in consort to realize the vision of the story. As subject matter it could not be more timely … The marriage of music, gesture, compositional form and theatrical excitement are so inexorably interwoven, that what we see is a procession of living paintings emblazoned on the stage.

Reprinted from J. Limón, 1955, "Composing a Dance," *Juilliard Review* 2(1). By permission of Limón Dance Company.

REFERENCES

www.limon.org/News/newsletter07.htm

www.answers.com/topic/jos-lim-n

www.washingtonpost.com/wp-dyn/content/article/2009/01/18/AR2009011802073.html

http://kclibrary.lonestar.edu/decade50.html

TEACHING STRATEGIES

The video clip should be viewed at least three times (see chapter 1). In the case where students are searching and observing from home, they will need to list the exact Web site so that teachers and other students can see the basis for the documentation.

Facilitate a class discussion using the discussion starters listed next. Have students use their recorded answers as a resource. Feel free to paraphrase and choose the questions that work best with your students.

Viewing: What Did You See?

Suggested discussion starters and questions: What is the first thing that strikes you about this dance? How would you describe this dance in three words? What are some of the ways the dancer expresses ideas?

Connecting: What Do You Know?

Suggested discussion starters and questions: Artists have used their art to comment on current events. What works of art do you know were created as a form of commentary? What was the artist's position on this event?

Responding: What Do You Think? What Do You Wonder?

Suggested discussion starters and questions: The following excerpts are from various reviews of *The Traitor.* How do these excerpts align with your impressions of this piece of choreography? Explain your thinking.

- "Tension abounds. There are fists, kicks, ducks, tosses, pouncing lunges, and silent screams. In this struggle of the heart, something sinister lurks, calling for self-examination."

  http://ballet-dance.com/200903/articles/limon_kennedy_20090116_morgan.html

- "Every gesture, step and movement is logical, expressive and connected in an active uninterrupted choreographic stream that tells a universal story."

  http://www.broadstreetreview.com/index.php/main/article/Jos_Limn_Dance_Company_at_Annenberg

- "…Judas expressed all the conflicting emotions of betrayal, rage, irony and doom."

  http://www.broadstreetreview.com/index.php/main/article/Jos_Limn_Dance_Company_at_Annenberg

- "There's no great need to 'act' in this work if you do the fullness of the movement—etch, flash, carve through the space using weight as a resistance."

  www.dancemagazine.com/issues/January-2008/Everything-Old-Is-New-Again

What questions do you have about this dance? Write them down and continue your research. Some of these questions can be answered through movement.

Performing: What Can You Do?

Choose both Re-create and Create, choose one of these two activities, or make your own performing work that you feel is most appropriate for your students.

Re-create   Choose movements from the dance that you feel represent one person's betrayal of another and recreate them.

Create   Create a short dance that reflects your view of a specific current world event.

*If you need music and don't have it among your resources, use the video.

FUN FACTS   Limón was born in Mexico and is known for using Mexican themes throughout his work.

WEB EXPLORATIONS   Key terms to search for include Jose Limon and The Traitor.

RECOMMENDED CLIPS

www.youtube.com/watch?v=4vCRQNw5P9c

From H. Scheff, M. Sprague, and S. McGreevy-Nichols, 2010, *Exploring dance forms and styles: A guide to concert, world, social, and historical dance* (Champaign, IL: Human Kinetics).

The Traitor

Name: _____ Class: _____ Date: _____

STUDENT KNOWLEDGE QUEST WORKSHEET

Name of Dance: *The Traitor*

1. Viewing: What did you see?
   Record your observations. Describe what you see. Be specific.

   _____

   _____

   _____

   _____

   _____

2. Connecting: What do you know?

   _____

   _____

   _____

   _____

   _____

3. Responding: What do you think? What do you wonder?

   _____

   _____

   _____

   _____

   _____

4. Performing: What can you do?

   _____

   _____

   _____

   _____

   _____

From H. Scheff, M. Sprague, and S. McGreevy-Nichols, 2010, *Exploring dance forms and styles: A guide to concert, world, social, and historical dance* (Champaign, IL: Human Kinetics).

KNOWLEDGE QUEST

INFORMATION AND TEACHING TIPS

Category M: Concert (Subcategory: Modern Dance)
Name of Dance: "Rainbow Repertory Etude" (excerpt from an American Dance Legacy Institute's [ADLI] Repertory Etude)

A choreographic masterwork, chain gangs,
rainbows, and a dance study (etude).

"Rainbow Repertory Etude"

BACKGROUND INFORMATION Before students view the video clip, share the following information with them.

- **Translation:** *Etude* is another word for a study. In dance, a study is an exploration of an idea through the creation of a short dance.

- **Country or culture of origin:** This work was conceived in the United States.

- **Timeline:** Donald McKayle's masterwork, *Rainbow 'Round My Shoulder,* was choreographed in 1959. The "Rainbow Repertory Etude" was commissioned by the American Dance Legacy Institute (ADLI) in 1996.

- **Function or reason:** Mr. McKayle choreographed the full dance, *Rainbow 'Round My Shoulder,* during the period of the Civil Rights movement. He felt that he was helping the cause by making this dance. Addressing social and political injustices was and is important to many artists. In showing the audience this character's inner thoughts and emotions as well as his physical distress, Donald McKayle was seeking to address a societal wrong, the inhumane conditions of being an inmate assigned to a chain gang.

- **Who does this dance:** "Rainbow Repertory Etude" is part of the American Dance Legacy Institute's *Repertory Etudes Dance Instructional Collection,* curated and directed by Carolyn Adams and Julie Adams Strandberg. The "Rainbow Repertory Etude" gives dance students access to the movement and ideas of this masterwork. Just as music students can learn technique and artistry from practicing simple versions of great composer's works, so can dance students learn from ADLI's *Repertory Etudes.*

- **Music and rhythms:** Several chain gang songs were originally collected for the full dance from the collection of John and Alan Lomax by Mr. McKayle, Robert de Cormier, and Milton Okun. The two songs used for "Rainbow Repertory Etude" were among these songs but were not chosen in 1959. African American sharecroppers (those who worked for a white landowner in order to live and work on a section of the land for themselves) worked as hard and long as the earlier slaves did even though they were free people. In order to keep the work pace up, they sang work songs. These songs evolved into chain gang songs, when prisoners had to keep up with the pace set by their prison guards. Both the work songs and the chain gang songs used the call and response model, but the chain gang songs focused on topics such as life in prison, missing family members, and yearning for freedom. A song leader would sing a phrase and the rest of the work crew would repeat that phrase, all the while keeping the cadence with each swing of the pick axe or other work implement.

- **Other information:** In the South, the system of sharecropping insured cheap labor for the white landowners. In order to deal with the shortage of laborers, after the Great Migration (when many African Americans took their families north), many landowners supported the institutions like Parchman Farm, really the Mississippi State Penitentiary. Parchman Farm operated like the plantations of old, complete with

From H. Scheff, M. Sprague, and S. McGreevy-Nichols, 2010, *Exploring dance forms and styles: A guide to concert, world, social, and historical dance* (Champaign, IL: Human Kinetics).

"Rainbow Repertory Etude"

slave labor now in the form of prisoners. These so-called *country farms* were also a way to control the African American population. It was common for black men to have trouble with the Jim Crow policies and laws and be sent to these institutions to work long and hard under the harsh sun with no hope of escape.

REFERENCES

Corey, M. 1996, rev. *Rainbow Etude: Resource guide and Labanotation score*. The American Dance Legacy Institute.

McGhee, D., and P. Sofras. 2003. *Roots and branches: Exploring an evolving dance legacy, volume II*. A consortium project directed by the American Dance Legacy Institute with the Harlem Dance Foundation, in collaboration with Brown University and the Southeast Center for Dance Education.

www.adli.us

http://northbysouth.kenyon.edu/2002/Music/Pages/worksongs.htm

TEACHING STRATEGIES

The video clip should be viewed at least three times (see chapter 1). After students record and discuss their observations and before the third viewing, use the discussion starters listed next to facilitate class discussion. Feel free to paraphrase and choose the questions that work best with your students.

Viewing: What Did You See?

Suggested discussion starters and questions: Which gesture was repeated most often? Describe the dancer's different ways of walking. What did you notice about the use of the levels?

Connecting: What Do You Know?

Suggested discussion starters and questions: Since this dance was about a man in a chain gang, select the movements that best show he was a prisoner. How did the gestures express the lyrics of the song?

Responding: What Do You Think? What Do You Wonder?

Suggested discussion starters and questions: Why was this man so concerned with the sun and the chance of rain? Describe which movements and energies support your answer.

Analyze how Donald McKayle portrayed the character's desperate situation through particular movements and gestures.

What questions do you have about this dance? Write them down and continue your research. Some of these questions can be answered through movement.

Performing: What Can You Do?

Choose both Re-create and Create, choose one of these two activities, or make your own performing work that you think is most appropriate for your students.

Re-create Watch and learn the hammering and hitting movements. Repeat each one many times. Reflect on how this movement makes you feel. Share this reflection with your class.

Create In small groups or partners, choreograph a short dance study based on the song lyrics from the etude. Listen especially to the section that is about swinging the hammer and the description of how the chain gang members swung the hammer. Your dance should include swinging movement and some different ways to swing a big, heavy sledgehammer. Use the levels of high, middle, and low and some traveling steps that represent sadness and ankles that are chained to someone else.

*If you need music and don't have it among your resources, use the video.

From H. Scheff, M. Sprague, and S. McGreevy-Nichols, 2010, *Exploring dance forms and styles: A guide to concert, world, social, and historical dance* (Champaign, IL: Human Kinetics).

"Rainbow Repertory Etude"

FUN FACTS   American Dance Legacy Institute has many other *Repertory Etudes* with lesson plans and videos that break the dances down so that students can learn and perform them. Please go to www.adli.us for more information and permission to perform these etudes.

WEB EXPLORATIONS

Key terms to search for include American Dance Legacy Institute, Donald McKayle, *Rainbow 'Round My Shoulder,* chain gangs, and call and response musical form.

From H. Scheff, M. Sprague, and S. McGreevy-Nichols, 2010, *Exploring dance forms and styles: A guide to concert, world, social, and historical dance* (Champaign, IL: Human Kinetics).

59

"Rainbow Repertory Etude"

Name: _____ Class: _____ Date: _____

STUDENT KNOWLEDGE QUEST WORKSHEET

Name of Dance: "Rainbow Repertory Etude"

1. Viewing: What did you see?
   Record your observations. Describe what you see. Be specific.

   _____

   _____

   _____

   _____

   _____

2. Connecting: What do you know?

   _____

   _____

   _____

   _____

   _____

3. Responding: What do you think? What do you wonder?

   _____

   _____

   _____

   _____

   _____

4. Performing: What can you do?

   _____

   _____

   _____

   _____

   _____

From H. Scheff, M. Sprague, and S. McGreevy-Nichols, 2010, *Exploring dance forms and styles: A guide to concert, world, social, and historical dance* (Champaign, IL: Human Kinetics).

KNOWLEDGE QUEST

INFORMATION AND TEACHING TIPS

Category M: Concert (Subcategory: Modern Dance)
Name of Dance: "Parsons Repertory Etude"
(excerpt from an American Dance
Legacy Institute's [ADLI] Repertory Etude)

"Parsons Repertory Etude"

A little of this and a little of that
makes a good soup and a great etude (dance study).

BACKGROUND INFORMATION   Before students view the video clip, share the following information with them.

- **Translation:** *Etude* is another word for a study. In dance, a study is an exploration of an idea through the creation of a short dance.

- **Country or culture of origin:** This dance was conceived in the United States.

- **Timeline:** In this excerpt from the "Parsons Repertory Etude" (1999) are dance motifs from the following dances choreographed by David Parsons: "Sleep Study" (1986), "Mood Swing" (1994), "The Almighty" (1996), "Destined," and "Anthem" (1998). David Parsons choreographed this etude while in residency with his company at the New York State Summer School of the Arts in the year 1999. The dance motifs and phrases were selected by Mr. Parsons himself. The Parsons Dance company members and the students of the summer program were part of the creation process.

- **Function or reason and who does this dance:** "Parsons Repertory Etude" is part of the *American Dance Legacy Institute's Repertory Etudes Dance Instructional Collection,* curated and directed by Carolyn Adams and Julie Adams Strandberg. The "Parsons Repertory Etude" gives dance students access to the movement and ideas from some of David Parsons' most memorable works. Just as music students can learn technique and artistry from practicing simple versions of great composers' works, dance students can learn from ADLI's dance etudes.

- **Music and rhythms:** The music for the "Parsons Repertory Etude" was put together by Tony Powell, who received permission from the original composer to devise an excerpt of a longer musical work, so the music is almost an etude as well.

- **Traditional clothing or costume:** The amazing dancer in the video clip, Elizabeth Koeppen, is wearing modern dancer's typical rehearsal clothing. When modern dancers rehearse they need to be able to move freely and the choreographer needs to see the movement clearly.

- **Other information:** A little of each of the following Parsons dances were combined to make the Parsons Etude.
  - "Sleep Study" (1986) uses common movements that everyone makes while they sleep.
  - "Mood Swing" (1994) is a commentary on our society's fast pace and the use of antidepressants.
  - "The Almighty" (1996) is a solo about how money can send one into madness.
  - "Anthem" (1998) is about (and danced to) actual fanfares and anthems and includes flag and ribbon dancing. Also included is some movement from another David Parsons dance called "Destined."

From H. Scheff, M. Sprague, and S. McGreevy-Nichols, 2010, *Exploring dance forms and styles: A guide to concert, world, social, and historical dance* (Champaign, IL: Human Kinetics).

"Parsons Repertory Etude"

REFERENCES

www.exploredance.com

https://media.wcu.edu/groups/dance/wiki/c0fb0/David_Parsons.html

www.thefreelibrary.com/David+Parsons:+the+challenge+of+a+higher+plateau.-a020645515

www.nytimes.com/1998/05/07/arts/dance-review-strobes-and-flags-as-more-than-gimmicks
.html?n=Top/Reference/Times%20Topics/Subjects/D/Dancing

TEACHING STRATEGIES   The video clip should be viewed at least three times (see chapter 1). After students record and discuss their observations and before the third viewing, use the discussion starters listed next to facilitate class discussion. Feel free to paraphrase and choose the questions that work best with your students.

Viewing: What Did You See?

Suggested discussion starters and questions: What everyday movement did you see in the beginning of the video clip? What kind of traveling or locomotor steps did you see? Describe the movement qualities that the dancer mostly used.

Connecting: What Do You Know?

Suggested discussion starters and questions: Mr. Parsons created a pattern of sleeping positions and then repeated them forward and backward at different speeds or tempos. What other art forms use patterns, repetition, and different speeds or tempos? Compare this modern dance with a classical ballet dance you have seen. (Teacher hint: A Venn diagram might be useful for this question.)

Responding: What Do You Think? What Do You Wonder?

Suggested discussion starters and questions: Much of the "Parsons Repertory Etude" uses powerful driving, quick movements that cover a lot of the space. If you were to make up a story for this dance, what would the plot be? How does this dance make you feel? Tell why you think this is so and defend this answer with details from the dance. Do you like this dance? Tell why you think this is so and defend this answer with details from the dance.

What questions do you have about this dance? Write them down and continue your research. Some of these questions can be answered through movement.

Performing: What Can You Do?

Choose both Re-create and Create, choose one of these two activities, or make your own performing work that you think is most appropriate for your students.

Re-create   Copy Mr. Parsons' sleeping positions and take four counts for each position. Practice this variation moving from the first position through the last and then reverse this order.

Create   Think about four or five of your favorite sleeping positions. Put them into a specific order, remembering that you must be able to change from position to position very quickly.

Practice and memorize this order, then practice and memorize how to do the positions backward. Design a count pattern that uses eight counts for each sleeping position, then four counts, and then two counts and set these counts for your sleeping position dance phrase. If you want a challenge, create a variation that uses similar sleeping positions but is done standing up.

*If you need music and don't have it among your resources, use the video.

From H. Scheff, M. Sprague, and S. McGreevy-Nichols, 2010, *Exploring dance forms and styles: A guide to concert, world, social, and historical dance* (Champaign, IL: Human Kinetics).

"Parsons Repertory Etude"

FUN FACTS   American Dance Legacy Institute has many other *Repertory Etudes* with lesson plans and videos that break the dances down so that students can learn and perform them. Please go to www.adli.us for more information and permission to perform these etudes.

WEB EXPLORATIONS   Key terms to search for include David Parsons Dance, David Parsons choreography, Sleep Study, and American Dance Legacy Institute.

From H. Scheff, M. Sprague, and S. McGreevy-Nichols, 2010, *Exploring dance forms and styles: A guide to concert, world, social, and historical dance* (Champaign, IL: Human Kinetics).

"Parsons Repertory Etude"

Name: _____ Class: _____ Date: _____

STUDENT KNOWLEDGE QUEST WORKSHEET

Name of Dance: "Parsons Repertory Etude"
(excerpt from an ADLI Repertory Etude)

1. Viewing: What did you see?
   Record your observations. Describe what you see. Be specific.

   _____

   _____

   _____

   _____

   _____

2. Connecting: What do you know?

   _____

   _____

   _____

   _____

   _____

3. Responding: What do you think? What do you wonder?

   _____

   _____

   _____

   _____

   _____

4. Performing: What can you do?

   _____

   _____

   _____

   _____

   _____

From H. Scheff, M. Sprague, and S. McGreevy-Nichols, 2010, *Exploring dance forms and styles: A guide to concert, world, social, and historical dance* (Champaign, IL: Human Kinetics).

KNOWLEDGE QUEST

INFORMATION AND TEACHING TIPS
Category M: Concert (Subcategory: Modern Dance)
Name of Dance: *Conflict*

Conflict

*A conflict can have more than one outcome;
consider understanding and friendship.*

BACKGROUND INFORMATION Before students view the video clip, share the following information with them.

- **Function or reason:** Modern dance is useful as an educational tool. As a form of communication, one can create a dance about anything. This is an example of such creative dance. Students have created all the movements; the teacher has supplied facilitation, some light guidance for organization, and a few suggestions on performance.

- **Who does this dance:** Public high school students who belong to an after-school dance group created and performed this dance.

- **Music and rhythms:** In this case, original music was created to fit this dance, but any appropriate music could be used. The music one chooses should enhance the effectiveness of the dance. A dance may also be performed without musical accompaniment.

- **Traditional clothing or costume:** Note that the costuming is very simple. Sweatpants and T-shirts are worn with the colors switched top and bottom to indicate two distinct groups in the first half of the dance. In the second half of the dance, everyone wearing the same two colors represents that there can be understanding and unity among individuals.

- **Other information:** The process of creation is modeled in the lesson in chapter 11 (page 277). After a discussion about the four aspects of conflict, students viewed the two suggested dances from *Fiddler on the Roof*. As an opening activity, students wrote about when they have experienced conflict. Each student created four movements they thought represented them as individuals. In partners, they then built dance phrases with the movements they could make look aggressive by emphasizing the fighting qualities of strength, suddenness, and bound (controlled) flow. The phrases were designed so that they could be repeated.

The choreographic structure of AB was chosen to represent the conflict section as A and the making-friends section as B. For the A section, a second choreographic structure of add-on was used. This structure could be represented in the following way: a movement was danced; this first movement was danced and then the second movement; the first two movements and then the third movement; the first three movements and then the fourth (1; 1 then 2; 1,2, then 3; 1,2,3, then 4). When all four of the movements in the phrase were danced, the add-on structure was stopped and the slow motion fight moves were added and performed with far distance (far reach) between the two dancers. Since the other two

From H. Scheff, M. Sprague, and S. McGreevy-Nichols, 2010, *Exploring dance forms and styles: A guide to concert, world, social, and historical dance* (Champaign, IL: Human Kinetics).

Conflict

dancers were absent during the development of the fight, the teacher chose to have the other two dancers remain in shapes during the fight. Oppositional staging was used in the conflict (A) section to represent the two different groups. A different ensemble staging was used in the making friends section (B) to represent a joining of the two groups. The two groups learned each other's movements that emphasized the qualities of lightness and sustained (not anxious) time and finished the dance with unison movement. This B section shows synthesis and change that grew out of the conflict of individual differences.

TEACHING STRATEGIES

The video clip should be viewed at least three times (see chapter 1). After students record and discuss their observations and before the third viewing, use the discussion starters listed next to facilitate class discussion. Feel free to paraphrase and choose the questions that work best with your students.

Viewing: What Did You See?

Suggested discussion starters and questions: In the first section, what was the pattern of repetition? Which movements showed aggression or conflict? How were the movement qualities in the second dance section changed to represent getting along with each other?

Connecting: What Do You Know?

Suggested discussion starters and questions: Compare this dance to conflicts and resolutions you may have experienced. Compare the movements used in the first and second sections. How are they different and what is similar?

Responding: What Do You Think? What Do You Wonder?

Suggested discussion starters and questions: As portrayed in this dance, what was the outcome of people not trying to understand and learn from each other? What was the outcome of people willing to learn from each other? Why do you think a choreographer would create such a dance?

What questions do you have about this dance? Write them down and continue your research. Some of these questions can be answered through movement.

Performing: What Can You Do?

Choose both Re-create and Create, choose one of these two activities, or make your own performing work that you think is most appropriate for your students.

Re-create   Choose and learn three movements from each of the two sections to make two mini dance phrases. Make sure to use the demonstrated qualities and energies. Discuss how each of the mini dance phrases felt in your body.

Create   Following your teacher's instructions, work with your classmates to create your own dance about conflict.

*If you need music and don't have it among your resources, use the video.

FUN FACTS

One does not have to be a trained dancer to perform creative or expressive dance. The performers in the video clip do not have formal technical dance training. They are regular high school students who are members of an after-school dance group.

WEB EXPLORATIONS

Key terms to search for include *Conflict,* conflict resolution, and Kanji listening (active listening).

From H. Scheff, M. Sprague, and S. McGreevy-Nichols, 2010, *Exploring dance forms and styles: A guide to concert, world, social, and historical dance* (Champaign, IL: Human Kinetics).

Name: _____ Class: _____ Date: _____

STUDENT KNOWLEDGE QUEST WORKSHEET

Conflict

Name of Dance: *Conflict*

1. Viewing: What did you see?
   Record your observations. Describe what you see. Be specific.

   _____

   _____

   _____

   _____

   _____

2. Connecting: What do you know?

   _____

   _____

   _____

   _____

   _____

3. Responding: What do you think? What do you wonder?

   _____

   _____

   _____

   _____

   _____

4. Performing: What can you do?

   _____

   _____

   _____

   _____

   _____

From H. Scheff, M. Sprague, and S. McGreevy-Nichols, 2010, *Exploring dance forms and styles: A guide to concert, world, social, and historical dance* (Champaign, IL: Human Kinetics).

Ta-Da!

KNOWLEDGE QUEST

INFORMATION AND TEACHING TIPS
Category M: Concert (Subcategory: Jazz or Musical Theater)
Name of Dance: *Ta-Da!*

Derbies and White Gloves—Tip Your Hats for Fosse

BACKGROUND INFORMATION   Before students view the video clip, share the following information with them.

- **Country or culture of origin:** This work was created in the United States. Bob Fosse got his break as a choreographer in 1954 for *Pajama Game*.

- **Timeline:** Bob Fosse's works are danced all over the world in films and Broadway shows that he choreographed. Before that he appeared as a dancer.

- **Function or reason:** Fosse had a passion for matching the dancers' abilities to his style. This particular dance was created to teach students the style and technique of Bob Fosse.

- **Who does this dance:** All ages and genders that study jazz dance can do this dance.

- **Music and rhythms:** Fosse worked with music that had catchy phrases with accented beats. There was always a bit of a surprise in the beat.

- **Traditional clothing or costume:** His hats—derby, bowler or top hat—were always tilted, sometimes covering the eyes. His dancers wore short white gloves.

- **Other information:** He used both hip and shoulder rolls as well as swiveling hips and strutting. He used backward exits. His snapping fingers (which is hard to do with gloves on) are present in many of his dances. He created a style that is recognizable in all his work throughout four decades on Broadway. The overall look of the technique displays a rounded shoulder, hip popping, elbow jutting, splayed hand, and derby.

REFERENCES

www.imdb.com/name/nm0002080/

www.pbs.org/wnet/broadway/stars/fosse_b.html

www.dancehelp.com/articles/jazz-dance/Bob-Fosse.aspx

Scheff, H., M. Sprague, and S. McGreevy-Nichols. 2005. *Experiencing dance: From student to dance artist*, p. 154. Champaign, IL: Human Kinetics.

TEACHING STRATEGIES   The video clip should be viewed at least three times (see chapter 1). After students record and discuss their observations and before the

From H. Scheff, M. Sprague, and S. McGreevy-Nichols, 2010, *Exploring dance forms and styles: A guide to concert, world, social, and historical dance* (Champaign, IL: Human Kinetics).

third viewing, use the discussion starters listed next to facilitate class discussion. Feel free to paraphrase and choose the questions that work best with your students.

Ta-Da!

Viewing: What Did You See?

Suggested discussion starters and questions: What did you notice about their accessories? Were their movements smooth or angular?

Connecting: What Do You Know?

Suggested discussion starters and questions: The hunched shoulders and the way the dancers rolled them back and forth are a signature for Fosse choreography. How is this viewed as different from many dances of the jazz form that you may have seen? The hands were also used in a distinct manner. What makes them different? The sharp music matches the angular movements of the dancers. Describe some of those movements.

Responding: What Do You Think? What Do You Wonder?

Suggested discussion starters and questions: Bob Fosse started formal dance training when he was only 13. He went to a school where he was the only boy. How would you act if you were one of a kind in a school situation?

Bob Fosse made permanent connections to many dancers, directors, and producers. How do you believe that these people have been able to keep his work and style alive long after his death?

What questions do you have about this dance? Write them down and continue your research. Some of these questions can be answered through movement.

Performing: What Can You Do?

Choose both Re-create and Create, choose one of these two activities, or make your own performing work that you think is most appropriate for your students.

Re-create   Borrow a hat. View the clip and carefully look at the posture with hat in hand and re-create the body position and the distinctive Fosse walk. *Note:* Use ideas from recorded observations from question 1 (What do you see?).

Create   Using the hat, plan a musical hat exchange with your peers. Use hip sways in rhythm with the hat sways.

*If you need music and don't have it among your resources, use the video.

FUN FACTS   Some people perceive that male dancers of all ages are physically weak. That is far from the truth.

> *"…Soon after he went to the Frederick Weaver Ballet School in Chicago, an academy where he was the only boy enrolled. He later recalled, 'I got a lot of jokes and I got whistled at a lot. But I beat up a couple of the whistlers and the rest sort of tapered off after a while.'"*
>
> www.fosse.com/features/fosse_an_introduction2.html

WEB EXPLORATIONS   Key terms to search for include Bob Fosse technique, *Pippin, Cabaret, Damn Yankees,* and *Pajama Game.*

From H. Scheff, M. Sprague, and S. McGreevy-Nichols, 2010, *Exploring dance forms and styles: A guide to concert, world, social, and historical dance* (Champaign, IL: Human Kinetics).

Ta-Da!

Name: _____ Class: _____ Date: _____

STUDENT KNOWLEDGE QUEST WORKSHEET

Name of Dance: *Ta-Da!*

1. Viewing: What did you see?
   Record your observations. Describe what you see. Be specific.

   _____

   _____

   _____

   _____

   _____

   _____

2. Connecting: What do you know?

   _____

   _____

   _____

   _____

   _____

   _____

3. Responding: What do you think? What do you wonder?

   _____

   _____

   _____

   _____

   _____

4. Performing: What can you do?

   _____

   _____

   _____

   _____

   _____

From H. Scheff, M. Sprague, and S. McGreevy-Nichols, 2010, *Exploring dance forms and styles: A guide to concert, world, social, and historical dance* (Champaign, IL: Human Kinetics).

KNOWLEDGE QUEST

INFORMATION AND TEACHING TIPS
Category M: Concert Dance (Subcategory: Jazz Dance After Jack Cole and Matt Mattox Styles)
Name of Dance: *Technically Difficult*

Technically Difficult

The legacy continues—from Cole to Mattox—it is worth the trip.

BACKGROUND INFORMATION   Before students view the video clip, share the following information with them.

- **Country or culture of origin:** This dance was created in the United States.

- **Timeline:** Jack Cole was choreographing in the mid-1930s. Matt Mattox first worked with Cole in 1948 and soon became his protégé.

- **Who does this dance:** Men, women, and students of jazz dance strive to master the Cole and Mattox style and technique, which is incorporated in the video clip.

- **Music and rhythms:** Both Cole and Mattox were comfortable creating dances for Broadway shows. Many of their pieces are set to rhythms of the East Indian dance form.

- **Traditional clothing or costume:** Appropriate dance clothes for the form could include tights, leotards, and shirts (fancy or plain). For productions, a costume designer creates what is appropriate for the production.

- **Other information:** This dance incorporates the extended style of the Jack Cole and Matt Mattox style of dance. **Jack Cole** is often called the father of theatrical jazz dance, or show dance. He developed his own style of dance based on his personal preference that was a combination of jazz, East Indian, and ballet.

His highly individual style emphasized **isolations** (moving one part of the body independently from another), angled foot placements (flexed foot), quick directional changes, and long knee slides (not to be tried by novice dancers). Cole was a master of India's Bharatanatyam, which influenced his style. (Compare with the video clip of the actual Indian dance.) Many people called his style the Cole style but he called it urban folk dance. Dancer Buzz Miller is quoted as saying, "Cole demanded a lot of isolations; for instance in an East Indian dance getting each finger to move quite separately, like a Buddha" was his aim.

From http://www.theatredance.com/choreographers/

From H. Scheff, M. Sprague, and S. McGreevy-Nichols, 2010, *Exploring dance forms and styles: A guide to concert, world, social, and historical dance* (Champaign, IL: Human Kinetics).

Technically Difficult

REFERENCES
www.theatredance.com/choreographers/

www.filmreference.com/Writers-and-Production-Artists-Ch-De/Cole-Jack

www.barbara-brune.de/teacher/mattox.htm

TEACHING STRATEGIES
The video clip should be viewed at least three times (see chapter 1). After students record and discuss their observations and before the third viewing, use the discussion starters listed next to facilitate class discussion. Feel free to paraphrase and choose the questions that work best with your students.

Viewing: What Did You See?

Suggested discussion starters and questions: Jack Cole and Matt Mattox both used Asian and Indian influences in their style and technique. Where did you see the use of this?

Connecting: What Do You Know?

Suggested discussion starters and questions: Four consecutive moves used both arms in a series of bent elbows, arms lifted, and opening out. What is the importance of the dancers being in sync? There are places in the dance where the dancers are not in sync on purpose. Describe what style of music this style reminds you of.

Responding: What Do You Think? What Do You Wonder?

Suggested discussion starters and questions: Dancers have to be strong. Where in this piece can you see this strength demonstrated? How do you think they build this strength?

What questions do you have about this dance? Write them down and continue your research. Some of these questions can be answered through movement.

Performing: What Can You Do?

Choose both Re-create and Create, choose one of these two activities, or make your own performing work that you think is most appropriate for your students.

Re-create
After viewing some of the arm movements, put them into an order. Begin and end the dance as the video clip does. *Note:* Use ideas from recorded observations from question 1 (What do you see?).

Create
Using the video clip as a guide, create a simple and short version of *Technically Difficult*. The name for this dance was titled by the choreographer. It is after the style of Jack Cole and Matt Mattox.

*If you need music and don't have it among your resources, use the video.

FUN FACTS
Matt Mattox prefers to call his style of dance *freestyle* rather than call it *jazz dance* but that doesn't mean he allows the dancers the freedom to do their own thing.

WEB EXPLORATIONS
Key terms to search for include Jack Cole, Matt Mattox, and jazz dance.

From H. Scheff, M. Sprague, and S. McGreevy-Nichols, 2010, *Exploring dance forms and styles: A guide to concert, world, social, and historical dance* (Champaign, IL: Human Kinetics).

Name: _____ Class: _____ Date: _____

STUDENT KNOWLEDGE QUEST WORKSHEET

Name of Dance: *Technically Difficult*

1. Viewing: What did you see?
   Record your observations. Describe what you see. Be specific.

   _____

   _____

   _____

   _____

   _____

2. Connecting: What do you know?

   _____

   _____

   _____

   _____

   _____

3. Responding: What do you think? What do you wonder?

   _____

   _____

   _____

   _____

   _____

4. Performing: What can you do?

   _____

   _____

   _____

   _____

   _____

From H. Scheff, M. Sprague, and S. McGreevy-Nichols, 2010, *Exploring dance forms and styles: A guide to concert, world, social, and historical dance* (Champaign, IL: Human Kinetics).

"Mambo in the Gym"

KNOWLEDGE QUEST

INFORMATION AND TEACHING TIPS
Video Clip Search
Category M: Concert (Subcategory: Musical Theater Dance)
Name of Dance: "Mambo in the Gym" (From *West Side Story*)

Romeo and Juliet, Tony and Maria—same story, different times.

DIRECTIONS Give the students the job of researching clips of and about the dance from the Internet. Many are available; have them choose one or two. They can do this in school if the Internet is available, at home, or at a library. Instruct them to take notes about the actual dancing so that they can complete the student worksheet.

BACKGROUND INFORMATION Before students view the video clip, share the following information with them and give them the KQ worksheets to complete as a homework assignment.

- **Country or culture of origin:** The musical is from the United States. The original dance form of the mambo is from Cuba.

- **Timeline:** The film version was made in 1961. The live musical opened in 1957 on Broadway in New York City. It has been reenvisioned and reproduced nationally and internationally. It is often used by high school drama groups and college or university theater programs.

- **Function or reason:** The dance is performed for entertainment, for education, and for showing a more current version of the heartbreaking romance of Romeo and Juliet.

- **Who does this dance:** This dance is performed by singers and dancers in the roles of high school students. They are at a school dance in the gym. Boys and girls dance as couples. They are from Latino families and from white immigrant families.

- **Music and rhythms:** The dance includes heavy Latino rhythms. The original Broadway show included Leonard Bernstein's music, Stephen Sondheim's lyrics, and Jerome Robbins' choreography.

- **Traditional clothing and costume:** For this number the dancers are dressed up in the dress of the 1960s. Most girls are in short prom dresses (in which they can move) and most boys are in suits.

- **Other information:** The story focuses on two gangs: the Jets, mostly young white men from immigrant families, and the Sharks, made up of members of the first American-born generation of Puerto Ricans. They clash over the turf in a neighborhood once called Hell's Kitchen.

REFERENCES:
www.wsu.edu/~brians/love-in-the-arts/west.html

www.lycos.com/info/chita-rivera--west-side-story.html

www.imdb.com/title/tt0055614/plotsummary

TEACHING STRATEGIES The video clip should be viewed at least three times (see chapter 1). In the case where students are searching and observing from home, they will need to list the exact Web site so that teachers and other students can see the basis for the documentation.

From H. Scheff, M. Sprague, and S. McGreevy-Nichols, 2010, *Exploring dance forms and styles: A guide to concert, world, social, and historical dance* (Champaign, IL: Human Kinetics).

Facilitate a class discussion using the discussion starters listed next. Have students use their recorded answers as a resource. Feel free to paraphrase and choose the questions that work best with your students.

Viewing: What Did You See?

Suggested discussion starters and questions: How do the dancers use the space? What did you see as the mood of the dancers? How did the change in music determine the change in attitude?

Connecting: What Do You Know?

Suggested discussion starters and questions: Research the following questions: The Mambo is a dance from what country? Where and why is it done today? How is the Mambo embellished from the traditional form to the stage version?

Responding: What Do You Think? What Do You Wonder?

Suggested discussion starters and questions: From watching this video clip, what do you think foreshadows the climax and outcome of the story? Do you wonder if the story line is made more exciting by the dancing? How?

What questions do you have about this dance? Write them down and continue your research. Some of these questions can be answered through movement.

Performing: What Can You Do?

Choose both Re-create and Create, choose one of these two activities, or make your own performing work that you think is most appropriate for your students.

Re-create Watch the video clip again. Re-create the Mambo step using the three-foot moves to four counts of music

Mambo step: Step out on count 1, hold and don't move on count 2, and step away using alternating feet on counts 3 and 4. Reverse the feet and change facings.

Create Take two groups of students. Each group should represent a different cultural group. Think of and make up some moves for each group that start off as fun and then become more and more hostile.

*If you need music and don't have it among your resources, use the video.

FUN FACTS This show has been performed all over the world and in many different languages. It has also been performed by a hearing impaired group. The dance remains the constant. Whether in Japan or Israel or Italy, a Mambo is a Mambo!

WEB EXPLORATIONS Key terms to search for include *West Side Story*, "Mambo in the Gym," Jerome Robbins choreography, Hell's Kitchen, New York City, Mambo.

RECOMMENDED CLIPS

- www.youtube.com/watch?v=II2uaRmlQNg
- www.youtube.com/watch?v=trqOojU_Y-w

From H. Scheff, M. Sprague, and S. McGreevy-Nichols, 2010, *Exploring dance forms and styles: A guide to concert, world, social, and historical dance* (Champaign, IL: Human Kinetics).

"Mambo in the Gym"

Name: _____ Class: _____ Date: _____

STUDENT KNOWLEDGE QUEST WORKSHEET

Name of Dance: "Mambo in the Gym" (From *West Side Story*)

1. Viewing: What did you see?
   Record your observations. Describe what you see. Be specific.

   _____

   _____

   _____

   _____

   _____

2. Connecting: What do you know?

   _____

   _____

   _____

   _____

   _____

3. Responding: What do you think? What do you wonder?

   _____

   _____

   _____

   _____

   _____

4. Performing: What can you do?

   _____

   _____

   _____

   _____

   _____

From H. Scheff, M. Sprague, and S. McGreevy-Nichols, 2010, *Exploring dance forms and styles: A guide to concert, world, social, and historical dance* (Champaign, IL: Human Kinetics).

KNOWLEDGE QUEST

INFORMATION AND TEACHING TIPS
Category M: Concert or Theatrical Dance (Subcategory: Tap)
Name of Dance: Soft Shoe

Soft Shoe

Light and easy—Fred Astaire lives on.

BACKGROUND INFORMATION   Before students view the video clip, share the following information with them.

- **Country or culture of origin:** This dance was conceived in the United States.
- **Timeline:** The soft shoe dates back to the pre-Vaudeville days. Variety shows would travel from town to town. Many performers got their start in Vaudeville, including Fred Astaire, Ray Bolger, Donald O'Connor, and many others.
- **Function or reason:** It enhances the dance portion of Vaudeville and theatrical presentations, including Broadway musicals.
- **Who does this dance:** Men, women, children, and old-time tappers do it.
- **Music and rhythms:** This dance is done in 4/4 time or 2/4 time.
- **Traditional clothing or costume:** The dancers wear costumes appropriate to the theatrical show in which the dance appears.
- **Other information:** The *Modern Tap Dance Dictionary* (Shipley 1976) says that soft shoe was originally done in soft shoes because taps were not affixed to tap shoes until around 1910. One form of soft shoe developed into the sand dance (done without taps and with sand sprinkled on the ground). In more recent forms, taps were added, especially in Vaudeville and on Broadway. The most famous soft shoe is probably "Tea For Two" from the Broadway musical *No, No, Nanette* (1925). This information was contributed by Bill Wilson, professor of theatre and dance at Rhode Island College and performer of the piece.

REFERENCES

www.ehow.com/how_4710097_soft-shoe-walk-tap-dancing.html

www.swinginhepcats.com/Swing_Dance/Videos/dances/slow_swing.html

www.britannica.com/EBchecked/topic/552464/soft-shoe

TEACHING STRATEGIES   The video clip should be viewed at least three times (see chapter 1). After students record and discuss their observations and before the third viewing, use the discussion starters listed next to facilitate class discussion. Feel free to paraphrase and choose the questions that work best with your students.

Viewing: What Did You See?

Suggested discussion starters and questions: What are the main body parts used for this dance? You see only one dancer in this section. What would it look like with many dancers doing this together?

From H. Scheff, M. Sprague, and S. McGreevy-Nichols, 2010, *Exploring dance forms and styles: A guide to concert, world, social, and historical dance* (Champaign, IL: Human Kinetics).

Soft Shoe

Connecting: What Do You Know?

Suggested discussion starters and questions: Where have you ever seen the soft shoe performed? What is the performance level? How did you know that the dancers were doing a good job?

Responding: What Do You Think? What Do You Wonder?

Suggested discussion starters and questions: This dance was named the soft shoe in the early days of its history. Why do you think that is so? Think of this dance as a man and woman duet and describe the interaction of the couple.

What questions do you have about this dance? Write them down and continue your research. Some of these questions can be answered through movement.

Performing: What Can You Do?

Choose both Re-create and Create, choose one of these two activities, or make your own performing work that you think is most appropriate for your students.

Re-create   Re-create your version of the soft shoe using the information from the instructions for **essence** and paddle step/turn that follow. Combine them or use singly added rhythms made with your hands to the beat of the music.

Essence

1. On the count of 1: Step L (to L side).
2. On the counts before 2: Flap R forward (in front of L; flap is a brush with the ball of the foot and putting it down).
3. On the count of 2: Step in place with the L.
4. On the count of 3: Step R to R side.
5. On the counts before 4: Flap L forward (in front of R).
6. On the count of 4: Step in place R.

Paddle Step/Turn

1. On the count of 1: Step L (to L side).
2. On the count of and 2: **Ball change** R-L.

These steps can be repeated over and over while turning.

Create   Using Internet and traditional library resources create a list of dancers who have performed the soft shoe in movies, on Broadway, and in Vaudeville. See how their backgrounds and dance training are similar or different. Steal a movement from each one and create a dance that is a tribute to those individuals.

*If you need music and don't have it among your resources, use the video.

FUN FACTS   This dance is known for the lightness of foot and body movement. Yet most of the dancers most famous for performing the soft shoe were men.

WEB EXPLORATIONS   Key terms to search for include Modern Tap Dance Dictionary, *No No, Nanette,* Fred Astaire, Ray Bolger, Donald O'Connor, Vaudeville, Gene Kelly, and Savion Glover.

From H. Scheff, M. Sprague, and S. McGreevy-Nichols, 2010, *Exploring dance forms and styles: A guide to concert, world, social, and historical dance* (Champaign, IL: Human Kinetics).

Name: _____ Class: _____ Date: _____

Soft Shoe

STUDENT KNOWLEDGE QUEST WORKSHEET

Name of Dance: Soft Shoe

1. Viewing: What did you see?
   Record your observations. Describe what you see. Be specific.

   _____

   _____

   _____

   _____

   _____

2. Connecting: What do you know?

   _____

   _____

   _____

   _____

   _____

3. Responding: What do you think? What do you wonder?

   _____

   _____

   _____

   _____

   _____

4. Performing: What can you do?

   _____

   _____

   _____

   _____

   _____

From H. Scheff, M. Sprague, and S. McGreevy-Nichols, 2010, *Exploring dance forms and styles: A guide to concert, world, social, and historical dance* (Champaign, IL: Human Kinetics).

Shim Sham

KNOWLEDGE QUEST

INFORMATION AND TEACHING TIPS

Category M: Concert or Theatrical Dance (Subcategory: Tap)
Name of Dance: Shim Sham or Shim Sham Shimmy

Word on the street is, Don't reinvent the wheel—steal.

BACKGROUND INFORMATION   Before students view the video clip, share the following information with them.

- **Translation:** Shim Sham has no translation per se, but the Shim Sham Shimmy refers to the shoulder action.

- **Country or culture of origin:** Two U.S. Vaudeville performers invented the Shim Sham as they were fooling around. The name of the dance was the Goofus before it became the Shim Sham. The posture of the old-time dancers relates back to African roots.

- **Timeline:** A social form (vernacular) of the Shim Sham started in the early 1900s and in 1927 became part of the tap genre. Several performers revised this dance over the years. One of the more famous ones was Frankie Manning, who danced and taught into his 90s.

- **Function or reason:** At social occasions dancers, novice and experienced, would dance side by side. In the theatrical setting it was used as a unifying culmination to the performance.

- **Who does this dance:** Everyone can learn this dance. It can be done alone or in groups.

- **Music or rhythms:** The rhythm of the dance uses syncopation and accented beats. Syncopation occurs with the placement of rhythmic accents on weak beats or portions of beats.

- **Traditional clothing or costume:** Dancers wear whatever the current style is for street wear at the time when the performance is set. If it is danced at the end of a performance, dancers wear whatever costume they last wore for the show.

- **Other information:** Historically, in the vernacular version, the torso is in a forward presentation and hips are extended back. The Shim Sham was an East Coast and Midwest phenomenon and didn't appear on the West Coast. Shim Sham dancers developed their own time and rhythmic signatures. Other dancers would steal these rhythmical patterns and steps. The practice was accepted and considered a compliment.

From H. Scheff, M. Sprague, and S. McGreevy-Nichols, 2010, *Exploring dance forms and styles: A guide to concert, world, social, and historical dance* (Champaign, IL: Human Kinetics).

REFERENCES

www.streetswing.com/histmain/z3shimsh.htm
www.youtube.com/watch?v=hubzPVG3f28

Shim Sham

TEACHING STRATEGIES

The video clip should be viewed at least three times (see chapter 1). After students record and discuss their observations and before the third viewing, use the discussion starters listed next to facilitate class discussion. Feel free to paraphrase and choose the questions that work best with your students.

Viewing: What Did You See?

Suggested discussion starters and questions: There are definite patterns of steps and then a **break** (a different step that is repeated). How many times does this happen during this dance? What does the dancer do with his arms?

Connecting: What Do You Know?

Suggested discussion starters and questions: The dancer uses his whole foot at some points and just his toes or heels at other times. What different types of sound could you hear? What other dances, games, or songs compose rhythms with their feet and hands?

Responding: What Do You Think? What Do You Wonder?

Suggested discussion starters and questions: When dancing the Shim Sham, the dancer makes rhythms and music. How can you identify the rhythmic and musical sounds made by the dancer? Shimmy refers to a shoulder movement. What does the dancer do with his shoulders?

What questions do you have about this dance? Write them down and continue your research. Some of these questions can be answered through movement.

Performing: What Can You Do?

Choose both Re-create and Create, choose one of these two activities, or make your own performing work that you think is most appropriate for your students.

Re-create Clap out the rhythm of the first set of steps. Chart it on paper. Give it to another student to read. *Note:* Use ideas from recorded observations from question 1 (What did you see?).

Create Create a clapping rhythm using eight counts. Put the sounds of the hand clapping into the feet, matching the sounds and pauses. When this has been accomplished the dancers create a cacophony of sound.

*If you need music and don't have it among your resources, use the video.

FUN FACTS In the heyday of Vaudeville all the entertainers would come on stage for the finale to do the Shim Sham. In more recent days at the Apollo Theatre audience members are called up to the dance floor for the final dance. The Shim Sham was an East Coast and Midwest phenomenon and didn't appear on the West Coast.

WEB EXPLORATIONS Key terms to search for include Shim Sham, Vaudeville, Apollo Theatre, early tap dance, and Frankie Manning.

From H. Scheff, M. Sprague, and S. McGreevy-Nichols, 2010, *Exploring dance forms and styles: A guide to concert, world, social, and historical dance* (Champaign, IL: Human Kinetics).

Shim Sham

Name: _____ Class: _____ Date: _____

STUDENT KNOWLEDGE QUEST WORKSHEET

Name of Dance: Shim Sham or Shim Sham Shimmy

1. Viewing: What did you see?
   Record your observations. Describe what you see. Be specific.

   _____

   _____

   _____

   _____

   _____

2. Connecting: What do you know?

   _____

   _____

   _____

   _____

   _____

3. Responding: What do you think? What do you wonder?

   _____

   _____

   _____

   _____

   _____

4. Performing: What can you do?

   _____

   _____

   _____

   _____

   _____

From H. Scheff, M. Sprague, and S. McGreevy-Nichols, 2010, *Exploring dance forms and styles: A guide to concert, world, social, and historical dance* (Champaign, IL: Human Kinetics).

KNOWLEDGE QUEST

INFORMATION AND TEACHING TIPS
Video Clip Search
Category M: Concert (Subcategory: Crossover)
Category A: Social (Subcategory: Alone in a group)
Category A: World (Subcategory: North America)
Name of Dance: Hip-Hop

Hip-Hop

"Expression takes many forms."

(http://knowledgerush.com/kr/encyclopedia/Definition_of_art/)

DIRECTIONS   Give the students the job of researching clips of and about hip-hop dance on the Internet. Many are available; they are to choose one or two. They can do this in school if the Internet is available, at home, or at a library. Instruct them to take notes about the actual dancing so that they can complete the student worksheet.

BACKGROUND INFORMATION   Before students view the video clip, share the following information with them and give them the KQ worksheets to complete as a homework assignment.

- **Country or culture of origin:** Hip-hop originated in the United States in the Bronx, New York.

- **Timeline:** In 1925, Earl Tucker (aka Snake Hips), a performer at the Cotton Club, invents a dance style similar to today's hip-hop moves. Similar moves would later inspire an element of hip-hop culture known as break dancing. In 1956, Clive Campbell is born in Kingston, Jamaica. Campbell would later become the father of hip-hop. In 1962, James Brown records *Live At The Apollo*. Brown's drummer, Clayton Fillyau, influences a sound that is now known as the break beat. In 1965, Muhammad Ali (born Cassius Clay) defeats Sonny Liston in the sixth round. Before the bout, however, Ali recited one of his earliest known rhymes which is said to be the start of rapping. In 1967, Clive Campbell migrates to the United States at the age of 11. Because of his size, kids at Alfred E. Smith High School nickname him Hercules. He later becomes a writer and changes his name to Kool Herc. In 1970, The Last Poets release their self-titled debut album on Douglas Records; it combines jazz instrumentations with heartfelt spoken word.

- **Function or reason:** According to J-Decibel, "Hip hop is the way of portraying skills, creativeness, teaching righteousness and feeding the listeners with knowledge of the self" (Hurwich 2009). In other words, hip-hop is a form of art, and, like other art forms, simply reflects the environment in which it was created. If anything, hip-hop may have slowed the violence on New York City streets by providing gangs with an alternative way to express sovereignty and gain respect instead of using guns. As Dave (aka DaveyD) Cook once wrote, the hip hop culture is "an accessible form of self expression capable of exciting positive affirmation from one's peers" (Hurwich 2009).

- **Who does this dance:** Boys and girls and young adults do hip-hop on the streets and more recently in concert and competition forms. Since it is a very athletic form of movement the dancers need to have flexibility and strength.

- **Music and rhythms:** This dance uses the break beat. "Rock Steady," recorded by Aretha Franklin on vocals and Bernard Purdie on drums is a great example.

From H. Scheff, M. Sprague, and S. McGreevy-Nichols, 2010, *Exploring dance forms and styles: A guide to concert, world, social, and historical dance* (Champaign, IL: Human Kinetics).

Hip-Hop

- **Traditional clothing or costume:** Anything goes, but generally the men wear loose, long pants (warm-up style) and oversized shirts and women wear the same thing but sometimes wear tighter-fitting warm-up suits. Often there is some kind of head gear.

- **Other information:** The B-boys and B-girls of New York City were largely influenced by Capoeira (a Brazilian form of self-defense disguised as dance), tap, the Lindy Hop, James Brown's Good Foot, Salsa, Afro-Cuban, and various African and Native American dances. West Coast funk dance styles, such as pop and lock, were similarly inspired by dances such as the Funky Chicken, Chubby Checker's Twist, James Brown's the Popcorn, and the Jerk; by cartoon animation; and by movement from everyday life.

REFERENCES

www.b-boys.com/classic/hiphoptimeline.html

http://rap.about.com/od/hiphop101/a/hiphoptimeline.htm

www.danz.org.nz/dancestyles.php

TEACHING STRATEGIES

The video clip should be viewed at least three times (see chapter 1). In the case where students are searching and observing from home, they will need to list the exact Web site so that teachers and other students can see the basis for the documentation.

Facilitate a class discussion using the discussion starters listed next. Have students use their recorded answers as a resource. Feel free to paraphrase and choose the questions that work best with your students.

Viewing: What Did You See?

Suggested discussion starters and questions: Quick moves, athletic steps, full use of entire body, choppy, high energy, strong moves, and angles are terms associated with hip-hop dances. Which of those do you see?

Connecting: What Do You Know?

Suggested discussion starters and questions: What kind of moves do the dancers use? Which parts of their bodies do they use most? Why are they wearing the type of dress that they are?

Responding: What Do You Think? What Do You Wonder?

Suggested discussion starters and questions: Some experts think that break dancing and hip-hop are linked to Capoeira. Check out the link on hip-hop and break dancing and the link on Capoeira listed on this form. Compare and contrast the moves and the energy.

What questions do you have about this dance? Write them down and continue your research. Some of these questions can be answered through movement.

Performing: What Can You Do?

Choose both Re-create and Create, choose one of these two activities, or make your own performing work that you think is most appropriate for your students.

Re-create Pick two moves from the hip-hop video clip. Also pick two moves from the suggested Capoeira clip. Re-create those moves to the best of your ability, thinking about what would be safe for you to do. Find similar moves in each dance form.

From H. Scheff, M. Sprague, and S. McGreevy-Nichols, 2010, *Exploring dance forms and styles: A guide to concert, world, social, and historical dance* (Champaign, IL: Human Kinetics).

Hip-Hop

Create   Make a short dance using the movement you chose to re-create. Change the facings and the energy level. Make the dance 24 counts long.

*If you need music and don't have it among your resources, use the video.

FUN FACTS   Parents were sure that this dance form would corrupt and build anger in their children; it turned out to be the opposite. The kids who danced learned to put their heart and soul into every move. Gangs found a way to compete in a non-violent way and to have respect for their own bodies.

WEB EXPLORATIONS   Key terms to search for include hip-hop, break dance, Michael Jackson, B-boys, B-girls, and rapping.

RECOMMENDED CLIPS

- www.youtube.com/watch?v=8FX_NFOgQUE
- http://vimeo.com/groups/3430/videos/3077823

From H. Scheff, M. Sprague, and S. McGreevy-Nichols, 2010, *Exploring dance forms and styles: A guide to concert, world, social, and historical dance* (Champaign, IL: Human Kinetics).

Hip-Hop

Name: _____ Class: _____ Date: _____

STUDENT KNOWLEDGE QUEST WORKSHEET

Name of Dance: Hip-Hop

1. Viewing: What did you see?
   Record your observations. Describe what you see. Be specific.

   _____

   _____

   _____

   _____

   _____

2. Connecting: What do you know?

   _____

   _____

   _____

   _____

   _____

3. Responding: What do you think? What do you wonder?

   _____

   _____

   _____

   _____

   _____

4. Performing: What can you do?

   _____

   _____

   _____

   _____

   _____

From H. Scheff, M. Sprague, and S. McGreevy-Nichols, 2010, *Exploring dance forms and styles: A guide to concert, world, social, and historical dance* (Champaign, IL: Human Kinetics).

KNOWLEDGE QUEST

INFORMATION AND TEACHING TIPS
Video Clip Search
Category M: Concert Dance (Crossover Style)
Name of Dance: Contemporary Dance

Contemporary Dance

Fusion and emotion fuels an expressive dance style.

DIRECTIONS   Give the students the job of researching clips of and about contemporary dance on the Internet. Many are available; have them choose one or two. They can do this in school if the Internet is available, at home, or at a library. Once they have viewed and chosen their favorite clips, share the following information with them. Instruct them to take notes about the actual dancing so that they can complete the student worksheet.

BACKGROUND INFORMATION   Before students view the video clip, share the following information with them.

- **Translation:** The word *contemporary* means modern. While the form of modern dance is often referred to as contemporary dance, for the purposes of this book, the term *contemporary dance* will mean the dance style that has emerged from lyrical dance. Many sources use the terms *contemporary* and *lyrical* interchangeably.

- **Country or culture of origin:** Some research states that contemporary dance started in Europe and was then transported to the United States.

- **Function or reason:** The main goal of a contemporary dance is to express, through movement and facial expression, the lyrics of a song or to represent the music's quality and tone. While some dance companies do perform in this style and some stage shows of contemporary music stars use this type of dance, contemporary dance is most often seen in the private sector (dance studios) and in dance competitions.

- **Who does this dance:** The most successful contemporary dancers, both male and female, have a high level of technical skill with a great deal of strength and flexibility. This style of dance includes a fusion of ballet, modern, and jazz moves, so the dancer should have technical skill in all these forms. Because of the emphasis on expression, one will often see older dancers (25-30 years old), who have had more life experience, performing this type of dance successfully.

- **Music and rhythms:** While a large range of music types can be used, many times contemporary dance uses songs by popular music artists.

- **Traditional clothing or costume:** Costuming is chosen to best express the topic of the song and to show the physique of the performers as they perform the technically difficult movements.

- **Other information:** Contemporary dance uses many modern dance elements, including contract–release, fall and recovery, floor work, and unusual supports and lifts in partnering. It also often includes improvisation (movement done without preplanning) expressing how the dancer feels at a particular moment.

REFERENCES

http://realitytv.about.com/od/soyouthinkyoucandance/ss/Choreographers_4.htm

www.theamericandancecompetition.com/jazzlyrical.htm

www.wisegeek.com/what-is-lyrical-dance.htm

www.dance.net/topic/5246209/1/Lyrical/Contemporary-Lyrical-What-s-the-difference.html&replies=22

www.ehow.com

From H. Scheff, M. Sprague, and S. McGreevy-Nichols, 2010, Exploring dance forms and styles: A guide to concert, world, social, and historical dance (Champaign, IL: Human Kinetics).

Contemporary Dance

TEACHING STRATEGIES   The video clip should be viewed at least three times (see chapter 1). In the case where students are searching and observing from home, they will need to list the exact Web site so that teachers and other students can see the basis for the documentation.

After students record and discuss their observations and before the third viewing, use the suggested questions and discussion starters listed next to facilitate class discussion. Feel free to paraphrase and choose the questions that work best with your students.

Viewing: What Did You See?

Suggested discussion starters and questions: What levels did you see the dancer(s) use? Which movements showed that the dancers needed to be both strong and flexible? What did you notice about their facial expressions?

Connecting: What Do You Know?

Suggested discussion starters and questions: What other kind of dance does this remind you of and why? How is it like that dance?

Responding: What Do You Think? What Do You Wonder?

Suggested discussion starters and questions: Fusion, or the blending of different dance forms and styles, has resulted in many popular dances. Why do many people consider contemporary dance a fusion of certain dance forms and styles? Compare it to another dance that could be considered a fusion dance style.

What questions do you have about contemporary dance? Write them down and continue your research. Some of these questions can be answered through movement.

Performing: What Can You Do?

Choose both Re-create and Create, choose one of these two activities, or make your own performing work that you feel is most appropriate for your students.

Re-create   View the chosen video and according to the topic of the dance. Select the six most expressive movements. Practice doing them. Do not forget to include the facial expressions. Perform them for your classmates.

Create   According to the topic or emotion of the dance video you chose, choreograph (create) six expressive movements. Put these movements in an order you like best. Perform these movements with improvised (movement done without preplanning) transitional movement sections between each of the choreographed movements. Perform this short study for your peers.

*If you need music and don't have it among your resources, use the video.

FUN FACTS   The immensely popular television show "So You Think You Can Dance" has highlighted contemporary dance and introduced it to wider audiences here in the United States and in Australia. One choreographer, Mia Michaels, has created some very memorable pieces. She has also choreographed for Celine Dion, Madonna, Ricky Martin, Gloria Estefan, and Prince.

WEB EXPLORATIONS   Key terms to search for include lyrical contemporary dance, lyrical dance, Mia Michaels contemporary dance, Wade Robson contemporary dance, and Mia Michaels Bench Dance.

From H. Scheff, M. Sprague, and S. McGreevy-Nichols, 2010, *Exploring dance forms and styles: A guide to concert, world, social, and historical dance* (Champaign, IL: Human Kinetics).

Contemporary Dance

RECOMMENDED CLIPS

- http://joiekoo.multiply.com/video/item/5
- http://joiekoo.multiply.com/video/item/1/Contemporary_Dance_by_Mia_Michaels
- http://video.google.com/videosearch?hl=en&q=mia+michaels+bench+dance&revid=412371099&ei=U34sSoCtFKTwMsGmvMkJ&resnum=0&um=1&ie=UTF-8&ei=vYAsSqjaGoKkNarN-OoJ&sa=X&oi=video_result_group&resnum=4&ct=title#
- http://video.google.com/videosearch?hl=en&q=mia+michaels+bench+dance&revid=412371099&ei=U34sSoCtFKTwMsGmvMkJ&resnum=0&um=1&ie=UTF-8&ei=vYAsSqjaGoKkNarN-OoJ&sa=X&oi=video_result_group&resnum=4&ct=title#q=wade+robeson+contemporary+dance&hl=en&emb=0

From H. Scheff, M. Sprague, and S. McGreevy-Nichols, 2010, *Exploring dance forms and styles: A guide to concert, world, social, and historical dance* (Champaign, IL: Human Kinetics).

Contemporary Dance

Name: _____ Class: _____ Date: _____

STUDENT KNOWLEDGE QUEST WORKSHEET

Name of Dance: Contemporary Dance

1. Viewing: What did you see?
   Record your observations. Describe what you see. Be specific.

   _____

   _____

   _____

   _____

   _____

2. Connecting: What do you know?

   _____

   _____

   _____

   _____

   _____

3. Responding: What do you think? What do you wonder?

   _____

   _____

   _____

   _____

   _____

4. Performing: What can you do?

   _____

   _____

   _____

   _____

   _____

From H. Scheff, M. Sprague, and S. McGreevy-Nichols, 2010, *Exploring dance forms and styles: A guide to concert, world, social, and historical dance* (Champaign, IL: Human Kinetics).

KNOWLEDGE QUEST

INFORMATION AND TEACHING TIPS
Video Clip Search
Category M: Concert (Subcategory: Crossover Style)
Category A: World (Subcategory: India)
Name of Dance: Bollywood Dance

Bollywood Dance

"Yes, in the moonlight. You and me. You'll dance with me, won't you?"

Slumdog Millionaire (2008)

DIRECTIONS   Give students the job of researching clips of and about Bollywood dance on the Internet. Many clips are available; have them choose one or two. They can do this in school if the Internet is available, at home, or at a library. Instruct them to take notes about the actual dancing so that they can complete the student worksheet.

BACKGROUND INFORMATION   Before students view the video clip, share the following information with them and give them the KQ worksheets to complete as a homework assignment.

- **Translation: Bollywood** is the informal term popularly used for the Mumbai-based Hindi language film industry in India.

- **Country or culture of origin:** Bollywood dance is used in many Indian films. It is a mixture of numerous styles, including Kathak, Indian folk, Western popular, jazz, and belly dancing.

- **Timeline:** The first silent feature film was made in India in 1913. By the 1930s, the industry was producing over 200 films per year and in the 1950s, lavish romantic musicals and melodramas were the staple fare at the cinema.

- **Function or reason:** A popular form of entertainment, Bollywood movies highlight elaborate dance sequences and original soundtracks. Melodrama and romance are common ingredients in Bollywood films.

- **Who does this dance:** Men, women, and children dance this dance.

- **Music and rhythms:** Songs from Bollywood movies are generally prerecorded by professional playback singers; the actors lip-synch the words to the song on screen, often while dancing. Bollywood dances usually follow songs. Songs typically comment on the action that takes place in the movie. Sometimes, a song is reflective of a character's thoughts.

- **Traditional clothing or costume:** Clothing and costume are an extremely important element of the Bollywood dance. Costumes can range anywhere from traditionally colorful Indian clothing to Western dress. To a great extent, the costume will determine the feel that the dance will have in the film.

- **Other information:** Over the years, Bollywood movies have developed their own signature style of song and dance, which combines the rich texture of India's many classical and folk dances and fuses them with elements of jazz, hip-hop, Arabic, and Latin forms. The hero or heroine often performs with a troupe of supporting dancers.

SOURCES

http://en.wikipedia.org/wiki/Bollywood

www.chandrakantha.com/articles/indian_music/nritya/bollywood.html

www.rhythm-india.com/WhatisBollywoodDance.html

From H. Scheff, M. Sprague, and S. McGreevy-Nichols, 2010, *Exploring dance forms and styles: A guide to concert, world, social, and historical dance* (Champaign, IL: Human Kinetics).

Bollywood Dance

TEACHING STRATEGIES   Have students view the video clip at least three times (see chapter 1 for details). In the case where students are searching and observing from home, they will need to list the exact Web site they used so that teachers and other students can see the basis for documentation.

Facilitate a class discussion using the discussion starters listed next. Have students use their recorded answers as a resource. Feel free to paraphrase and choose the questions that work best with your students.

Viewing: What Did You See?

Suggested discussion starters and questions: What is the first thing that strikes you about this dance? Describe this dance in three words. How do the dancers relate to one another? How do the dancers move around the floor?

Connecting: What Do You Know?

Suggested discussion starters and questions: When have you ever seen a dance like this performed? How was it like this dance? How was it different?

Responding: What Do You Think? What Do You Wonder?

Suggested discussion starters and questions: Working with a large number of dancers as in Bollywood dances can be challenging. One way to deal with it is to place the dancers in a variety of formations such as lines or circles. What did you notice about the way the choreographer moved the dancers around and placed them in the performance space?

What questions do you have about this dance? Write them down and continue your research. Some of these questions might be answered through movement.

Performing: What Can You Do?

Choose both Re-Create and Create, choose one of these two activities, or make your own performing work that you think is most appropriate for your students.

Re-Create   Choose three arm movements from the video to re-create in a sequence. Teach the class this sequence and have them perform it as a whole group.

Create   Divide the class up into small groups. Have each group create a 16-count movement sequence in the style of Bollywood dance. Decide on a formation to place the dancers in (e.g., circles, lines, clusters) and then add movement to enter and exit the performance space. Perform as a group dance with one group following after the other.

*If you need music and don't have it among your resources, use the video.

FUN FACTS   With the success of films such as the Oscar-winning *Slumdog Millionaire*, Bollywood films and dance have now come into the global spotlight.

WEB EXPLORATIONS   Key terms to search for include Bollywood, India film industry, *Slumdog Millionaire*, and *Bend It Like Beckham*.

RECOMMENDED CLIPS

- http://pinoysphere.com/tag/slumdog-millionaire-dance-scene-on-youtube
- www.youtube.com/watch?v=vewp4vJojac
- www.youtube.com/watch?v=8IVhtt6KX5w
- www.youtube.com/watch?v=hqtILz_IGSk

From H. Scheff, M. Sprague, and S. McGreevy-Nichols, 2010, *Exploring dance forms and styles: A guide to concert, world, social, and historical dance* (Champaign, IL: Human Kinetics).

Name: _____ Class: _____ Date: _____

STUDENT KNOWLEDGE QUEST WORKSHEET

Name of Dance: Bollywood Dance

1. Viewing: What did you see?
   Record your observations. Describe what you see. Be specific.

   _____

   _____

   _____

   _____

   _____

2. Connecting: What do you know?

   _____

   _____

   _____

   _____

   _____

3. Responding: What do you think? What do you wonder?

   _____

   _____

   _____

   _____

   _____

4. Performing: What can you do?

   _____

   _____

   _____

   _____

   _____

From H. Scheff, M. Sprague, and S. McGreevy-Nichols, 2010, *Exploring dance forms and styles: A guide to concert, world, social, and historical dance* (Champaign, IL: Human Kinetics).

CHAPTER 6

World Dance

"The truest expression of a people is in its dances and its music. Bodies never lie."

Agnes De Mille (The Dance Notebook 1984)

World dance can be defined as a category of dance that represents the traditions, beliefs, and values of a specific community and its people. It has also been referred to as ethnic, cultural, and folk dance. Within this category exist many subcategories. Of the myriad world dances that exist, we have selected 25 that are included on the DVD. Under this category are the common geographic subcategories of North America, South and Central America, Europe, Asia, Africa, and Oceania.

Purposes of World Dance

The world dances discussed in this chapter are also social in nature. When performed for an audience, they become theatrical dance. These subcategories affect their purposes. One social purpose is to commune for a celebration, a ritual, or other social occasion. World dances reflect the cultural traditions of the country where they were developed. These dances are usually passed down through generations of families and communities. They bring a sense of pride, community, and identity to the people of that culture. Dancing brings people together which is an important characteristic of world dance.

A theatrical purpose of world dance is to expose dances to the public for entertainment, education, or personal fulfillment. Viewing these dances might rekindle an interest in personal heritage. National and international companies such as the Chuck Davis African American Dance Ensemble (from North Carolina), Beta Dance Troupe (from Israel), the Moiseyev Dance Company (from Russia), and

Riverdance (from Ireland) are just a few of the world dance companies that tour annually to many parts of the world. Many of these companies have DVDs of full-length works for sale online. Watching these videos gives the viewer a basic understanding of different cultures.

Sacredness of World Dances

Some cultures have sacred dances that they do not want people outside their culture to learn and perform. For example, the Maori Haka dance has been exploited in advertising, Hollywood films, cartoons, and by non-Maori sporting organizations. The Maori people have expressed that these groups are culturally insensitive and the public displays have undermined the Haka's traditional sacred significance. In February of 2009 the Maori people won a court battle that prompted the New Zealand government to assign intellectual property rights in one style of the traditional Maori Haka called the Ka Mate, to Ngati Toa, a North Island tribal group.

When observing and re-creating world dances, it is important to study the cultural contexts associated with those dances. Teach your students to research and be conscientious of people's traditions and beliefs. An innocent movement in one dance or dance form could translate into a spiritual or even offensive gesture in another.

Changes in World Dance

Traditional dance forms are not static. Over the years the dance steps may change, but the intent and essence endure. A look at the **Dabkee** is a good example. This dance is danced differently in different countries, including Greece, Syria, Egypt, Israel, and Jordan. The Dabkee looks very different when you see it danced in different countries. All versions use the grapevine step traveling counterclockwise but the accented beats and stomps occur in different parts of the movement patterns. When comparing the Freilach from Eastern Europe with the Dabkee and the Armenian village dance, the Bod, the grapevine step appears in all three.

When viewing different world dances one can often see glimpses of similar stylistic movements. This similarity is most prevalent when the countries are in close proximity. For your reference, you can go to the Information and Teaching Tips pages on the Knowledge Quest forms or video clips on the DVD to compare stylistic movements in similar dances. In Slavic countries the heavy stomping of the men in boots is clearly evident from one land to another. The arm movements and heelwork in the Flamenco are similar to movements in the dances of the Gypsies that traveled throughout the Middle East and Spain. The twisting and rotating hand movements in Flamenco dance are also prevalent in Middle Eastern dances. The hip sway in Flamenco dance also appears in other Latin dance forms, including Salsa and Perico Ripiao (a faster version of the Merengue).

Styles and techniques are sometimes linked to the topography of the country. For example, male dancers from Georgia (the country) seem to have strong legs. The need for leg strength may originate from moving across the mountainous terrain. When one views these dancers performing, the visual impression is that they are flying through the air and have springs in their legs.

Summary

All around the world, people dance and have danced for celebrations, for rites of passage, to create a sense of community, for fun, in protest, and as a way to preserve their heritage. As well as being an art form, dance is a part of culture.

The following pages contain the Knowledge Quest worksheets for the following dances, unless otherwise noted. Those with a DVD icon next to them have video clips that appear on the DVD.

North America

- (DVD) Native American dances (women's eastern blanket dance and men's eastern war dance)
- (DVD) Virginia Reel
- Hip-hop (see KQ worksheet in chapter 5)
- (DVD) Break dancing (see KQ worksheet in chapter 7)

South and Central America

- Capoeira
- (DVD) Perico Ripiao
- (DVD) Salsa (see KQ worksheet in chapter 7)
- (DVD) El Fon de la Negra (Mexican folkloric, from a different part of Mexico than El Tilingo Lingo)
- (DVD) El Tilingo Lingo (Mexican folkloric; from a different part of Mexico than El Fon de la Negra)
- (DVD) La Bomba
- Tinku (a dance from Bolivia)

Europe

- (DVD) Der Unterwestner
- Flamenco (also a concert dance)
- Cossack dancing (also a concert dance)
- Irish dancing (also a concert and social dance)
- (DVD) Freilach (also a social dance)
- (DVD) Polka (see KQ Worksheet in chapter 7)
- Cancan (also a concert dance)
- Contra dancing (see KQ worksheet in chapter 7)

Asia

- (DVD) Kathak
- (DVD) Hmong dance
- (DVD) Raqs al Balas
- Barong dance (a dance from Bali)
- (DVD) Bharatanatyam
- (DVD) Dabkee (also a social dance)

Africa

- Gumboot dance (also a social dance)
- ⊙DVD Raks Assaya
- ⊙DVD Tiriba (also a social dance)

Oceania

- ⊙DVD Hula
- ⊙DVD Tahitian dance
- Maori Haka dance

KNOWLEDGE QUEST

INFORMATION AND TEACHING TIPS
Category M: World (Subcategory: North America)
Category A: Social (Subcategory: Alone in a group)
Names of Dances: Women's Eastern Blanket Dance; Men's Eastern War Dance

Native American Dances

War and Peace—A Native American Tale

BACKGROUND INFORMATION Before students view the video clip, share the following information with them.

- **Country or culture of origin:** Many communities of Native North Americans (sometimes called Nations) exist in the United States. The women's blanket dance has its origins with the Narragansett Indians of Rhode Island. Other Nations may have their own versions. Many Nations have their version of the war dance but this one is from the Narragansett nation in Rhode Island.

- **Timeline:** Documentation of both dances goes back to the early 1800s.

- **Function or reason:** The men's eastern war dance is a warrior dance and represents a man's victory, courage and honor. The women's eastern blanket dance is an eastern North American style dance and is performed with a woman's personal blanket.

- **Who does this dance:** Men and boys do the war dance and women and girls do the blanket dance.

- **Music and rhythms:** The dances are done to drum beats and chanting. The woman's dance can be a slow, graceful walk or a bouncy double step according to the life and age of the woman.

- **Traditional clothing or costume:** Clothing and hairstyles are slightly different from Nation to Nation. Mohegan women wear knee-length skirts or straight-line dresses and the men wear loin cloths or leggings. Shirts are not worn during warmer weather, but those tribes that are in colder climates wear deerskin tunics or loose-fitting shirts. Men and women both wear earrings in their ears and some have painted faces. Their feet are covered by moccasins, which are ankle length or came up over their calves. Not all Nations wear the long headdresses. The men often have chest decoration for when they dance the war dances. They are made of beads or pieces of wood bark.

- **Other information:** Among other reasons for Native Americans dancing is the belief that these dances are for good hunting, for bountiful harvest, for good outcomes to wars, and to assure a good life. The younger, unmarried women use their dance as a courtship dance and they each show off their blanket. At the end of the dance they drop the blanket to their feet. The dance represents a woman's stages of life. The war dance has

From H. Scheff, M. Sprague, and S. McGreevy-Nichols, 2010, *Exploring dance forms and styles: A guide to concert, world, social, and historical dance* (Champaign, IL: Human Kinetics).

Native American Dances

its origins with the Eastern Woodland Indian tribes but many Nations have their own version that is very similar.

REFERENCES

www.inquiry.net/OUTDOOR/native/dance/index.htm

www.sbgmusic.com/html/teacher/reference/cultures/nativedance.html

www.native-languages.org/clothing.htm

TEACHING STRATEGIES

The video clip should be viewed at least three times (see chapter 1). After students record and discuss their observations and before the third viewing, use the discussion starters listed next to facilitate class discussion. Feel free to paraphrase and choose the questions that work best with your students.

Viewing: What Did You See?

Suggested discussion starters and questions: How did the dancers move? Did the dancers use props during their dances? Did you see movement patterns?

Connecting: What Do You Know?

Suggested discussion starters and questions: Native Americans dance for many reasons. What reasons can you talk or write about? What makes the dancers speed up or slow down? Did you notice the movement of the two women in the blanket dance? How are the men's steps different from the women's steps?

Responding: What Do You Think? What Do You Wonder?

Suggested discussion starters and questions: The women are standing upright. Why might they be in that posture? The men are hunched over. Why might they assume that position?

What questions do you have about this dance? Write them down and continue your research. Some of these questions can be answered through movement.

Performing: What Can You Do?

Choose both Re-create and Create, choose one of these two activities, or make your own performing work that you think is most appropriate for your students.

Re-create   Re-create the blanket dance and warrior dance. *Note:* Use ideas from recorded observations from question 1 (What do you see?).

Create   Plan a floor pattern to create a path for the dances. Put both sets of dancers on the floor at the same time, making sure that they do not travel the same path or bump into each other.

*If you need music and don't have it among your resources, use the video.

FUN FACTS

If you want to learn more about Native American dance, do some more research. A source of interesting, detailed information is in a book called *Native American Dance Steps* by Bessie Evans and May G. Evans. It was published by Dover Publications, Inc., of Mineola, NY, in 2003.

WEB EXPLORATIONS

Key terms to search for include Native American dances, Indian war dances, Eastern Woodlands Indian dances, Pueblo dances, Blanket dances, and Native American dance.

From H. Scheff, M. Sprague, and S. McGreevy-Nichols, 2010, *Exploring dance forms and styles: A guide to concert, world, social, and historical dance* (Champaign, IL: Human Kinetics).

Name: _____ Class: _____ Date: _____

STUDENT KNOWLEDGE QUEST WORKSHEET

Name of Dance: Women's Eastern Blanket Dance; Men's Eastern War Dance

1. Viewing: What did you see?
   Record your observations. Describe what you see. Be specific.

   _____

   _____

   _____

   _____

   _____

2. Connecting: What do you know?

   _____

   _____

   _____

   _____

   _____

3. Responding: What do you think? What do you wonder?

   _____

   _____

   _____

   _____

   _____

4. Performing: What can you do?

   _____

   _____

   _____

   _____

   _____

From H. Scheff, M. Sprague, and S. McGreevy-Nichols, 2010, *Exploring dance forms and styles: A guide to concert, world, social, and historical dance* (Champaign, IL: Human Kinetics).

Virginia Reel

KNOWLEDGE QUEST

INFORMATION AND TEACHING TIPS
Category M: World (Subcategory: North America)
Category A: Social (Subcategory: Dances done in a line)
Category A: Historical (Subcategory: Baroque)
Name of Dance: Virginia Reel

Everyone is a leader—no kings and queens.

BACKGROUND INFORMATION Before students view the video clip, share the following information with them.

- **Translation:** One theory is that since this dance was so very popular in the southeastern United States, it was named after the state of Virginia.

- **Country or culture of origin:** This dance was originally from England and made popular by Sir Roger de Coverley. It was used as a finale in court balls. It later came to the United States.

- **Timeline:** Introduced to the United States in the late 1600s, it was most popular between the 1830s and 1890s and is still danced today.

- **Function or reason:** The Virginia Reel was danced at social functions that called for dancing and now it is a popular contra and square dance.

- **Who does this dance:** All ages and both genders can dance this dance.

- **Music and rhythms:** Most times the accompaniment is a fiddler and a caller (as in square dancing). The dancers carry out the instructions of the calls.

- **Traditional clothing or costume:** According to the time period and venue, clothing was as follows: For formal occasions in colonial Virginia they would wear their most dressy outfits. In country settings, women wore full skirts and men wore casual, or country dress.

- **Other information:** This social dance is called a progressive dance in that the couples are in double lines and respond to a caller. Some common names of the steps are sashay (which comes from the French word *chassé* meaning chase), swing your partner, do-si-do, and elbow turn. The partners move in and back, cross over, and swing each other and sashay up and down the inner space. The head couple separate from each other by going to the outside of the lines (the figure or the particular movement section was called "cast off" in court dance) and moving to the end of the lines to make an arch. The other couples go under the arch and a new head couple begins the dance figures all over again. Virginia Reel was a democratic, new world response to the court dances and their formal patterns or figures, where the king and queen were always the head couple. Here in the Virginia Reel, the head couple changes until every couple gets a chance to be spotlighted as the leader. Also, reels were thought to show the movement of the spools of thread or

From H. Scheff, M. Sprague, and S. McGreevy-Nichols, 2010, *Exploring dance forms and styles: A guide to concert, world, social, and historical dance* (Champaign, IL: Human Kinetics).

yarn, called reels, in the weaving process. The movement of the head couple when they turn around each other, then turn around the other dancers, then turn around themselves again, is called the reel.

REFERENCES

www.wisegeek.com/what-is-the-virginia-reel.htm

TEACHING STRATEGIES   The video clip should be viewed at least three times (see chapter 1). After students record and discuss their observations and before the third viewing, use the discussion starters listed next to facilitate class discussion. Feel free to paraphrase and choose the questions that work best with your students.

Viewing: What Did You See?

Suggested discussion starters and questions: Did you notice the movement they were doing when they held hands? At what point in the dance does this happen? With each new head couple, how do the movements repeat, and in what order? Do the men ever do anything different from the woman?

Connecting: What Do You Know?

Suggested discussion starters and questions: What did you notice about the patterns of repeated movements the dancers made as they progressed through the dance? How does this dance look similar to and different from traditional square dances? What other dances do you know that have repeating movement patterns? What floor patterns do you notice? How did the dancers connect with each other?

Responding: What Do You Think? What Do You Wonder?

Suggested discussion starters and questions: How much could the repeated movement pattern, formation (lines), and types of steps change without making it a completely different dance? How would you compare these steps with those of the Quadrille (do a video clip search)? How does the music help the dance? This dance was sometimes done to Waltz music. How would using this music change how the dance was done (its quality)?

What questions do you have about this dance? Write them down and continue your research. Some of these questions can be answered through movement.

Performing: What Can You Do?

Choose both Re-create and Create, choose one of these two activities, or make your own performing work that you think is most appropriate for your students.

Re-create   Working in small groups, use the information that you recorded on this answer sheet and the video clip to re-create a section or two of the Virginia Reel.

Create   Working in a small group, first put some locomotor movements together in a phrase that can be done with a partner and repeated. Then design a floor pattern that works well with your locomotor partner pattern and allows for a change of the head couple.

*If you need music and don't have it among your resources, use the video.

FUN FACTS   The classic 1939 movie *Gone With the Wind,* includes a short example of the Virginia Reel in the bazaar scene.

WEB EXPLORATIONS   Key terms to search for include square dance, country dance, barn dance, and Quadrille.

From H. Scheff, M. Sprague, and S. McGreevy-Nichols, 2010, *Exploring dance forms and styles: A guide to concert, world, social, and historical dance* (Champaign, IL: Human Kinetics).

Virginia Reel

Name: _____ Class: _____ Date: _____

STUDENT KNOWLEDGE QUEST WORKSHEET

Name of Dance: Virginia Reel

1. Viewing: What did you see?
   Record your observations. Describe what you see. Be specific.

   _____

   _____

   _____

   _____

   _____

   _____

2. Connecting: What do you know?

   _____

   _____

   _____

   _____

   _____

3. Responding: What do you think? What do you wonder?

   _____

   _____

   _____

   _____

   _____

4. Performing: What can you do?

   _____

   _____

   _____

   _____

   _____

From H. Scheff, M. Sprague, and S. McGreevy-Nichols, 2010, *Exploring dance forms and styles: A guide to concert, world, social, and historical dance* (Champaign, IL: Human Kinetics).

KNOWLEDGE QUEST

INFORMATION AND TEACHING TIPS
Video Clip Search
Category M: World (Subcategory: South America)
Category A: Historical (Subcategory: 18th and 19th Century)
Name of Dance: Capoeira

Capoeira

"Capoeira cannot exist without black men but its birthplace is Brazil."

Salvano

DIRECTIONS   Give the students the job of researching clips of and about Capoeira on the Internet. Many are available; have them choose one or two. They can do this in school if the Internet is available, at home, or at a library. Instruct them to take notes about the actual dancing so that they can complete the student worksheet.

BACKGROUND INFORMATION   Before students view the video clip, share the following information with them and give them the KQ worksheets to complete as a homework assignment.

- **Translation:** The origin of the word *capoeira* is debated. The Portuguese word *capão* means capon, or a castrated rooster, and could mean that the style appears similar to two roosters fighting. Kongo scholar K. Kia Bunseki Fu-Kiau also suggested *capoeira* could be derived from the Kikongo word *kipura*, which describes a rooster's movements in a fight. Afro-Brazilian scholar Carlos Eugenio has suggested that the dance took its name from a large round basket called a capa, commonly worn on the head by urban slaves. Others claim the term derives from the Tupi-Guarani words *kaá* (meaning leaf or plant) and *puéra* (past aspect marker), meaning formerly a forest. Another claim is that given that *capoeira* in Portuguese literally means chicken coop, it could simply be a derisive term used by slave owners to refer to the displays as chicken fights.

- **Country or culture of origin:** Capoeira's origins are not entirely clear. While many believe that the form displays a combination of African and Brazilian martial arts, historians are divided between those who believe it is a direct descendant of African fighting styles and those who believe it is a uniquely Brazilian dance form distilled from various African and Brazilian influences.

- **Timeline:** The earliest historical record of Capoeira as a martial art is approximately 1770, long after early years of slavery. No further accounts of Capoeira are found until the early 1800s in the form of various police records from Rio de Janeiro.

- **Function or reason:** Capoeira was practiced by captured slaves as a method of defending themselves against their violent overlords. Because of their predicament, these enslaved people had to disguise their training as recreational song and dance.

- **Who does this dance:** Men and women do Capoeira.

- **Music and rhythms:** Music is integral to Capoeira. It sets the tempo and style of the dance that is to be played within the roda. The roda (hoh-dah) or roda de Capoeira is the circle of people within which Capoeira is performed. Its circular shape is maintained to keep focus on the players and musicians and retain the energy created by the Capoeira dance. The music is composed of instruments and song. The tempos differ from very slow (Angola) to very fast (São Bento regional). Many of the songs are sung in a call and response format while others are in the form of a narrative.

From H. Scheff, M. Sprague, and S. McGreevy-Nichols, 2010, *Exploring dance forms and styles: A guide to concert, world, social, and historical dance* (Champaign, IL: Human Kinetics).

Capoeira

- **Traditional clothing or costume:** Everyday clothing is worn for Capoeira.
- **Other information:** Capoeira is an Afro-Brazilian art form that involves movements from martial arts, games, and dance. In Capoeira, contact is generally not made but rather feigned or done theatrically. Some movements include the following:
  - The ginga (literally, rocking back and forth; to swing): This is a fundamental movement in Capoeira. Ginga is accomplished by maintaining both feet approximately shoulder-width apart and then moving one foot backward and then back to the base, describing a triangular step on the ground. This movement is done to prepare the body for other movements.
  - Attacks: Capoeira primarily attacks with kicks, sweeps, and head strikes.
  - Defenses: Capoeira defenses consist of evasive moves and rolls. A series of ducks, called esquivas (which literally means escape), are also a staple of a Capoeirista's defensive vocabulary.
  - Styles of moves that combine both elements of attack and defense: An example is the au batido. The move begins as an evasive cartwheel, which then turns into a blocking kick. Two kicks called meia-lua-de-frente and armada are often combined to create a double spinning kick.

REFERENCES

http://en.wikipedia.org/wiki/Capoeira

www.capoeira.htmlplanet.com/capoeira_hist.htm

www.ithaca.edu/capoeira/pages/history.html

www.capoeirasa.co.za/history.asp

TEACHING STRATEGIES   The video clip should be viewed at least three times (see chapter 1). In the case where students are searching and observing from home, they will need to list the exact Web site used so that teachers and other students can see the basis for their documentation.

Facilitate a class discussion using the discussion starters listed next. Have students use their recorded answers as a resource. Feel free to paraphrase and choose the questions that work best with your students.

Viewing: What Did You See?

Suggested discussion starters and questions: What is the first thing that strikes you about this dance? How would you describe this dance in three words? What are the main body parts that are used?

Connecting: What Do You Know?

Suggested discussion starters and questions: How do the dancers relate to one another? How do the dancers move around the floor?

Responding: What Do You Think? What Do You Wonder?

Suggested discussion starters and questions: Capoeira predates break dancing. Watch a video clip of break dancing. Do you think that Capoeira has had an influence on the development of break dancing? Why or why not?

What questions do you have about this dance? Write them down and continue your research. Some of these questions can be answered through movement.

From H. Scheff, M. Sprague, and S. McGreevy-Nichols, 2010, *Exploring dance forms and styles: A guide to concert, world, social, and historical dance* (Champaign, IL: Human Kinetics).

Performing: What Can You Do?

Choose both Re-create and Create, choose one of these two activities, or make your own performing work that you think is most appropriate for your students.

Re-create   View the video and re-create the basic preparation footwork that is used *before* performing any acrobatic movements.

Create   Capoeira is a dance that combines martial arts, acrobatics, and rhythmic footwork. Create a dance that has aspects of those three components.

*If you need music and don't have it among your resources, use the video.

FUN FACTS   The law that prohibited the practice of Capoeira was still in effect until 1920 so its practice was disguised as a folk dance. In their hidden places, Capoeiristas did their best to keep the tradition alive. By presenting it as a folk art, they made the practice of Capoeira more acceptable to the society.

WEB EXPLORATIONS   Key terms to search for include Capoeira, Brazilian dance, and Palmares + runaway slaves + dance.

RECOMMENDED CLIPS

- www.youtube.com/watch?v=DdZXp0Tq6Jk
- www.youtube.com/watch?v=51q1VB_dDik
- www.youtube.com/watch?v=5lfbW7K6u2Q

From H. Scheff, M. Sprague, and S. McGreevy-Nichols, 2010, *Exploring dance forms and styles: A guide to concert, world, social, and historical dance* (Champaign, IL: Human Kinetics).

Capoeira

Name: _____ Class: _____ Date: _____

STUDENT KNOWLEDGE QUEST WORKSHEET

Name of Dance: Capoeira

1. Viewing: What did you see?
   Record your observations. Describe what you see. Be specific.

   _____

   _____

   _____

   _____

   _____

2. Connecting: What do you know?

   _____

   _____

   _____

   _____

   _____

3. Responding: What do you think? What do you wonder?

   _____

   _____

   _____

   _____

   _____

4. Performing: What can you do?

   _____

   _____

   _____

   _____

   _____

From H. Scheff, M. Sprague, and S. McGreevy-Nichols, 2010, *Exploring dance forms and styles: A guide to concert, world, social, and historical dance* (Champaign, IL: Human Kinetics).

KNOWLEDGE QUEST

INFORMATION AND TEACHING TIPS
Category M: World (Subcategory: North America)
Category A: Social (Subcategory: Partners)
Name of Dance: Perico Ripiao

Polly doesn't want a cracker, he wants to dance a Merengue!

BACKGROUND INFORMATION   Before students view the video clip, share the following information with them.

- **Translation:** The term *perico ripiao* means ripped, plucked, or deboned parrot, because this bird may have been served as food at the establishment where this dance was popular. The more polite name of this dance is Merengue Tipico (meaning traditional, typical) or Meringue Cibaeño (a Merengue from the northern rural region of Cibao).

- **Country or culture of origin:** This dance is considered the national dance of the Dominican Republic. It is thought to have originated in the northern region of the Dominican Republic, called Cibao. Perico Ripiao is the oldest style of Merengue that is still played and danced.

- **Timeline:** Merengue, the dance form under which Perico Ripiao is a style, was already popular in the 1870s. This Merengue Tipico, or folk Merengue, found its form in 1910 and continues to this day.

- **Function or reason:** This dance is done at celebrations and other social events. It is thought to have originated in the northern region of the Dominican Republic, called Cibao. Perico Ripiao is the oldest style of Merengue that is still played and danced.

- **Who does this dance:** Everyone, young and old, dances this dance.

- **Music or rhythms:** African and Spanish rhythms are mixed in a Caribbean blend. The traditional ensemble symbolizes this blend. The güiro, originating from the native Taino people is a metal scraper. The tambora, from Africa, is a two-headed drum. The accordion was added when Germans traded the instruments for tobacco.

- **Traditional clothing or costume:** Men wear their pants with cuffs rolled up (in the past, to keep pants clean when people hiked cross country from different plantations to get to the social functions) and wear white dress shirts. Sometimes they wear straw hats. Women wear long skirts that they manipulate in a way similar to Spanish Flamenco dance.

- **Other information:** Some people tried to ban the Perico Ripiao because they did not think this dance was proper. This may be because of the use of the fast-swaying hips used in the dance.

REFERENCES

www.merengue-ripiao.com/survey.htm

www.nationmaster.com/encyclopedia/Perico-Ripiao

Manuel, P. 2006. *Caribbean currents: Caribbean music from rumba to reggae.* Philadelphia, PA: Temple University Press.

www.iasorecords.com/merengue.cfm

From H. Scheff, M. Sprague, and S. McGreevy-Nichols, 2010, *Exploring dance forms and styles: A guide to concert, world, social, and historical dance* (Champaign, IL: Human Kinetics).

109

Perico Ripiao

TEACHING STRATEGIES   The video clip should be viewed at least three times (see chapter 1). After students record and discuss their observations and before the third viewing, use the discussion starters listed next to facilitate class discussion. Feel free to paraphrase and choose the questions that work best with your students.

Viewing: What Did You See?

Suggested discussion starters and questions: What simple traveling steps were used mostly in this dance? Describe the partnering moves in this dance. Describe some of the ways the female dancers used their skirts. Which of the dancers' movements reflected rhythms of the music?

Connecting: What Do You Know?

Suggested discussion starters and questions: What other dances are partner dances and how are they similar to or different from the Perico Ripiao? How do the skirt movements add to this dance? Compare the particular importance of this skirt work to another dance in which clothing is a basic part of the dance movement.

Responding: What Do You Think? What Do You Wonder?

Suggested discussion starters and questions: Some people wanted to ban this dance. Historically, why have some people tried to control other people's actions and art forms?

What aspects does this dance share with African, Spanish Flamenco, and other European court dances? Why do you think this is so? If Perico Ripiao is the national dance of the Dominican Republic, which dance do you think should be the national dance of the United States? Explain why you chose this dance.

What questions do you have about this dance? Write them down and continue your research. Some of these questions can be answered through movement.

Performing: What Can You Do?

Choose both Re-create and Create, choose one of these two activities, or make your own performing work that you think is most appropriate for your students.

Re-create   With a partner, and using the Merengue step (a fast walking step with a swaying of the hips), copy some of the partnering moves of the couples on the video clip.

Create   In the Perico Ripiao the skirt work is very important to the character of this dance. By yourself, choose a piece of clothing that can be used to make dance movement. Design a small dance from movements that use the piece of clothing in a special, distinctive way.

*If you need music and don't have it among your resources, use the video.

FUN FACTS   In the 1930s Dominican Republic dictator, Rafael Trujillo, brought Merengue accordion players with him on his first campaign for president. Later, as president, he insisted that these folk Merengues be played at all high society ballrooms to get back at the elite who did not support him. Many of the lyrics for these dances were about him and what he had done for the good of the country.

WEB EXPLORATIONS   Key terms to search for include Perico Ripiao, Merengue Tipico, Dominican Republic, Merengue dance, and Merengue music.

From H. Scheff, M. Sprague, and S. McGreevy-Nichols, 2010, *Exploring dance forms and styles: A guide to concert, world, social, and historical dance* (Champaign, IL: Human Kinetics).

Name: _____ Class: _____ Date: _____

STUDENT KNOWLEDGE QUEST WORKSHEET

Name of Dance: Perico Ripiao

1. Viewing: What did you see?
   Record your observations. Describe what you see. Be specific.

   _____

   _____

   _____

   _____

   _____

2. Connecting: What do you know?

   _____

   _____

   _____

   _____

   _____

3. Responding: What do you think? What do you wonder?

   _____

   _____

   _____

   _____

   _____

4. Performing: What can you do?

   _____

   _____

   _____

   _____

   _____

From H. Scheff, M. Sprague, and S. McGreevy-Nichols, 2010, *Exploring dance forms and styles: A guide to concert, world, social, and historical dance* (Champaign, IL: Human Kinetics).

El Fon de la Negra

KNOWLEDGE QUEST

INFORMATION AND TEACHING TIPS
Category M: World (Subcategory: North America)
Category A: Concert
Name of Dance: El Fon de la Negra

Stomping and skirt swings—a folkloric tradition.

BACKGROUND INFORMATION Before students view the video clip, share the following information with them.

- **Translation:** No direct translation exists for this dance title.
- **Country or culture of origin:** This dance comes from the Mexican state of Jalisco.
- **Timeline:** Dances of the region date back to pre-Aztec times.
- **Function or reason:** This is a celebratory dance done at festivals and community gatherings and in formal performances.
- **Who does this dance:** Both men and women dance this dance.
- **Music and rhythms:** In Jalisco, the traditional zapateado step is danced to a three-beat rhythm or 3/4 time. Traditional folkloric music is played by a mariachi band. They sing while they play.
- **Traditional clothing or costume:** Women wear skirts made of three circles of fabric. They often have a shawl or scarf and hair is adorned with flowers. Men wear fitted trousers, boleros, and sombreros (hats with large brims).
- **Other information:** This is one of the bailes regionales (regional dances). These dances are social in origin. The community performs them at community events and semi-professional troupes have staged theatrical performances. Each geographic or cultural area in Mexico has dances that they call their own tradition. The word *zapateados* refers to the traditional footwork that includes stomping in a definite pattern. The accompaniment for traditional dances is the traditional folk music from a mariachi band. Enormous energy and movement are involved in the

From H. Scheff, M. Sprague, and S. McGreevy-Nichols, 2010, *Exploring dance forms and styles: A guide to concert, world, social, and historical dance* (Champaign, IL: Human Kinetics).

songs from Jalisco. The word *faldeo* (fahl-day-o) refers to a movement of the skirt that the female dancer creates with her hand or hands. Skirts are very important for female dancers and can be seen in many Hispanic dance forms. Male dancers keep their hands behind the back or holding the front corners of their jackets (boleros).

REFERENCES

http://uniqueweddings.net/lapaloma/html/history.html

www.photohouston.com/Mexican-folk-dance/ballet-folklorico-stock-photos.html

http://en.wikipedia.org/wiki/Jarabe_tapat%C3%ADo

TEACHING STRATEGIES

The video clip should be viewed at least three times (see chapter 1). After students record and discuss their observations and before the third viewing, use the discussion starters listed next to facilitate class discussion. Feel free to paraphrase and choose the questions that work best with your students.

Viewing: What Did You See?

Suggested discussion starters and questions: What did you notice about the handling of the skirts throughout the dance? What patterns were created with their dance movement?

Connecting: What Do You Know?

Suggested discussion starters and questions: Did the girls in the dance always twirl both sides of their skirts? Do you know of any other dances where the women use skirts in the same or similar way?

Responding: What Do You Think? What Do You Wonder?

Suggested discussion starters and questions: What do you believe to be the strongest parts of the dance? From viewing this video and others online, what can you say about the costumes and the colors?

What questions do you have about this dance? Write them down and continue your research. Some of these questions can be answered through movement.

Performing: What Can You Do?

Choose both Re-create and Create, choose one of these two activities, or make your own performing work that you think is most appropriate for your students.

Re-create   Use the travel patterns that you see on the video clip. Be sure to start and end in the same spot and pose.

Create   Work with fellow students to achieve a similar sound of the stomping and heel beats of the feet. *Note:* Use ideas from recorded observations from question 1 (What do you see?).

*If you need music and don't have it among your resources, use the video.

FUN FACTS

Each of the 31 Mexican states (and the Federal District) has its typical zapateados. This means that there is lots of heelwork and footwork. Imagine if representatives of all these districts or states came together for a grand festival! Wow!

WEB EXPLORATIONS

Key terms to search for include PELINKS4U, Ballet Folklorico de Mexico, and Jalisco dances.

From H. Scheff, M. Sprague, and S. McGreevy-Nichols, 2010, *Exploring dance forms and styles: A guide to concert, world, social, and historical dance* (Champaign, IL: Human Kinetics).

**El Fon
de la Negra**

Name: _____ Class: _____ Date: _____

STUDENT KNOWLEDGE QUEST WORKSHEET

Name of Dance: El Fon de la Negra

1. Viewing: What did you see?
   Record your observations. Describe what you see. Be specific.

   _____

   _____

   _____

   _____

   _____

2. Connecting: What do you know?

   _____

   _____

   _____

   _____

   _____

3. Responding: What do you think? What do you wonder?

   _____

   _____

   _____

   _____

   _____

4. Performing: What can you do?

   _____

   _____

   _____

   _____

   _____

From H. Scheff, M. Sprague, and S. McGreevy-Nichols, 2010, *Exploring dance forms and styles: A guide to concert, world, social, and historical dance* (Champaign, IL: Human Kinetics).

KNOWLEDGE QUEST

INFORMATION AND TEACHING TIPS
Category M: World (Subcategory: North America)
Category A: Concert
Name of Dance: El Tilingo Lingo (From Veracruz)

El Tilingo Lingo

Adapt, Adjust, Alter—The many dances of Mexico—Triple A

BACKGROUND INFORMATION Before students view the video clip, share the following information with them.

- **Translation:** No direct translation exists for this dance title.

- **Country or culture of origin:** This dance is from Veracruz, Mexico. It follows the Spanish heritage because everything from Spain had to pass through the port of Veracaruz.

- **Timeline:** This dance was being done in the 18th century, during the time of the American Revolutionary War.

- **Function or reason:** Veracruz is considered to be one of the liveliest and happiest areas of Mexican folklorico dance. These dances help to make celebrations lively.

- **Who does this dance:** The whole population takes part in this dance.

- **Music and rhythms:** In Veracruz, the traditional zapateado step is danced to a 4/4 rhythm. The name given to Mexican Folk melodies is *sóns*. They are sometimes referred to as *fandangos*. We hear the influence of African drum beats along with the Spanish. Each area in Mexico has dances that they call their own tradition. The accompaniment of the traditional folk music for this dance is the mariachi band. Enormous energy and movement are involved in the sóns from Veracruz.

- **Traditional clothing or costume:** Dancers perform their dynamic steps in white costumes, which are supposed to reflect the heat of this subtropical climate. Their hair is up on their heads and adorned with flowers. They often carry fans to help with the heat. The men wear white shirts, white pants, and straw hats.

- **Other information:** Mexican folkloric dances can be divided into three categories: (1) Danza—Indigenous dances often performed in ritual and community

From H. Scheff, M. Sprague, and S. McGreevy-Nichols, 2010, *Exploring dance forms and styles: A guide to concert, world, social, and historical dance* (Champaign, IL: Human Kinetics).

El Tilingo Lingo

settings. (2) Mestizo—Indigenous dances reflecting European influences in either steps, theme, instrumentation, or a combination of the three. (3) Bailes regionales—Regional dances which are social dances performed in community and theatrical settings. A main feature of the foot patterns is a three-stamp introduction to a new step. It is as if a drummer were signaling a new step as they do in African dance.

REFERENCES

www.alegria.org/modules/content/index.php?id=2

www.thailandgrandfestival.com/festival.asp?festID=647

www.travelbymexico.com/veracruz/video/index2.php

www.veracruz.gob.mx

TEACHING STRATEGIES

The video clip should be viewed at least three times (see chapter 1). After students record and discuss their observations and before the third viewing, use the discussion starters listed next to facilitate class discussion. Feel free to paraphrase and choose the questions that work best with your students.

Viewing: What Did You See?

Suggested discussion starters and questions: What did you notice about head movement throughout the dance? They were using their feet to make steps. How many different steps did they do?

Connecting: What Do You Know?

Suggested discussion starters and questions: The dancers held their skirts with both hands. How does this compare with other Hispanic dances and the use of the skirt? How would you describe the skirt movement?

Responding: What Do You Think? What Do You Wonder?

Suggested discussion starters and questions: The women are dressed in white. Why do you think they are? View the La Bomba clip on the DVD. What does that clip have in common with this one? Compare and contrast them.

What questions do you have about this dance? Write them down and continue your research. Some of these questions can be answered through movement.

Performing: What Can You Do?

Choose both Re-create and Create, one of these two activities, or make your own performing work that you think is most appropriate for your students.

Re-create   Make a short dance study including head movements that you saw in the video clip and include the three-stomp step before starting another footwork pattern.

Create   After listening to the music on the DVD, create a percussion pattern with your feet using toes and heels separately.

*If you need music and don't have it among your resources, use the video.

FUN FACTS

Once upon a time, Veracruz was home to many pirates. In 1519, Hernando Cortes (some call him a pirate for his own cause) made landfall on the Mexican coast. He gets credit for naming the city La Villa Rica de la Vera Cruz, the Rich Town of the True Cross, which was shortened to Veracruz.

WEB EXPLORATIONS

Key terms to search for include Mexican folkloric dance traditions and Veracruz.

From H. Scheff, M. Sprague, and S. McGreevy-Nichols, 2010, *Exploring dance forms and styles: A guide to concert, world, social, and historical dance* (Champaign, IL: Human Kinetics).

Name: _____ Class: _____ Date: _____

STUDENT KNOWLEDGE QUEST WORKSHEET

Name of Dance: El Tilingo Lingo

El Tilingo Lingo

1. Viewing: What did you see?
   Record your observations. Describe what you see. Be specific.

   _____
   _____
   _____
   _____
   _____

2. Connecting: What do you know?

   _____
   _____
   _____
   _____
   _____

3. Responding: What do you think? What do you wonder?

   _____
   _____
   _____
   _____
   _____

4. Performing: What can you do?

   _____
   _____
   _____
   _____
   _____

From H. Scheff, M. Sprague, and S. McGreevy-Nichols, 2010, *Exploring dance forms and styles: A guide to concert, world, social, and historical dance* (Champaign, IL: Human Kinetics).

La Bomba

KNOWLEDGE QUEST

INFORMATION AND TEACHING TIPS
Category M: World (Subcategory: North America)
Category A: Historical (Subcategory: Baroque)
Category A: Social (Subcategory: Alone in a group)
Name of Dance: La Bomba

A dynamic conversation, the dancer calls and the drummer responds.

BACKGROUND INFORMATION Before students view the video clip, share the following information with them.

- **Translation:** It is thought that La Bomba was originally an African religious practice.

- **Country or culture of origin:** La Bomba's roots are found in the Ashanti people of West Africa who were imported to Puerto Rico as slaves.

- **Timeline:** La Bomba was probably developed during the late 17th century. It is thought that the dance developed in Loiza, Puerto Rico, where there had been many West African slaves living and working on the sugar cane plantations.

- **Function or reason:** Bailes de Bombas, or Bomba dances, were held to celebrate baptisms, marriages, and even to plan rebellions.

- **Who does this dance:** While men also used to dance La Bomba, now women usually dance accompanied by musicians, with the subidor drum player, who responds to the dancer's movements.

- **Music and rhythms:** Usually La Bomba begins with a woman (laina) singing a phrase to which a chorus makes a response to the call. The time signature can be 2/4 or 6/8. Typical instruments are the buleador (the low-sounding drum that gives the basic beat), the subidor (which responds to the dancer's movements), palitos (sticks), and one maraca.

- **Traditional clothing or costume:** The female dancers often raise their long skirts to show their petticoats. It is thought that the slaves would do this to make fun of the ladies of the plantation.

- **Other information:** Since the slaves in Puerto Rico were not allowed to worship in their old way, they mixed their African traditions with the worship of St. James. During the festivals for St. James, Bomba music was allowed and vejigantes (traditional masks) were worn in order to frighten away evil spirits and even pirates.

REFERENCES

Manuel, P. 2006. *Caribbean currents: Caribbean music from rumba to reggae.* Philadelphia, PA: Temple University Press.

www.reddpr.tripod.com/plena/history.htm

www.prfdance.org/bomba.htm

www.musicofpuertorico.com/index.php/genre/bomba/

From H. Scheff, M. Sprague, and S. McGreevy-Nichols, 2010, *Exploring dance forms and styles: A guide to concert, world, social, and historical dance* (Champaign, IL: Human Kinetics).

La Bomba

TEACHING STRATEGIES   The video clip should be viewed at least three times (see chapter 1). After students record and discuss their observations and before the third viewing, use the discussion starters listed next to facilitate class discussion. Feel free to paraphrase and choose the questions that work best with your students.

Viewing: What Did You See?

Suggested discussion starters and questions: How did La Bomba start? What did the dancer do with her skirt? What body parts did the dancer use the most? Describe some of the movements.

Connecting: What Do You Know?

Suggested discussion starters and questions: What did you notice about the relationship between the dancer and the drummer? How did the conversation between the dancer and the drummer resemble your conversations? Compare this dancer–musician relationship to any other dance you have seen or know about.

Responding: What Do You Think? What Do You Wonder?

Suggested discussion starters and questions: Watch the La Bomba video clip again, looking closely at the movements and dancer's clothing and listening to the music. What evidence can you find for both African and European influences on the dance? Support your answers. Explain why you think the slaves used the Bomba dances to disguise the planning of rebellions.

What questions do you have about this dance? Write them down and continue your research. Some of these questions can be answered through movement.

Performing: What Can You Do?

Choose both Re-create and Create, choose one of these two activities, or make your own performing work that you think is most appropriate for your students.

Re-create   Choose three or four movements from the video clip of La Bomba. Perform them one at a time, letting your partner respond to each of your movements by clapping the rhythm of your movements. Reverse your roles. *Note:* To help you perform the movements more clearly, use the answers from question 1 on your Knowledge Quest worksheet and the video clip.

Create   La Bomba uses the traditional call and response choreographic form. Choreograph two or three short dance sentences (phrases) to use for a call section. After watching each of your dance sentences, have a partner improvise (make up on the spot) response movements. If you want to make your dance a bit longer, reverse roles where you respond to your partner's choreographed dance sentences.

*If you need music and don't have it among your resources, use the video.

FUN FACTS   La Bomba dance starts with a short walk (paseo) and includes sudden jerks called ponche, small hops, and free movements called piquetes. These and other movements are used as vocabulary for improvisational conversations with the lead drummer.

WEB EXPLORATIONS   Key terms to search for include La Bomba dance and vejigante masks of Puerto Rico.

From H. Scheff, M. Sprague, and S. McGreevy-Nichols, 2010, *Exploring dance forms and styles: A guide to concert, world, social, and historical dance* (Champaign, IL: Human Kinetics).

La Bomba

Name: _____ Class: _____ Date: _____

STUDENT KNOWLEDGE QUEST WORKSHEET

Name of Dance: La Bomba

1. Viewing: What did you see?
   Record your observations. Describe what you see. Be specific.

   _____

   _____

   _____

   _____

   _____

2. Connecting: What do you know?

   _____

   _____

   _____

   _____

   _____

3. Responding: What do you think? What do you wonder?

   _____

   _____

   _____

   _____

   _____

4. Performing: What can you do?

   _____

   _____

   _____

   _____

   _____

From H. Scheff, M. Sprague, and S. McGreevy-Nichols, 2010, *Exploring dance forms and styles: A guide to concert, world, social, and historical dance* (Champaign, IL: Human Kinetics).

KNOWLEDGE QUEST

INFORMATION AND TEACHING TIPS
Video Clip Search
Category M: World Dance (Subcategory: South America)
Name of Dance: Tinku

Tinku

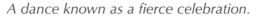

A dance known as a fierce celebration.

DIRECTIONS   Give the students the job of researching clips of and about the Tinku dance on the Internet. Many are available; have them choose one or two. They can do this in school if the Internet is available, at home, or at a library. Instruct them to take notes about the actual dancing so that they can complete the student worksheet.

BACKGROUND INFORMATION   Before students view the video clip, share the following information with them and give them the KQ worksheets to complete as a homework assignment.

- **Translation:** The Quechua word *tinku* means encounter or duel.

- **Country or culture of origin:** Tinkus occur between different communities and moieties (kinship or social groups). These events are prearranged and usually take place in the small towns of southern Bolivia.

- **Timeline:** The Tinku is thought to date back to the time of the Moche culture. A tradition of Andean culture since before they first had contact with Europeans, some anthropologists claim that ancient Andes culture would have Tinkus instead of battles. This form of dance would help limit the aggression between different groups and also act as a form of entertainment, similar to football games in the United States.

- **Function or reason:** "Today Tinku takes place on specified holidays, when both male and female members of moieties fight hand-to-hand with those of the other moiety. In Bolivia, the Tinku is held around May 3rd and lasts for a few days. Although the conflict is largely symbolic and ceremonial, the brawl may inflict real, serious physical harm that can sometimes be fatal. Status of a specific moiety is determined by this conflict" (http://wapedia.mobi/en/Tinku).

- **Who does this dance:** Men and women take part in Tinku.

- **Music and rhythms:** Tinkus use traditional Andes music. Instruments include panpipes, called siku or zampoñas; the charango, which resembles a small guitar with 10 strings; and the bombo, a drum made from a hollowed tree trunk with hide skins stretched across the top and bottom, usually sheep or llama hide at one end, and cow hide on the other.

- **Traditional clothing or costumes:** "The male ceremonial Tinku outfit includes a helmet designed to protect the head from lateral blows. The jacket shirt is of bright color. The pants are either black or white with decorations embroidered near the feet. Wide belts and aguayos (native weavings) are tied around the waist and stomach for greater protection from hand strikes. The woman really doesn't participate in the ceremonial Tinku because it is a fight among men. In the festive Tinku the women take part in the simulated fight. Their main garment is of a bright-colored single piece with a long skirt and wide belt (chumpi). The female hat has colorful ribbons hanging down the front and decorative feathers on top. Both men and women wear the traditional abarcas (walking sandals) to cover their feet" (excerpt from www.lossambos.com/dances/PDFs/Tinku-English.pdf).

From H. Scheff, M. Sprague, and S. McGreevy-Nichols, 2010, *Exploring dance forms and styles: A guide to concert, world, social, and historical dance* (Champaign, IL: Human Kinetics).

Tinku

- **Other information:** One of the steps in the dance looks as if they were marching like soldiers ready to encounter the opponent. At times the dance position is bent down at the waist, and the arm and hand gestures provoke fighting just as in the ritual of their origin.

REFERENCES

www.lossambos.com/dances/PDFs/Tinku-English.pdf

www.worldartswest.org/main/edf_performer.asp?i=93

www.madison.com/communities/boliviamanta/

TEACHING STRATEGIES The video clip should be viewed at least three times (see chapter 1). In the case where students are searching and observing from home, they will need to list the exact Web site used so that teachers and other students can see the basis for their documentation.

Facilitate a class discussion using the discussion starters listed next. Have students use their recorded answers as a resource. Feel free to paraphrase and choose the questions that work best with your students.

Viewing: What Did You See?

Suggested discussion starters and questions: What is the first thing that strikes you about this dance? How would you describe this dance in three words? What are the main body parts that are used? How would you describe the most repeated movement?

Connecting: What Do You Know?

Suggested discussion starters and questions: Given the overall purpose of the dance, what types of movements and behaviors do the dancers perform that suggest the combative nature of the dance?

Responding: What Do You Think? What Do You Wonder?

Suggested discussion starters and questions: Many cultures use dance as a way to intimidate their opponents. The Maori people use the Haka to do just that. Research and view a video clip of this dance. Why do these dances look the way they do? Explain and give examples.

What questions do you have about this dance? Write them down and continue your research. Some of these questions can be answered through movement.

Performing: What Can You Do?

Choose both Re-create and Create, choose one of these two activities, or make your own performing work that you think is most appropriate for your students.

Re-create Identify and re-create three distinct rhythmic movements used in this dance.

Create Divide the class into two groups and have a dance-off between the two. Each group should create several eight-count rhythmic combinations that demonstrate aggressive behavior (without touching the other group) and might scare off the other.

*If you need music and don't have it among your resources, use the video.

FUN FACTS In the movie *Happy Feet* the penguins do their version of the Tinku. Check it out on YouTube; just enter Happy Feet + Tinku.

From H. Scheff, M. Sprague, and S. McGreevy-Nichols, 2010, *Exploring dance forms and styles: A guide to concert, world, social, and historical dance* (Champaign, IL: Human Kinetics).

Tinku

WEB EXPLORATIONS
Key terms to search for include Tinku and Bolivian dance.

RECOMMENDED CLIPS

- www.youtube.com/watch?v=eEsqqsAbLXo
- www.youtube.com/watch?v=Nv6ojemF2ZE
- www.truveo.com/BONANZA-TINKU-Tinkus-Cochabamba-BOLIVIA/id/1941383045

From H. Scheff, M. Sprague, and S. McGreevy-Nichols, 2010, *Exploring dance forms and styles: A guide to concert, world, social, and historical dance* (Champaign, IL: Human Kinetics).

123

Tinku

Name: _____ Class: _____ Date: _____

STUDENT KNOWLEDGE QUEST WORKSHEET

Name of Dance: Tinku

1. Viewing: What did you see?
   Record your observations. Describe what you see. Be specific.

   _____

   _____

   _____

   _____

   _____

2. Connecting: What do you know?

   _____

   _____

   _____

   _____

   _____

3. Responding: What do you think? What do you wonder?

   _____

   _____

   _____

   _____

   _____

4. Performing: What can you do?

   _____

   _____

   _____

   _____

   _____

From H. Scheff, M. Sprague, and S. McGreevy-Nichols, 2010, *Exploring dance forms and styles: A guide to concert, world, social, and historical dance* (Champaign, IL: Human Kinetics).

KNOWLEDGE QUEST

INFORMATION AND TEACHING TIPS
Category M: World (Subcategory: Europe)
Category A: Social (Subcategory: Partner)
Name of Dance: Der Unterwestner (Clapping Dance)

How complicated can a clapping game get?

BACKGROUND INFORMATION   Before students view the video clip, share the following information with them.

- **Translation:** Der Unterwestner is also called the Clapping Dance by the performers in the video clip. It is a Bavarian Schuhplattler dance. In German the word *Schuhplattler* means shoe-slapping dance.

- **Country or culture of origin:** This dance originates from the southern part of Germany. The region is also called Bavaria.

- **Timeline:** An early form of this dance was described in a monk's poem that was written in 1050. A men-only dance, Burschentanz was danced between the 11th and 14th centuries. Later, in the 18th century, a version was meant to demonstrate the men's physical ability and strength to the women; this type of movement developed into the shoe slapping.

- **Function or reason:** One of the main reasons for dancing this dance is to maintain tradition and to represent the region's culture. Some dances were created to represent professions such as the Mühlradl (miller's dance), the Bergknaben Tanz (the miner's dance), the Holzhacker (woodcutter's dance), the Glockenplattler (bell dance that represents the shepherd), and the Ambosstanz (dance of the anvil of the blacksmith). Animals are imitated in certain dances such as the Auerhahn (a bird) and the Gamerlsprung (mountain goat spring or leap). There are also flirting dances, such as Figurentanz (figure dance) and Austrian Steirer. There are even dances that honor places, such as the Haushammer, Reit im Wink'l, Rhupoldinger, Wendelstoana, and Ammerseer.

- **Who does this dance:** At first the Schulplattler was only for men, but in later years women were allowed to participate as well. While the men jump, clap, and slap their shoes and legs, the women spin around like so many toy tops without appearing to get dizzy. Their skirts spin out so that they look like bells. Periodically during the dance, the men and women pair off to waltz, before repeating the pattern of men slapping and clapping and the women spinning.

- **Music and rhythms:** Bavarian dances of the 18th and 19th centuries strongly influenced the folk music, which depended on the specific dances for the various structures, speeds, and styles. The time signatures are either 2/4 and 4/4 (even time) or 3/4. The 3/4-time Bavarian dances include the Landler, the Waltzer, the Mazurka,

From H. Scheff, M. Sprague, and S. McGreevy-Nichols, 2010, *Exploring dance forms and styles: A guide to concert, world, social, and historical dance* (Champaign, IL: Human Kinetics).

Der Unterwestner

the Polonaise, and the Menuetten, whereas the Polkas, the Schottische, the Galopp, the Boarischer, and the Marsch are all in even time. The structures are usually similar to a rondo (ABAC. . .) in that they have repeating parts. In this video clip, the 3/4-time music is played by a single accordionist but it is usually played by several musicians.

- **Traditional clothing or costume:** People from Bavaria honor their past and keep their customs. Mirroring this value is the local or regional clothing or Tracht, which isn't much changed from the clothing of 200 years ago. The men's Tracht includes Lederhosen (leather pants), a trachten shirt (with rolled-up sleeves), suspenders, Allgauer hat with a Gamsbart (a brush-like ornament worn on the right side of the hat), knee socks, and trachten shoes. The women's Tracht includes a skirt, white trachten blouse, Mieder or bodice, an apron, and black trachten shoes (with white hosiery).

- **Other information:** The roots of this dance form go back to rural people such as farmers, hunters, and woodsmen. The type of dance in this video clip is thought to have been an imitation of a male bird, the Auerhahn, who during his mating ritual, flaps his wings, kicks his feet, and spins in a circle. As was documented in 1838, when the empress of Russia visited the region, the plattling was more free-form or improvised and the women spun separately until it was time for the waltzing. Gradually, the dances became more set and the group dancing, or group **plattling** emerged. Clubs and societies were formed and according to regional differences approximately 150 different Schuhplattler dances were created. While preserving traditional culture is important to the Bavarian people, new Schuhplattler dances are being created today.

REFERENCES

http://bva.rochesfergerman.com/Tanz/Tutorial1.html

www.marquise.de/en/ethno/bayern/baydic.shtml

www.tsvallgau.org/TSV/Our_Tracht.html

www.gtvalmrausch.org/schuhplattler.htm

www.schwuhplattler.de/geschichte/geschichte.en.htm

www.economy-point.org/s/schuhplattler.html

www.zither.us/solo.interpretations.bavarian.folk.music

TEACHING STRATEGIES   The video clip should be viewed at least three times (see chapter 1). After students record and discuss their observations and before the third viewing, use the discussion starters listed next to facilitate class discussion. Feel free to paraphrase and choose the questions that work best with your students.

Viewing: What Did You See?

Suggested discussion starters and questions: What floor pattern (imaginary shapes drawn on the floor with dancers' footsteps) and formation was used in this dance? What locomotor (movement that travels) step did the dancers use? What nonlocomotor (movement that stays in one place) movements did the dancers use?

Connecting: What Do You Know?

Suggested discussion starters and questions: What rhythmic or clapping games and dances do you know? How are they similar to this Schuhplattler? How are they different?

From H. Scheff, M. Sprague, and S. McGreevy-Nichols, 2010, *Exploring dance forms and styles: A guide to concert, world, social, and historical dance* (Champaign, IL: Human Kinetics).

Responding: What Do You Think? What Do You Wonder?

Suggested discussion starters and questions: Traditionally this dance was done during village festivals and social gatherings. The young men would show their physical strength and athletic abilities during the plattling section of the dance. Why do you think this was so? Support your answer with details from the dance. In the video clip, dancers of all ages are dancing together. This is normal for the German and Bavarian clubs and societies. In the United States, the generations do not usually socialize together very often. How does an emphasis on traditional culture and dance create a tighter social bond between the generations? Could this work in the United States?

What questions do you have about this dance? Write them down and continue your research. Some of these questions can be answered through movement.

Performing: What Can You Do?

Choose both Re-create and Create, choose one of these two activities, or make your own performing work that you think is most appropriate for your students.

Re-create   Learn the simple clapping section done between the partners. Clap behind your back (count 1), clap in front of yourself (count 2), and clap your partner's hands (count 3). For a challenge learn all or part of the men's plattling. (Teacher hint: Learning the more complicated patterns may require many replays.)

Create   Create your own hand clapping and slapping pattern. Write it down and teach it to a small, even-numbered group of students in your class. After all have learned this pattern, combine it with a locomotor movement that will move people to a new partner.

*If you need music and don't have it among your resources, use the video.

FUN FACTS   The Holzhackertanz, the wood chopper's dance, actually alternates the plattling with chopping and sawing a log in time with the music. To see an example, try searching the words *video of Holzhackertanz* on the Web.

WEB EXPLORATIONS   Key terms to search for include Bavarian Schuhplatter, Bavarian folk music, Bavarian Trachten, Bavarian folk costume, and Bavarian dances.

From H. Scheff, M. Sprague, and S. McGreevy-Nichols, 2010, *Exploring dance forms and styles: A guide to concert, world, social, and historical dance* (Champaign, IL: Human Kinetics).

Der Unterwestner

Name: _____ Class: _____ Date: _____

STUDENT KNOWLEDGE QUEST WORKSHEET

Name of Dance: Der Unterwestner (Clapping Dance)

1. Viewing: What did you see?
   Record your observations. Describe what you see. Be specific.

   _____

   _____

   _____

   _____

   _____

2. Connecting: What do you know?

   _____

   _____

   _____

   _____

   _____

3. Responding: What do you think? What do you wonder?

   _____

   _____

   _____

   _____

   _____

4. Performing: What can you do?

   _____

   _____

   _____

   _____

   _____

From H. Scheff, M. Sprague, and S. McGreevy-Nichols, 2010, *Exploring dance forms and styles: A guide to concert, world, social, and historical dance* (Champaign, IL: Human Kinetics).

KNOWLEDGE QUEST

INFORMATION AND TEACHING TIPS
Video Clip Search
Category M: World (Subcategory: Europe)
Category A: Concert
Name of Dance: Flamenco

Flamenco

Percussive feet, angular arms, but a long, sleek torso—all at the same time.

DIRECTIONS   Give the students the job of researching clips of and about traditional Flamenco dance on the Internet. Many are available; have them choose one or two. They can do this in school if the Internet is available, at home, or at a library. Instruct them to take notes about the actual dancing so that they can complete the student worksheet.

BACKGROUND INFORMATION   Before students view the video clip, share the following information with them and give them the KQ worksheets to complete as a homework assignment.

- **Translation:** There are many translations of the word *flamenco*. One accepted version translates *flamenco* as Spanish for the Flemish soldiers of the Spanish-Belgian territories. They were self-confident and full of pride, qualities that speak to the character of Gypsies. The term *flamenco* came to be synonymous with *gitano* (Gypsy) in Spanish Romany argot.

- **Country or culture of origin:** This dance form is known to have come from Andalusia (pronounced Andaluthia), which is now the country of Spain.

- **Timeline:** Flamenco dancing appears to have its roots in the last half of the 18th century. Schools of Flamenco dance appeared and each had its own twist and style.

- **Function or reason:** Flamenco dancing may be of different styles depending on the intention of the dance—-to entertain (as in concert dance), to pursue a lover (as in social dance), or to comfort those in need (community building).

- **Who does this dance:** Both men and women do Flamenco dancing. They have traditional steps that stem from the various regions in Spain from the mountains to the shore. They dance as solos, duets, and groups.

- **Music and rhythms:** Originally the dancing was set to no instrumental music, only singing and toque de palmas (the clapping of hands). These actions were not done by the dancers but by the support staff sitting behind or on the sidelines. Eventually the use of the guitar and other instruments was introduced. A musical style in Flamenco, known as *palos,* encompasses a wide range of cultural and social contexts, as well as simple rhythmic and stylized differences. The dancers used castanets (small handheld percussive instruments) to accent their heel work.

- **Traditional clothing and costume:** Women are always skirted in three tiers, diagonally cut flounces, or sporting a long train that is loaded with ruffles. The fabric was usually chosen for the bright colors and design. The torso part of the costume is always fitted tightly and can be embellished with shawls, a large flower, or a ruffle at the top of the bodice. The men wear tight-fitting trousers, sometimes with a cummerbund to accentuate the torso. The blouson part of the outfit could be a shirt with very full sleeves and tight cuffs, a vest, or a bolero. Both men and women wear shoes with heels that can make loud sounds. Men often have hollowed-out heels on their shoes to make them sound louder. They sometimes wear castanets to help make more percussive sounds.

From H. Scheff, M. Sprague, and S. McGreevy-Nichols, 2010, *Exploring dance forms and styles: A guide to concert, world, social, and historical dance* (Champaign, IL: Human Kinetics).

Flamenco

- **Other information:** Flamenco dancing is one of the three integral parts of the art of Flamenco. This was heavily influenced by the local Gypsy population, the Gitanos (the Rom people). Many of the musical stylings and dance movements of Flamenco come from the Jewish tradition, as well as from Moorish and East Indian cultures. There are also many different musical instruments that are used. These include the human voice, hand clapping, finger snapping, guitars, and other strummed instruments and most recently drumming on a wide variety of percussion instruments. Often the music is what drives the dancers. They determine speed and intensity of the performers.

REFERENCES

www.inquisitivetraveler.com/pages/artlib/flamenco.html

www.centralhome.com/ballroomcountry/flamenco_history.htm

TEACHING STRATEGIES

The video clip should be viewed at least three times (see chapter 1). In the case where students are searching and observing from home, they will need to list the exact Web site used so that teachers and other students can see the basis for their documentation.

Facilitate a class discussion using the discussion starters listed next. Have students use their recorded answers as a resource. Feel free to paraphrase and choose the questions that work best with your students.

Viewing: What Did You See?

Suggested discussion starters and questions: What are the feet doing in the dance? How are the dancers connected in the group dances? How do the dancers work with the rhythm and music?

Connecting: What Do You Know?

Suggested discussion starters and questions: What are the differences between the men's dancing and the women's dancing? What other dances from other countries use their skirts? How is the use of the skirt different? How are they the same?

Responding: What Do You Think? What Do You Wonder?

Suggested discussion starters and questions: Because of the migration habits of the Gypsies, Flamenco dance has a very strong resemblance to East Indian dances such as Kathak and Bharatanatyam. View a video clip of either of these dances. Where do you think the Indian influence plays out in Flamenco dance?

What questions do you have about this dance? Write them down and continue your research. Some of these questions can be answered through movement.

Performing: What Can You Do?

Choose both Re-create and Create, choose one of these two activities, or make your own performing work that you think is most appropriate for your students.

Re-create Using a toe-heel, toe-heel repetitive footwork step as a means of travel, do the following:

1. Make a floor pattern taken from a video clip.
2. Take the positions from your chosen video. Add the toe-heel movement to get from one position to another.

From H. Scheff, M. Sprague, and S. McGreevy-Nichols, 2010, *Exploring dance forms and styles: A guide to concert, world, social, and historical dance* (Champaign, IL: Human Kinetics).

Create   Create a movement phrase using only the arm movements of the dancers you observed. Make sure it is 24 counts (count from 1 to 24 as you move your arms).

*If you need music and don't have it among your resources, use the video.

FUN FACT   Hindu dancers were hired as entertainers for the festivals. Dance was incorporated into local processions and religious festivals. The ancestors of the Gypsies (Rom) originated in Northern India. As they traveled through west Asia to Europe, they continued this practice of being paid to entertain.

WEB EXPLORATIONS   Key terms to search for include heel work (bulerias, zapateado), castanets, Spanish skirts, Spanish guitar, Cabo San Lucas Flamenco dancing, and Alegrias 3 Rosa De Las Heras.

RECOMMENDED CLIPS

- www.dailymotion.com/video/x1610v_flamenco-dance-show-seville-spain_music
- www.youtube.com/watch?v=bTvG_8QLZwM
- www.youtube.com/watch?v=BWhBGE_oKXE&feature=related
- www.youtube.com/watch?v=Z3r5L1wHJSU&feature=related

From H. Scheff, M. Sprague, and S. McGreevy-Nichols, 2010, *Exploring dance forms and styles: A guide to concert, world, social, and historical dance* (Champaign, IL: Human Kinetics).

Flamenco

Name: _____ Class: _____ Date: _____

STUDENT KNOWLEDGE QUEST WORKSHEET

Name of Dance: Flamenco

1. Viewing: What did you see?
    Record your observations. Describe what you see. Be specific.

    _____

    _____

    _____

    _____

    _____

2. Connecting: What do you know?

    _____

    _____

    _____

    _____

    _____

3. Responding: What do you think? What do you wonder?

    _____

    _____

    _____

    _____

    _____

4. Performing: What can you do?

    _____

    _____

    _____

    _____

    _____

From H. Scheff, M. Sprague, and S. McGreevy-Nichols, 2010, *Exploring dance forms and styles: A guide to concert, world, social, and historical dance* (Champaign, IL: Human Kinetics).

KNOWLEDGE QUEST

INFORMATION AND TEACHING TIPS
Video Clip Search
Category M: World (Subcategory: Europe)
Category A: Concert
Name of Dance: Cossack Dance

Cossack Dance

Dancing from the heart keeps the body warm in cold climates.

DIRECTIONS   Give the students the job of researching clips of and about Cossack dance on the Internet. Many are available; have them choose one or two. They can do this in school if the Internet is available, at home, or at a library. Instruct them to take notes about the actual dancing so that they can complete the student worksheet.

BACKGROUND INFORMATION   Share the following information with them and give them the KQ worksheets to complete as a homework or movement assignment.

- **Translation:** Kazaki are better known outside of Russia as Cossacks. The name *kazak* comes from the Turkish word for outlaw, adventurer, freebooter, or freeman.

- **Country or culture of origin:** Cossack dance comes from Russia and the Ukraine.

- **Timeline:** The first official record of Russian dancing is documented in the year 907 when Great Russian Prince Oleg (Vechshiy Oleg) was victorious over the Greeks in Kiev. Cossack dance was seen in southern Russia and the Ukraine from the 15th to early 20th centuries. Russian and Hungarian (or Slavic) dancing was popular in the United States, especially in Vaudeville, as early as 1900. The immigrants who came from Slavic nations were eager to share their heritage with their fellow Americans and the producers of Vaudeville were eager to employ cheap labor

- **Function or reason:** Cossack army men danced to show their strength. The folk dances were significant to the culture of all the Slavic countries. Some of the dances show that the dance steps were borrowed and adapted from country to country. Cossack dancers were always called to entertain at social and state functions.

- **Who does this dance:** A Ukrainian-Russian folk dance called Hopak was originally a dance for men only. The Hopak has no fixed pattern of steps. Men competitively improvise steps, high leaps, squatting kicks, and turns; women dance simple steps, sway, clap, or circle. Most of the women walk to perfection; it is a very rare art, that of walking gracefully and simply, while being watched.

- **Music and rhythms:** The wandering minstrels of the 16th and 17th centuries who accompanied their songs about the brave accomplishments of the Cossacks, played the kozba, a lute-like instrument. The bandura, a larger instrument with up to 45 strings, replaced the kozba in the 18th century. The introduction of the balalaika, also a strummed instrument, added another layer of interest. For concert performances, singers often accompany the musicians on stage.

- **Traditional clothing or costume:** Traditional Cossack costumes for both men and women were very colorful and covered with embroidered ribbons. It is said that this is the way their homes were, bright and cheerful. The men wore huge baggy pants tucked into their boots. The women's skirts or dresses were full and they wore many petticoats underneath.

From H. Scheff, M. Sprague, and S. McGreevy-Nichols, 2010, *Exploring dance forms and styles: A guide to concert, world, social, and historical dance* (Champaign, IL: Human Kinetics).

Cossack Dance

- **Other information:** The original dancers were serfs. The movement that Cossack dancers do is made up of jumps and leaps. Raising the arms and using many hefty sounds when greeting each other is also common.

REFERENCES

www.sara-artists.com/cossacks/cossacks_eng.htm

www.streetswing.com/histmain/z3cosck1.htm

www.barynya.com/barynya/Cossack%27s_Dance.htm

TEACHING STRATEGIES The video clip should be viewed at least three times (see chapter 1). In the case where students are searching and observing from home, they will need to list the exact Web site used so that teachers and other students can see the basis for their documentation.

Facilitate a class discussion using the discussion starters listed next. Have students use their recorded answers as a resource. Feel free to paraphrase and choose the questions that work best with your students.

Viewing: What Did You See?

Suggested discussion starters and questions: What is the first thing that strikes you about this dance? How would you describe this dance in three words? What are the main body parts that are used?

Connecting: What Do You Know?

Suggested discussion starters and questions: Cossack army men danced to show their strength. What movements demonstrate the strength of the dancers? What are the purposes of the use of their voices that are coordinated with their movement?

Responding: What Do You Think? What Do You Wonder?

Suggested discussion starters and questions: Look at old maps of the Slavic countries. Research dances done in those countries. Cossacks were warriors and traveled from country to country. How has that fact impacted the Cossack dances?

What questions do you have about this dance? Write them down and continue your research. Some of these questions can be answered through movement.

Performing: What Can You Do?

Choose both Re-create and Create, choose one of these two activities, or make your own performing work that you think is most appropriate for your students.

Re-create One of the most difficult steps is the kazatsky. Try to re-create this step. Bend both knees into a plié, or deep knee bend. Fold your arms in front of you and sit straight up while keeping your knees bent. While keeping the supporting leg bent, stick one leg out in front of you with the knee as straight as you can and toe pointed to the ceiling. Quickly change feet. Repeat and repeat and repeat. When you first try this movement you might want to have a helper on each side to support your weight. Once you can balance, you should be able to do three or four in a row. You might have a contest to see who can last the longest.

Create Cossack dances use heavy footed moves and giant jumps and leaps. Research and study how to do some of these steps. Then create your own Cossack dance. You can go to many sites and listen to Russian music or play the music from the video clip to give your dance a finishing touch.

*If you need music and don't have it among your resources, use the video.

From H. Scheff, M. Sprague, and S. McGreevy-Nichols, 2010, *Exploring dance forms and styles: A guide to concert, world, social, and historical dance* (Champaign, IL: Human Kinetics).

Cossack Dance

FUN FACTS   Kazaki (Cossacks) are first mentioned in the 15th century as freedom-loving ex-serfs, Tatars, and descendants of Scythian warriors living on the open plains of southern Ukraine and Russia's Don River basin. Many Hollywood movies depict fearless, captivating warriors, quite lively, dancing with their sabers.

WEB EXPLORATIONS   Key terms to search for include hopak, troika, tsars, Cossack and Russian dances, and dances from the Ukraine.

RECOMMENDED VIDEO CLIPS

- www.youtube.com/watch?v=ZmskmfM5hx8
- www.barynya.com/mp3/barynya_trio.stm

From H. Scheff, M. Sprague, and S. McGreevy-Nichols, 2010, *Exploring dance forms and styles: A guide to concert, world, social, and historical dance* (Champaign, IL: Human Kinetics).

Cossack Dance

Name: _____ Class: _____ Date: _____

STUDENT KNOWLEDGE QUEST WORKSHEET

Name of Dance: Cossack Dance

1. Viewing: What did you see?
   Record your observations. Describe what you see. Be specific.

   _____

   _____

   _____

   _____

   _____

2. Connecting: What do you know?

   _____

   _____

   _____

   _____

   _____

3. Responding: What do you think? What do you wonder?

   _____

   _____

   _____

   _____

   _____

4. Performing: What can you do?

   _____

   _____

   _____

   _____

   _____

From H. Scheff, M. Sprague, and S. McGreevy-Nichols, 2010, *Exploring dance forms and styles: A guide to concert, world, social, and historical dance* (Champaign, IL: Human Kinetics).

KNOWLEDGE QUEST

INFORMATION AND TEACHING TIPS
Video Clip Search
Category M: World (Subcategory: Europe)
Category A: Social (Subcategory: Alone in a group)
Category A: Concert
Name of Dance: Irish Dancing

Irish Dancing

Soft shoe, hard shoe, it is all Irish dancing.

DIRECTIONS   Give the students the job of researching clips of and about Irish dancing on the Internet. Many are available; have them choose one or two. They can do this in school if the Internet is available, at home, or at a library. Instruct them to take notes about the actual dancing so that they can complete the student worksheet.

BACKGROUND INFORMATION   Before students view the video clip, share the following information with them and give them the KQ worksheets to complete as a homework assignment.

- **Country or culture of origin:** From the early history of Irish dance we find a constant shifting of the people because of their traveling from one area to another and because of invasions. As with many other cultural dance forms, each of these peoples had their preferences for different types of dance and music. It is believed that these early dancers were the Druids, who danced as a religious ritual to honor the oak tree and the sun. Their circular dances are seen in the ring dances.

- **Timeline:** Through writings of the 16th century, frequently mentioned dances are the following: the Irish Hey, the Rinnce Fada (long dance), and the Trenchmore. During the mid-16th century, dances were performed at formal occasions. During the 16th century, through the practice of English invaders adopting and adapting dances, the English brought back these dances to Queen Elizabeth's court. Skip several generations and we come to the current one. The worldwide success of Riverdance and Lord of the Dance has placed Irish dance on the international stage for all to enjoy as concert dance and is commonly referred to as Irish step dancing. Two people lead the trend: Michael Flatley and Jean Butler.

- **Function or reason:** Irish people have kept this part of their culture alive to celebrate and to not forget their heritage. Dance is part of funerals as well as celebrations. Irish dance in its many forms still has a part in social functions.

- **Who does this dance:** Women and girls, men and boys, experienced dancers and novices do Irish dance. There are simpler dances for the novices.

- **Music and rhythms:** Accompanying musical instruments are bagpipes, fiddles, and harps. Traditional practice in a country-dance setting is for the fiddler to play a lively tune to get the people to the dance floor. Sometimes it takes three or four times through the tune to get people up and dancing. Some names of the music, which also refers to the names of the dances, are the reel, the light jig, the heavy jig, the single jig, and the hornpipe.

- **Traditional clothing or costume:** Three types of shoes are worn for dancing: a hard shoe and two different soft shoes. The hard shoe looks like a tap shoe but has no metal on it. Early shoes had wooden taps or nails pounded into the heels. Today a fiberglass material is used instead, making the shoes a lighter weight yet able to produce wonderful sound. The soft shoes, which are called *ghillies*, resemble black

From H. Scheff, M. Sprague, and S. McGreevy-Nichols, 2010, *Exploring dance forms and styles: A guide to concert, world, social, and historical dance* (Champaign, IL: Human Kinetics).

Irish Dancing

ballet shoes. Ghillies are worn only by women and girls. Men and boys wear black leather shoes called **reel shoes.** They are also black with a soft front and a hard heel. In early years people wore their "go to meeting" clothes, their Sunday best. There are now intricate and detailed costumes for performances and competions. Different schools and competition teams have special designs for the fronts of their dresses.

- **Other information:** It was the concept and practice of Irish dance masters touring around the country that brought Irish dance in its many forms to other communities. Dancing was also performed during wakes. The mourners followed each other in a ring around the coffin to bagpipe music. Irish step dancing is primarily done in competitions, public performances, or other formal settings. There are rules that have to be followed in competitions, but within those rules there is room for variation, making the choreography interesting. More recently the rules for costumes have become exact. Irish step dancing schools have sprung up internationally. Step dance competitions are very popular and guided by the Irish Dancing Commission. Circa 1780, visiting royalty were treated to young women dancing native dances in proper costumes. When King James visited, he was welcomed by dancers. On special occasions such as this, the lineup would be three people standing side by side. Each person would hold the ends of a white handkerchief. Dancing couples, also holding a handkerchief between them, would follow.

REFERENCES

www.irelandseye.com/dance.html

http://en.wikipedia.org/wiki/Irish_dance

TEACHING STRATEGIES

The video clip should be viewed at least three times (see chapter 1). In the case where students are searching and observing from home, they will need to list the exact Web site used so that teachers and other students can see the basis for their documentation.

Facilitate a class discussion using the discussion starters listed next. Have students use their recorded answers as a resource. Feel free to paraphrase and choose the questions that work best with your students.

Viewing: What Did You See?

Suggested discussion starters and questions: The dancers were light on their feet. What makes them look that way? Does it matter if they were wearing soft or heavy shoes? How did they carry their arms for Irish step dancing?

Connecting: What Do You Know?

Suggested discussion starters and questions: Research both Irish dance and Irish step dancing. What is the difference between Irish dance and Irish step dancing?

Responding: What Do You Think? What Do You Wonder?

Suggested discussion starters and questions: Can you name other dance forms that come to mind when you look at Irish dance? Explain why you think that Lord of the Dance and Riverdance gained such popularity.

What questions do you have about this dance? Write them down and continue your research. Some of these questions can be answered through movement.

From H. Scheff, M. Sprague, and S. McGreevy-Nichols, 2010, *Exploring dance forms and styles: A guide to concert, world, social, and historical dance* (Champaign, IL: Human Kinetics).

Performing: What Can You Do?

Choose both Re-create and Create, choose one of these two activities, or make your own performing work that you think is most appropriate for your students.

Re-create   After watching your clip again, re-create the passing of dancers in the dance around, behind, between, and beside the other dancers. Try walking it and then doing one of the steps you create.

Create   For Irish step dancing many women wear a front piece to their formal costume that represents something about their family or part of the country from which they come. Design and draw such a front piece for your family. Attach it to what you are wearing. See how wearing it makes you stand even straighter than usual.

*If you need music and don't have it among your resources, use the video.

FUN FACTS   When you watch Irish step dancers you will see that they use very few arm movements. The arms are either straight up or straight down. The history behind this is that when the dance was first being performed the stage space was very tight. The groups had no room to hold their arms in any other fashion.

WEB EXPLORATIONS   Key terms to search for include ghillies, hornpipe dance, Yellow-Haired Goat, Single Time, Shoe the Donkey, Irish dancing, Irish step dancing, and Irish dances.

RECOMMENDED CLIPS

- www.youtube.com/watch?v=W22gpBv00gg
- www.youtube.com/watch?v=iQmBHHvmrD4&feature=related
- www.youtube.com/watch?v=MSGqxSdsC4w

From H. Scheff, M. Sprague, and S. McGreevy-Nichols, 2010, *Exploring dance forms and styles: A guide to concert, world, social, and historical dance* (Champaign, IL: Human Kinetics).

Irish Dancing

Name: _____ Class: _____ Date: _____

STUDENT KNOWLEDGE QUEST WORKSHEET

Name of Dance: Irish Dancing

1. Viewing: What did you see?
   Record your observations. Describe what you see. Be specific.

   _____

   _____

   _____

   _____

   _____

2. Connecting: What do you know?

   _____

   _____

   _____

   _____

   _____

3. Responding: What do you think? What do you wonder?

   _____

   _____

   _____

   _____

   _____

4. Performing: What can you do?

   _____

   _____

   _____

   _____

   _____

From H. Scheff, M. Sprague, and S. McGreevy-Nichols, 2010, *Exploring dance forms and styles: A guide to concert, world, social, and historical dance* (Champaign, IL: Human Kinetics).

KNOWLEDGE QUEST

INFORMATION AND TEACHING TIPS
Category M: World (Subcategory: Europe)
Category A: Social (Subcategory: Dances done in a circle)
Name of Dance: Freilach (or Freylach)

Freilach

Circles have no beginning and no end;
a perfect formation for the culture of community.

BACKGROUND INFORMATION Before students view the video clip, share the following information with them.

- **Translation:** The word *freilach* means joy, happiness, festive, and spirited.

- **Country or culture of origin:** This dance comes from shtetls, which were Jewish settlements in Eastern European villages. The dances of the Eastern European Jews were made up of movements that the residents borrowed from Poland, Russia, Romania, and Hungary.

- **Timeline:** This dance was popular from the late 1800s and up to the Holocaust. Now it is being revived and saved by Jews all over the world. Few Jews are left in Eastern Europe. They were either exterminated by the Nazis or fled to other areas of the world for safety.

- **Function or reason:** It is currently performed at celebrations and rites of passage such as weddings, anniversaries, and bar and bat mitzvahs. In the 1800s it was danced at any and many social events in the towns (shtetls).

- **Who does this dance:** Men, women, boys, and girls do this dance, each to their own ability.

- **Music and rhythms:** The music is counted in eights. There is a Slavic undertone with accents on beats 2 and 4 instead of on 1 and 3.

- **Traditional clothing and costume:** The women would wear skirts that came down to their ankles and as fancy a blouse as they could find. They would often wear a scarf around their shoulders. Married women would have their heads covered by a babushka (kerchief), and girls could be bareheaded. Men would wear their dressier trousers, suspenders, a plain shirt, and maybe a vest. Their heads would be covered with a hat or a kippah (circular skullcap).

Photo courtesy of LNDesigns.

From H. Scheff, M. Sprague, and S. McGreevy-Nichols, 2010, *Exploring dance forms and styles: A guide to concert, world, social, and historical dance* (Champaign, IL: Human Kinetics).

Freilach

- **Other information:** It is said that people in concentration camps would dance when "lights out" was called. This kept the dance alive. The people who escaped from the **pogroms** brought the dance and the music with them in their hearts and heads to whatever new land they made home. When the dancer was put in a chair and then the chair was lifted it signified that he or she was the last son or daughter to be married off. Today when the Freilach is performed at weddings, both the bride and the groom are lifted. The lifters will often get close enough so that the couple can dance together.

REFERENCES

www.angelfire.com/ns/helenwinkler/assorted.html

www.jimgold.com/downLoadFile.aspx?fileName=music/Freilach.pdf

http://dance.lovetoknow.com/Traditional_Jewish_Dance

TEACHING STRATEGIES
The video clip should be viewed at least three times (see chapter 1). After students record and discuss their observations and before the third viewing, use the discussion starters listed next to facilitate class discussion. Feel free to paraphrase and choose the questions that work best with your students.

Viewing: What Did You See?

Suggested discussion starters and questions: What did you notice about their head coverings for most women and men? What are the basic movements in this dance?

Connecting: What Do You Know?

Suggested discussion starters and questions: Did you notice which people are holding the handkerchief between them? What formation did they use most in the dance? What other steps do you know that move sideways?

Responding: What Do You Think? What Do You Wonder?

Suggested discussion starters and questions: What are the dancers doing when they take turns coming into the center of the circle? Is this movement different from the movement they were doing before? Why do you think anyone would want to do this? Have you seen any other dances that use this dancing in the center idea?

What questions do you have about this dance? Write them down and continue your research. Some of these questions can be answered through movement.

Performing: What Can You Do?

Choose both Re-create and Create, choose one of these two activities, or make your own performing work that you think is most appropriate for your students.

Re-create   Make a human chain and use the grapevine step (see figure on the next page) to move around the room. You can also reverse the direction. *Note:* Use ideas from recorded observations from question 1 (What did you see?).

Create   Make a dance that celebrates community. Use a circle form.

*If you need music and don't have it among your resources, use the video.

From H. Scheff, M. Sprague, and S. McGreevy-Nichols, 2010, *Exploring dance forms and styles: A guide to concert, world, social, and historical dance* (Champaign, IL: Human Kinetics).

Freilach

FUN FACTS   Klezmer music is traditional for all the dances of Eastern European villages. The instruments used could include a violin, accordion, clarinet, snare drum, trombone, and bass. Itzhak Perlman, a world-class violinist, toured Poland and Romania to learn how to fiddle with klezmer musicians. The word comes from the Hebrew term *klei zemir,* meaning instruments of song.

WEB EXPLORATIONS   Key terms to search for include villages of Eastern Europe, early 1900s to WWII, Jewish dances in Eastern Europe, and klezmer music.

Count 1	Count 2	Count 3	Count 4	Count 1

Right foot steps out sideways.	Left foot crosses in front of right foot.	Right foot steps out sideways.	Left foot crosses behind right foot.	Right foot steps out sideways.

From H. Scheff, M. Sprague, and S. McGreevy-Nichols, 2010, *Exploring dance forms and styles: A guide to concert, world, social, and historical dance* (Champaign, IL: Human Kinetics).

Freilach

Name: _____ Class: _____ Date: _____

STUDENT KNOWLEDGE QUEST WORKSHEET

Name of Dance: Freilach (or Freylach)

1. Viewing: What did you see?
   Record your observations. Describe what you see. Be specific.

   _____

   _____

   _____

   _____

   _____

2. Connecting: What do you know?

   _____

   _____

   _____

   _____

   _____

3. Responding: What do you think? What do you wonder?

   _____

   _____

   _____

   _____

   _____

4. Performing: What can you do?

   _____

   _____

   _____

   _____

   _____

From H. Scheff, M. Sprague, and S. McGreevy-Nichols, 2010, *Exploring dance forms and styles: A guide to concert, world, social, and historical dance* (Champaign, IL: Human Kinetics).

KNOWLEDGE QUEST

INFORMATION AND TEACHING TIPS
Video Clip Search
Category M: World (Subcategory: Europe)
Category A: Concert
Name of Dance: Cancan

Cancan

Ooh la la!

DIRECTIONS   Give the students the job of researching clips of and about the Cancan on the Internet. Many are available; have them choose one or two. They can do this in school if the Internet is available, at home, or at a library. Instruct them to take notes about the actual dancing so that they can complete the student worksheet.

BACKGROUND INFORMATION   Before students view the video clip, share the following information with them and give them the KQ worksheets to complete as a homework assignment.

- **Translation:** Throughout most of the 19th century in France, the dance was also known as the *chahut*. Both words are French; *cancan* means tittle-tattle or scandal, hence a scandalous dance, while *chahut* means noise or uproar.
- **Country or culture of origin:** France
- **Timeline:** The Cancan first appeared in the working-class ballrooms of Montparnasse in Paris around 1830.
- **Function or reason:** It is a physically demanding music hall dance.
- **Who does this dance:** While both sexes originally danced the Cancan, the French Cancan is now primarily danced by women.
- **Music and rhythms:** The "Galop" from Jacques Offenbach's *Orpheus in the Underworld* is the tune most associated with the Cancan.
- **Traditional clothing or costume:** Female dancers wear costumes with long skirts, petticoats, and black stockings, which date back to the fashions of the 1890s.
- **Other information:** The Cancan was a more lively version of the Galop, a dance in quick 2/4 time, which often featured as the final figure in the Quadrille. The Cancan was, therefore, originally a dance for couples, who indulged in high kicks and other gestures with arms and legs. It is thought that they were influenced by the antics of a popular entertainer of the 1820s, Charles Mazurier, who was well known for his acrobatic performances, which included the grand écart (jump splits), which was later a popular feature of the Cancan. The main moves are the high kick or battement, the rond de jambe (quick rotary movement of lower leg with knee raised and skirt held up), the port d'armes (turning on one leg while grasping the other leg by the ankle and holding it almost vertical), the cartwheel, and the grand écart. It has become common practice for dancers to scream and yelp while performing the Cancan, but it is by no means essential.

REFERENCES

http://en.wikipedia.org/wiki/Can-can

www.streetswing.com/histmain/z3cancan.htm

www.economicexpert.com/a/Can:can.htm

From H. Scheff, M. Sprague, and S. McGreevy-Nichols, 2010, *Exploring dance forms and styles: A guide to concert, world, social, and historical dance* (Champaign, IL: Human Kinetics).

Cancan

TEACHING STRATEGIES The video clip should be viewed at least three times (see chapter 1). In the case where students are searching and observing from home, they will need to list the exact Web site so that teachers and other students can see the basis for the documentation.

Facilitate a class discussion using the discussion starters listed next. Have students use their recorded answers as a resource. Feel free to paraphrase and choose the questions that work best with your students.

Viewing: What Did You See?

Suggested discussion starters and questions: What is the first thing that strikes you about this dance? How would you describe this dance in three words? What are the main body parts that are used?

Connecting: What Do You Know?

Suggested discussion starters and questions: When have you ever seen a dance like this performed? How was it like this dance? How was it different?

Responding: What Do You Think? What Do You Wonder?

Suggested discussion starters and questions: The Cancan is a hybrid of the Polka and the Quadrille. Research these two dances on the Internet. Where do you see the connections between these dances?

What questions do you have about this dance? Write them down and continue your research. Some of these questions can be answered through movement.

Performing: What Can You Do?

Choose both Re-create and Create, choose one of these two activities, or make your own performing work that you feel is most appropriate for your students.

Re-create Choose two or three movements from the Cancan and organize into a shortened version of the dance.

Create Create a chorus line routine for 10 or more dancers.

*If you need music and don't have it among your resources, use the video.

FUN FACTS French painter Henri de Toulouse-Lautrec produced several paintings and a large number of posters of Cancan dancers. Other painters to have treated the Cancan as a subject include Georges Seurat, Georges Rouault, and Pablo Picasso.

WEB EXPLORATIONS Key terms to search for include Cancan, Can Can, and Can-Can.

RECOMMENDED CLIPS

- www.youtube.com/watch?v=lK0gYi1YEZ8
- www.youtube.com/watch?v=mA2avYxfaFU&feature=related
- www.youtube.com/watch?v=Lks7YtP4984&feature=related

From H. Scheff, M. Sprague, and S. McGreevy-Nichols, 2010, *Exploring dance forms and styles: A guide to concert, world, social, and historical dance* (Champaign, IL: Human Kinetics).

Name: _____ Class: _____ Date: _____

STUDENT KNOWLEDGE QUEST WORKSHEET

Name of Dance: Cancan

1. Viewing: What did you see?
   Record your observations. Describe what you see. Be specific.

   _____

   _____

   _____

   _____

   _____

2. Connecting: What do you know?

   _____

   _____

   _____

   _____

   _____

3. Responding: What do you think? What do you wonder?

   _____

   _____

   _____

   _____

   _____

4. Performing: What can you do?

   _____

   _____

   _____

   _____

   _____

From H. Scheff, M. Sprague, and S. McGreevy-Nichols, 2010, *Exploring dance forms and styles: A guide to concert, world, social, and historical dance* (Champaign, IL: Human Kinetics).

Kathak

KNOWLEDGE QUEST

INFORMATION AND TEACHING TIPS
Category M: World (Subcategory: Asia)
Name of Dance: Kathak

Dance is Divine

from Hindu mythology

BACKGROUND INFORMATION   Before students view the video clip, share the following information with them.

Note: There are two video clips: One demonstrates the basic 16-count rhythmic foot pattern and the other demonstrates one version of this dance integrating the footwork.

- **Translation:** The Sanskrit word *kathak* means to tell a story.

- **Country or culture of origin:** One of the main styles of Indian classical dance, Kathak originated in northern India.

- **Timeline:** Nearly 2000 years old, the Kathak dance began to acquire its distinctive shape and features after the 16th century.

- **Function or reason:** Kathak dance emphasizes the telling of stories through the portrayal of a variety of traditional characters and themes. Performed originally in the temples to express epic stories of the Hindu gods, it eventually made its way to the royal courts.

- **Who does this dance:** Both men and women perform this dance as solo dancers.

- **Music and rhythms:** Rhythmical sounds are made from hundreds of bells on the dancers' ankles. The main instruments are tabla (two-drum ensemble), pakahawaj (a barrel-shaped drum with two heads), sarangi (a stringed instrument played with a bow), a flute, and sometimes a violin and a sitar. Many times it is accompanied by song or poetry.

- **Traditional clothing or costume:** Women wear a flared knee-length dress over churidar (tight-fitting trousers) with a dupatta (long scarf) draping the head and shoulders. Men wear a Persian costume of wide shirts and round caps.

- **Other information:** Kathak is known for its fast footwork and spins, called chakkaras, which, combined with hand positions (mudras), steps, expression, and mime, are used to tell the story. The ankle bells (ghungroo) turn the feet into musical instruments. Kathak comes from an oral tradition, and has been passed down from gurus to students for hundreds of years. The four basic elements that must be mastered in Kathak dance are tayari (technique with precision), layakari (mastery of rhythm), khubsurti (beauty), and

From H. Scheff, M. Sprague, and S. McGreevy-Nichols, 2010, *Exploring dance forms and styles: A guide to concert, world, social, and historical dance* (Champaign, IL: Human Kinetics).

nazakut (delicacy). Traditional storylines, themes, and emotions being expressed revolve around the following: shringar (beauty and attraction), karuna (compassion and sadness), vira (heroic pride and confidence), raudra (anger and ferocity), bibhatsa (disgust and aversion), hasya (laughter and joy), bhayanaka (fear and fright), adbhuta (surprise and wonder), and shanti (peace).

Kathak

REFERENCES

http://en.wikipedia.org/wiki/Kathak

www.geocities.com/kathakdance/kathak.htm

http://dances.iloveindia.com/classical-dances/kathak.html

TEACHING STRATEGIES   The video clip should be viewed at least three times (see chapter 1). After students record and discuss their observations and before the third viewing, use the discussion starters listed next to facilitate class discussion. Feel free to paraphrase and choose the questions that work best with your students.

Viewing: What Did You See?

Suggested discussion starters and questions: What are the main body parts used? What are some key movements used? How is sound used in this dance? What do you notice about the way the feet are used? What do you notice about the way the hands are used in this dance? What do you notice about the facial expressions?

Connecting: What Do You Know?

Suggested discussion starters and questions: What other dances do you know that tell a story? What are some of the ways the dancer moves to create different sounds with the bells? How is speed represented in this dance? Look at a clip of Flamenco dance (do a Web search for one). What similarities and differences can you see between these two world dance forms?

Responding: What Do You Think? What Do You Wonder?

Suggested discussion starters and questions: What idea or emotion do you think this dance is expressing? What is the role of facial expressions in this dance? Why do you think that Kathak dance might sometimes be referred to as a whirling dance? Why do you think there is such a strong similarity between Flamenco and Kathak dances?

What questions do you have about this dance? Write them down and continue your research. Some of these questions can be answered through movement.

Performing: What Can You Do?

Choose both Re-create and Create, choose one of these two activities, or make your own performing work that you think is most appropriate for your students.

Re-create

1. In small groups, students re-create the basic 16-count rhythmic pattern of the feet demonstrated in the first video clip.

   - Count 1: Stamp right.
   - Count 2: Stamp left.
   - Count 3: Stamp right.
   - Count 4: Stamp left.
   - Count 5: Stamp left.
   - Count 6: Stamp right.

From H. Scheff, M. Sprague, and S. McGreevy-Nichols, 2010, *Exploring dance forms and styles: A guide to concert, world, social, and historical dance* (Champaign, IL: Human Kinetics).

- Count 7: Stamp left.
- Count 8: Stamp right.
- Count 9: Stamp right.
- Count 10: Stamp left.
- Count 11: Stamp right.
- Count 12: Stamp left.
- Count 13: Stamp right.
- Count 14: Stamp right.
- Count 15: Stamp left.
- Count 16: Stamp right.

2. Try to speed up the tempo of the movement.
3. Replicate some of the arm and hand movements.

Create   Create an original dance using repeating patterns of gestures, facial movements, and body movements that express one of the following traditional Kathak dance themes:

- Beauty and attraction
- Compassion and sadness
- Pride and confidence
- Anger and ferocity
- Disgust and aversion
- Laughter and joy
- Fear and fright
- Surprise and wonder
- Peace

*If you need music and don't have it among your resources, use the video.

FUN FACTS   There are many striking similarities between Kathak and the Flamenco dances of the Spanish Gitanos, most notably in the lack of much deviation from the vertical axis, percussive footwork, and dependence on a sometimes complex rhythmic cycle.

WEB EXPLORATIONS   Key terms to search for include Kathak dance, Indian dance, and Gitanos.

From H. Scheff, M. Sprague, and S. McGreevy-Nichols, 2010, *Exploring dance forms and styles: A guide to concert, world, social, and historical dance* (Champaign, IL: Human Kinetics).

Name: _____ Class: _____ Date: _____

STUDENT KNOWLEDGE QUEST WORKSHEET

Name of Dance: Kathak

1. Viewing: What did you see?
   Record your observations. Describe what you see. Be specific.

   _____

   _____

   _____

   _____

   _____

2. Connecting: What do you know?

   _____

   _____

   _____

   _____

   _____

3. Responding: What do you think? What do you wonder?

   _____

   _____

   _____

   _____

   _____

4. Performing: What can you do?

   _____

   _____

   _____

   _____

   _____

From H. Scheff, M. Sprague, and S. McGreevy-Nichols, 2010, *Exploring dance forms and styles: A guide to concert, world, social, and historical dance* (Champaign, IL: Human Kinetics).

Hmong Dance

KNOWLEDGE QUEST
INFORMATION AND TEACHING TIPS
Category M: World (Subcategory: Asia)
Name of Dance: Hmong Dance

Almost lost but not forgotten.

BACKGROUND INFORMATION   Before students view the video clip, share the following information with them.

- **Country or culture of origin:** The Hmong are hill tribe people from Laos. They migrated from China in the 1800s to Laos to escape Chinese oppression and persecution. The Hmong traditions come from a history that was not recorded through the written word; instead Hmong history and traditions are passed down through story telling, music, dance and, of late, story cloths called pa ndau.

- **Timeline:** While no one knows exactly where the Hmong people originated, evidence of the Hmong can be traced to settlements along the Yellow River in China thousands of years ago. Dance has always been part of their culture.

- **Function or reason:** Dance in the Hmong culture takes place at community gatherings such as the New Year. During the New Year celebration, Hmong dress in traditional clothing and enjoy Hmong traditional foods, dance, music, bull fights, and other forms of entertainment. Hmong New Year celebrations frequently occur in November and December (traditionally at the end of the harvest season when all work is done), serving as a thanksgiving holiday for the Hmong people. Traditional dance is also associated with meaningful events and is an important expression of the cultural identity.

- **Who does this dance:** Both males and females of all ages do this dance.

- **Music and rhythms:** The unique music used in Hmong dance has both indigenous and foreign influences, which have given it a character of its own. For example, at the New Year festival, as a way to bridge Hmong and North American culture, the stage is shared by musicians performing traditional Hmong music and current North American hits. Rock bands and qeej (traditional wood and bamboo mouth instrument) players both attract crowds.

- **Traditional clothing and costume:** The girls wear very elaborate costumes. Usually, mothers make the shirts and aprons for them. However, the making of a

traditional skirt takes about one year to complete, so it is easier for Hmong living in the United States to order traditional dresses and costumes from Laos, Vietnam, or Thailand.

- **Other information:** This traditional Hmong dance is influenced by the Laos and Thai culture, from where the majority of U.S. Hmong immigrated. Many other types of Hmong dances exist, but it's hard to distinguish exactly which one is the original Hmong dance because their origins are uncertain.

REFERENCES

www.arts.wa.gov/folk-arts/hmong/dance.shtml

www.tcdailyplanet.net/node/3858

www.postcrescent.com/apps/pbcs.dll/article?AID=/20071207/APC06/712070538/1036

www.hmongstudies.org/Dance_Student_s_survey_Chart.pdf

http://henry.mpls.k12.mn.us/sites/40ffb804-cceb-41db-92d5-ed0b7a6eb987/uploads/seexeng-lee-sig.pdf

TEACHING STRATEGIES   The video clip should be viewed at least three times (see chapter 1). After students record and discuss their observations and before the third viewing, use the discussion starters listed next to facilitate class discussion. Feel free to paraphrase and choose the questions that work best with your students.

Viewing: What Did You See?

Suggested discussion starters and questions: What are the main body parts used? What are some key movements used? What do you notice about the way the feet are used? What do you notice about the way the hands are used in this dance? How do the dancers change positions?

Connecting: What Do You Know?

Suggested discussion starters and questions: How do the dancers relate to one another? What do you notice about the floor pattern? What do you notice about the rhythm of the movement?

Responding: What Do You Think? What Do You Wonder?

Suggested discussion starters and questions: The Hmong people have been forced to move from place to place over time. Where do you see influences of other cultures in their dance and music? Where do you see a commitment to stay true to their culture?

What questions do you have about this dance? Write them down and continue your research. Some of these questions can be answered through movement.

Performing: What Can You Do?

Choose both Re-create and Create, choose one of these two activities, or make your own performing work that you think is most appropriate for your students.

Re-create   View the video clip on the DVD again. As the video is playing, try to learn and reproduce either just some of the arm and hand movements or just some of the foot movements. Once you get comfortable with this try to coordinate a small section of hand and foot movements. Work with a group and try to perform the movements using various formations. *Note:* Use ideas from recorded observations from question 1 (What did you see?).

From H. Scheff, M. Sprague, and S. McGreevy-Nichols, 2010, *Exploring dance forms and styles: A guide to concert, world, social, and historical dance* (Champaign, IL: Human Kinetics).

Hmong Dance

Create   Hmong paj ntaub story cloths play an important role in Hmong everyday and ceremonial life. Story cloths depict narratives of ancient legends and traditional life in peaceful times. They also often depict their recent experiences of warfare, loss of homeland, the hopeless future of Thai refugee camps, and for some, their departure to an uncertain new life in North America. Find images of Hmong story cloths on the Internet. Choose one and use it as an inspiration for an original dance that expresses the ideas, emotions, and story represented in the story cloth.

*If you need music and don't have it among your resources, use the video.

FUN FACTS   In a recent survey, when asked if they think taking dance class at Hmong Cultural Center has helped them do better in any classes at school, 23 of 30 Hmong girls said yes!

WEB EXPLORATIONS   Key terms to search for include Hmong dance, Hmong music, and Hmong story cloths.

Name: _____ Class: _____ Date: _____

STUDENT KNOWLEDGE QUEST WORKSHEET

Hmong Dance

Name of Dance: Hmong Dance

1. Viewing: What did you see?
   Record your observations. Describe what you see. Be specific.

   _____

   _____

   _____

   _____

   _____

2. Connecting: What do you know?

   _____

   _____

   _____

   _____

   _____

3. Responding: What do you think? What do you wonder?

   _____

   _____

   _____

   _____

   _____

4. Performing: What can you do?

   _____

   _____

   _____

   _____

   _____

From H. Scheff, M. Sprague, and S. McGreevy-Nichols, 2010, *Exploring dance forms and styles: A guide to concert, world, social, and historical dance* (Champaign, IL: Human Kinetics).

Raqs al Balas

KNOWLEDGE QUEST

INFORMATION AND TEACHING TIPS

Category M: World (Subcategory: North Africa and Middle East)
Name of Dance: Raqs al Balas (Ballas or Balaise)

It is not always easy to get a drink of water.

BACKGROUND INFORMATION Before students view the video clip, share the following information with them.

- **Translation:** The word *raqs* means dance and the word *balas* means water jug.

- **Country or culture of origin:** Raqs al Balas could represent Upper Egypt. There are also versions from Tunisia (men's dance) and North Africa.

- **Timeline:** The Raqs al Balas is a folkloric dance and may be quite old. It is still performed today.

- **Who does this dance:** Fellahen (farmer girls) of Upper Egypt dance this country dance. In Tunisia, both men and women perform this dance at weddings.

- **Music and rhythms:** If you are watching a version from Upper Egypt, Saidi music is used. Saidi rhythms are named for where they originated, Upper Egypt, between Gizeh and Edfu. The time signature is 4/4 and the makloub rhythm could be heard as dom-tak, dom-dom-tak. Instrumentation includes traditional instruments such as the rababa (an ancestor of the violin), the mizmar (a horn), and dumbek and tabla beledi drums. Of course, if the dance version is from Tunisia, traditional Tunisian music is used.

- **Traditional clothing or costume:** Galabiya fellahi are granny dresses with large, full skirts, often with ruffles. The dancer in the video clip is wearing one of these dresses.

From H. Scheff, M. Sprague, and S. McGreevy-Nichols, 2010, *Exploring dance forms and styles: A guide to concert, world, social, and historical dance* (Champaign, IL: Human Kinetics).

- **Other information:** Since women carrying water jugs on their shoulders or heads are still seen today in rural areas, it is easy to believe that this dance is based on work movement. The movement of the balas (water jug) is an important part of the dance. The jug can be balanced on either shoulder, used for scooping and pouring movements, balanced on the head, or moved in a figure-eight pattern, which indicates the water of the Nile. The Tunisian men's version includes balancing multiple water jugs on the head.

REFERENCES

Lihs, H.R. 2002. *Appreciating dance: A guide to the world's liveliest art,* third edition. Highstown, NJ: Princeton Book Company Publishers.

Richards T., (ed.). 2000. *The belly dance book: Rediscovering the oldest dance.* Concord, CA: Backbeat Press.

www.princessfarhana.com/articles/propbalance.htm

www.gildedserpent.com/art43/gamilaniledance2jug.htm

TEACHING STRATEGIES   The video clip should be viewed at least three times (see chapter 1). After students record and discuss their observations and before the third viewing, use the discussion starters listed next to facilitate class discussion. Feel free to paraphrase and choose the questions that work best with your students.

Viewing: What Did You See?

Suggested discussion starters and questions: What did the dancer do with the water jug? Describe the special way she often walked. How did she use her skirt and veil? What did you notice about how movement was repeated?

Connecting: What Do You Know?

Suggested discussion starters and questions: Since both this version of the water jug dance and the cane dance are from Upper Egypt, how are they similar? Choose the movements that represent the work of getting water and explain why you chose them. What other dances represent working?

Responding: What Do You Think? What Do You Wonder?

Suggested discussion starters and questions: How did a simple chore like going to get water become a dance? How does a dance travel or become popular in more than one country? (Remember, versions of this dance exist in many of the North African and Middle Eastern countries.)

   What questions do you have about this dance? Write them down and continue your research. Some of these questions can be answered through movement.

Performing: What Can You Do?

Choose both Re-create and Create, choose one of these two activities, or make your own performing work that you think is most appropriate for your students.

Re-create   In the video clip is a step called kashlimar. In order to do this step the dancer has to alternate feet while stepping forward, stepping in place, stepping backward, and stepping in place (forward, step, back, step). Practice this step. Then do one kashlimar toward each of the four walls (front wall, side wall, back wall, and the other side wall). Once you can do these direction changes, add a shoulder shimmy (front and back alternating movements of the shoulders). You can use the video clip to check your work.

From H. Scheff, M. Sprague, and S. McGreevy-Nichols, 2010, *Exploring dance forms and styles: A guide to concert, world, social, and historical dance* (Champaign, IL: Human Kinetics).

157

Raqs al Balas

Create Using a plastic bowl or pitcher, create some movements. Organize them in a way you like. Practice, then show another student or the class.

*If you need music and don't have it among your resources, use the video.

FUN FACTS There are other dances that call for balancing different objects on one's head. Some of these objects are a sword, a candelabra or candles, a tray, bottles, and glasses.

WEB EXPLORATIONS Key terms to search for include Water Jug dance, Raqs al Balas, Raqs al Ballas, and Raqs al Balaise.

From H. Scheff, M. Sprague, and S. McGreevy-Nichols, 2010, *Exploring dance forms and styles: A guide to concert, world, social, and historical dance* (Champaign, IL: Human Kinetics).

Name: _____ Class: _____ Date: _____

STUDENT KNOWLEDGE QUEST WORKSHEET

Name of Dance: Raqs al Balas (Ballas or Balaise)

1. Viewing: What did you see?
   Record your observations. Describe what you see. Be specific.

   _____

   _____

   _____

   _____

   _____

2. Connecting: What do you know?

   _____

   _____

   _____

   _____

   _____

3. Responding: What do you think? What do you wonder?

   _____

   _____

   _____

   _____

   _____

4. Performing: What can you do?

   _____

   _____

   _____

   _____

   _____

From H. Scheff, M. Sprague, and S. McGreevy-Nichols, 2010, *Exploring dance forms and styles: A guide to concert, world, social, and historical dance* (Champaign, IL: Human Kinetics).

Barong Dance

KNOWLEDGE QUEST
INFORMATION AND TEACHING TIPS
Video Clip Search
Category M: World (Subcategory: Asia)
Category A: Concert
Name of Dance: Barong Dance (A Balinese Dance)

A fight between good and evil

DIRECTIONS   Give the students the job of researching clips of and about the Barong dance on the Internet. Many are available; have them choose one or two. They can do this in school if the Internet is available, at home, or at a library. Instruct them to take notes about the actual dancing so that they can complete the student worksheet.

BACKGROUND INFORMATION   Before students view the video clip, share the following information with them and give them the KQ worksheets to complete as a homework assignment.

- **Translation:** Barong is a character in the mythology of Bali. He is the king of the spirits, leader of the hosts of good, and enemy of Rangda in the mythological traditions of Bali. Because Bali has an abundance of myths and legends, several versions of the Barong dance exist, including Barong Ket (Lion Barong), Barong Asu (Dog Barong), Barong Macan (Tiger Barong), Barong Bangkal (Pig Barong), Barong Gajah (Elephant Barong), and others.

- **Country or culture of origin:** This dance comes from Bali.

- **Timeline:** Balinese dance has been evolving for almost 1,000 years.

- **Function or reason:** The Barong is probably the most well known dance in Bali. It is a story-telling dance, narrating the fight between good and evil. This dance is the classic example of the Balinese way of acting out mythology—blending myth and history into one.

- **Who does this dance:** Men and women do the Barong.

- **Music and rhythms:** The traditional Balinese orchestra, known as gamelan, is composed of various forms of percussion, among which notes overlap. Also included are a number of string and woodwind instruments. Most of the players, which can range from a few to several dozen, sit behind various kinds of metallophones, gongs, and xylophones. Each gamelan has its own tuning, which prevents instruments from being interchanged from one gamelan to another (www.anomcottages.com/culture/music.html).

- **Traditional clothing or costumes:** The Barong Ket is a lion-like creature. The mask of a Barong Ket costume is borrowed from Hindu-inspired sculpture while the two-person dancing body was probably inspired by the dancing lions and unicorns of Chinese festivals. The Barong's mask is believed to be inhabited by a spirit. During rituals and when not in use, the mask is given an honored place in a village temple.

- **Other information:** Go to www.inm-asiaguides.com/Bali/ebarong.htm to read an excerpt from one of the Barong stories.

REFERENCES
www.inm-asiaguides.com/Bali/ebarong.htm
www.geocities.com/bali_info_4u/bali_dances.htm
www.baliholiday.com/balinese_dance_and_drama.htm
www.anomcottages.com/culture/music.html

From H. Scheff, M. Sprague, and S. McGreevy-Nichols, 2010, *Exploring dance forms and styles: A guide to concert, world, social, and historical dance* (Champaign, IL: Human Kinetics).

TEACHING STRATEGIES The video clip should be viewed at least three times (see chapter 1). In the case where students are searching and observing from home, they will need to list the exact Web site used so that teachers and other students can see the basis for their documentation.

Facilitate a class discussion using the discussion starters listed next. Have students use their recorded answers as a resource. Feel free to paraphrase and choose the questions that work best with your students.

Viewing: What Did You See?

Suggested discussion starters and questions: What is the first thing that strikes you about this dance? How would you describe this dance in three words? What are some of the ways the dancer expresses ideas? What might the costumes say about the dance or performers?

Connecting: What Do You Know?

Suggested discussion starters and questions: When have you ever seen a dance that tells a story like this performed? How was it like this dance? How was it different?

Responding: What do You Think? What Do You Wonder?

Suggested discussion starters and questions: In this story are good characters and evil characters. How might you move as an evil character? How might you move as a good character?

What questions do you have about this dance? Write them down and continue your research. Some of these questions can be answered through movement.

Performing: What Can You Do?

Choose both Re-create and Create, choose one of these two activities, or make your own performing work that you think is most appropriate for your students.

Re-create Working in trios, two students create a Barong character using a bed sheet so that the two dancers look like one creature. The third becomes the monkey character. The trio entertains the audience.

Create Create a story dance about good and evil. Make and use masks to define characters.

*If you need music and don't have it among your resources, use the video.**

FUN FACTS Balinese dance is a part of daily life of Balinese people and carries great religious importance. The commercial performances for tourists that are today offered on a daily basis in several places of Bali do not have the same religious significance and atmosphere of a dance that is performed at a real temple festival.

WEB EXPLORATIONS Key terms to search for include Balinese dance and Barong dance.

RECOMMENDED CLIPS

- www.youtube.com/watch?v=AtxiA-YhRfw
- www.youtube.com/watch?v=2ZoK4xCieXg
- www.youtube.com/watch?v=kPx02UcSwcY

From H. Scheff, M. Sprague, and S. McGreevy-Nichols, 2010, *Exploring dance forms and styles: A guide to concert, world, social, and historical dance* (Champaign, IL: Human Kinetics).

Barong Dance

Name: _____ Class: _____ Date: _____

STUDENT KNOWLEDGE QUEST WORKSHEET
Name of Dance: Barong Dance (A Balinese Dance)

1. Viewing: What did you see?
   Record your observations. Describe what you see. Be specific.

   _____

   _____

   _____

   _____

   _____

2. Connecting: What do you know?

   _____

   _____

   _____

   _____

   _____

3. Responding: What do you think? What do you wonder?

   _____

   _____

   _____

   _____

   _____

4. Performing: What can you do?

   _____

   _____

   _____

   _____

   _____

From H. Scheff, M. Sprague, and S. McGreevy-Nichols, 2010, *Exploring dance forms and styles: A guide to concert, world, social, and historical dance* (Champaign, IL: Human Kinetics).

KNOWLEDGE QUEST

INFORMATION AND TEACHING TIPS
Category M: World (Subcategory: Asia)
Category A: Concert
Name of Dance: Bharatanatyam

Bharatanatyam

Dance of the Gods

BACKGROUND INFORMATION Before students view the video clip, share the following information with them.

- **Translation:** The word *bharatanatyam* is derived from three terms—*bha* meaning bhava or abhinaya (expression), *ra* meaning raga (melody) and *ta* meaning tala (rhythm). In short, the dance form is a communion of expression, melody, and rhythm.

- **Country or culture of origin:** Bharatanatyam is a classic dance form originating in South India and is known as the national dance of India.

- **Timeline:** Bharatanatyam traces its origins back 3,000 years.

- **Function or reason:** Bharatanatyam dance expresses a variety of feelings, sentiments, and actions. From interpreting scriptures to narrating myths and legends, the movements portray ideas such as praising the gods or they express moods and emotions relating to love, humor, heroism, fear, courage, disaster, compassion, wonder, peace, and anger.

- **Who does this dance:** Women perform this dance the most; many think men cannot adequately portray this dance.

- **Music and rhythms:** Bharatanatyam is usually accompanied by the classical Carnatic music. Basic accompaniments are vocals, mridangam, violin, natuvanga, veena, and flute. The musicians sit in the corner of a stage or in a place in front of the stage.

- **Traditional clothing:** The Bharatanatyam costume is actually based on what the bride wears when she gets married. The sari is ankle length. The dhoti is wrapped around the legs, and the end of it covers the back and comes to the front from the right shoulder of the dancer. This end is secured tightly on the waist of the dancer with the help of a golden or decorated belt. Between both legs another piece of cloth is stitched and looks like a Chinese fan that opens up when the dancer bends or spreads her legs during the dance. The entire jewelry and headpiece that you see is what a bride would wear once she gets married. Jingles are a must.

- **Other information:** The basic techniques of Bharatanatyam are called karana (which means doing, also called karanam) and hasta mudras. *Karana* refers to the conscious and systematic movements in Indian classical dance; Bharatanatyam has 108-125 of these dance postures and transitional movements. *Hasta mudras* refers to the different ways of holding the hands (single and double hand gestures).

REFERENCES

http://en.wikipedia.org/wiki/Bharatanatyam

www.geocities.com/Tokyo/Shrine/3155/bnatyam.html

http://in.geocities.com/medhahari/bharatanatyam/bharatanatyam.html

From H. Scheff, M. Sprague, and S. McGreevy-Nichols, 2010, *Exploring dance forms and styles: A guide to concert, world, social, and historical dance* (Champaign, IL: Human Kinetics).

Bharatanatyam

TEACHING STRATEGIES   The video clip should be viewed at least three times (see chapter 1). After students record and discuss their observations and before the third viewing, use the discussion starters listed next to facilitate class discussion. Feel free to paraphrase and choose the questions that work best with your students.

Viewing: What Did You See?

Suggested discussion starters and questions: What are the main body parts used? What are some key movements used? What do you notice about the way the feet are used? What do you notice about the way the hands are used in this dance? What do you notice about the facial expressions?

Connecting: What Do You Know?

Suggested discussion starters and questions: What are some of the ways the dancer expresses ideas? What are some ways the dancer transitions from one position to the next? What might the costume say about the dance and performer?

Responding: What Do You Think? What Do You Wonder?

Suggested discussion starters and questions: Bharatanatyam dance expresses a variety of feelings, sentiments, and actions. From interpreting scriptures to narrating myths and legends, the movements portray ideas such as praising the gods or they express moods and emotions relating to love, humor, heroism, fear, courage, disaster, compassion, wonder, peace, and anger. How do the various poses and hand movements suggest any of these themes? Support your argument with examples.

What questions do you have about this dance? Write them down and continue your research. Some of these questions can be answered through movement.

Performing: What Can You Do?

Choose both Re-create and Create, choose one of these two activities, or make your own performing work that you think is most appropriate for your students.

Re-create   View the video again. As the video is playing, try to learn and reproduce either just some of the arm and hand movements or just some of the foot movements. Once you get comfortable with doing this, try to coordinate a small section of hand and foot movements.

Create   In a small group or individually, create your own version of the Bharatanatyam by creating the following:

- Three original dance postures (karanas)
- Two original hand gestures (hasta mudras)
- One facial or eye gesture
- Transitional movements to connect the postures and gestures.

*If you need music and don't have it among your resources, use the video.

FUN FACTS   Many of the ancient sculptures in Hindu temples are based on Bharatanatyam dance postures.

WEB EXPLORATIONS   Key terms to search for include Bharatanatyam, dances of India, karanas, and hasta mudras.

From H. Scheff, M. Sprague, and S. McGreevy-Nichols, 2010, *Exploring dance forms and styles: A guide to concert, world, social, and historical dance* (Champaign, IL: Human Kinetics).

Name: _____ Class: _____ Date: _____

STUDENT KNOWLEDGE QUEST WORKSHEET

Bharatanatyam

Name of Dance: Bharatanatyam

1. Viewing: What did you see?
   Record your observations. Describe what you see. Be specific.

   _____

   _____

   _____

   _____

   _____

2. Connecting: What do you know?

   _____

   _____

   _____

   _____

   _____

3. Responding: What do you think? What do you wonder?

   _____

   _____

   _____

   _____

   _____

4. Performing: What can you do?

   _____

   _____

   _____

   _____

   _____

From H. Scheff, M. Sprague, and S. McGreevy-Nichols, 2010, *Exploring dance forms and styles: A guide to concert, world, social, and historical dance* (Champaign, IL: Human Kinetics).

Dabkee

KNOWLEDGE QUEST
INFORMATION AND TEACHING TIPS
Category M: World (Subcategory: Asia and Middle East)
Category A: Social (Subcategory: Dances done in a line)
Name of Dance: Dabkee

What's in a name? The Dabkee by any other spelling is just as fun!

BACKGROUND INFORMATION Before students view the video clip, share the following information with them.

- **Translation:** In Arabic, the word *dabkeh* means the stomping of the feet.
- **Country or culture of origin:** The Dabkee came from the people of the Levant region, which includes Lebanon, Syria, Palestine, and parts of Iraq and Jordan.
- **Timeline:** Although two Lebanese composers, Assi and Mansour Rahbani, made the Dabkee music well known in the 20th century, its roots are folkloric and based on the music that helped the work of stomping to compact the dirt and straw on the roofs.
- **Function or reason:** This dance is performed at community social events or celebrations such as family parties or weddings. There are also Dabkee competitions.
- **Who does this dance:** This dance is danced by men and women, young and old.
- **Music and rhythms:** The word *dabkee* can also refer to the type of music as well as the dance form. The rhythms of the dance are as varied as the countries and people who dance it.
- **Traditional clothing or costume:** Today people dance the Dabkee in modern-day clothing. Folkloric groups perform in more traditional clothing. Women wear full-length dresses with pants underneath and long veils on their heads that cover their hair. Men wear boots, full-legged pants, vests, and Arab-type headdresses. The dancers in the video clip are not wearing the traditional clothing.
- **Other information:** The Dabkee is a line dance. The dancers hold hands and usually travel in a counterclockwise direction, in a circular pathway. The leader,

Dabkee

called raas (head) or lawweeh (waver), can be at the front of the line or out in front of the line directing the change of steps and perhaps improvising variations. The leader usually swings a scarf or a string of beads or masbha, which is like a rosary. Some of the variations of the steps can be very complicated patterns of stomping, hopping, and stepping. The dancers in the video clip are performing a simple version of a Lebanese step.

REFERENCES

http://al-juthoor.com/about.htm

http://en.wikipedia.org/wiki/Dabke

TEACHING STRATEGIES

The video clip should be viewed at least three times (see chapter 1). After students record and discuss their observations and before the third viewing, use the discussion starters listed next to facilitate class discussion. Feel free to paraphrase and choose the questions that work best with your students.

Viewing: What Did You See?

Suggested discussion starters and questions: Describe the shoulder movement and tell how it was relating to the music. What formation was used? What floor pattern was used? What was the lead dancer doing with the scarf? What were the dancers doing with their arms and hands?

Connecting: What Do You Know?

Suggested discussion starters and questions: Many cultures, including in the United States, have line dances; what are the usual characteristics? Name some line dances you know.

Responding: What Do You Think? What Do You Wonder?

Suggested discussion starters and questions: Why do you think so many cultures have line dances? How do the characteristics of line dances work so well for social occasions?

What questions do you have about this dance? Write them down and continue your research. Some of these questions can be answered through movement.

Performing: What Can You Do?

Choose both Re-create and Create, choose one of these two activities, or make your own performing work that you think is most appropriate for your students.

Re-create   Learn the simple version of the Dabkee from the video clip. Dance this with your classmates. Take turns being the leader. (This repeating phrase could be written as follows: Touch left foot front, step on the left foot, and repeat this with the right foot. Cross left foot over right, step side with right foot, and repeat this pattern again.)

Create   Make your own traveling line dance by including sideways locomotor (traveling) steps, stomping steps, and toe or heel touches on the floor. Make sure that the movement and rhythmic pattern can be easily repeated. Use the choreographic form of AB by (A) dancing the simple Dabkee step learned in the Re-create activity, then (B) dancing your stomping line dance step. This AB dance can itself be repeated many times.

*If you need music and don't have it among your resources, use the video.

From H. Scheff, M. Sprague, and S. McGreevy-Nichols, 2010, *Exploring dance forms and styles: A guide to concert, world, social, and historical dance* (Champaign, IL: Human Kinetics).

Dabkee

FUN FACTS   The world record for a Dabkee line is currently 2,743 people; it was established in 2007 by Arab Israelis.

WEB EXPLORATIONS   Key terms to search for include Dabkee Falstenyee, Debkah, Dabkeh, Dabka, Dabkee, Adam Basma Dabkee-Debkah dance, and Lebanese Dabkee.

From H. Scheff, M. Sprague, and S. McGreevy-Nichols, 2010, *Exploring dance forms and styles: A guide to concert, world, social, and historical dance* (Champaign, IL: Human Kinetics).

Name: _____ Class: _____ Date: _____

STUDENT KNOWLEDGE QUEST WORKSHEET

Name of Dance: Dabkee

1. Viewing: What did you see?
   Record your observations. Describe what you see. Be specific.

   _____

   _____

   _____

   _____

   _____

2. Connecting: What do you know?

   _____

   _____

   _____

   _____

   _____

3. Responding: What do you think? What do you wonder?

   _____

   _____

   _____

   _____

   _____

4. Performing: What can you do?

   _____

   _____

   _____

   _____

   _____

From H. Scheff, M. Sprague, and S. McGreevy-Nichols, 2010, *Exploring dance forms and styles: A guide to concert, world, social, and historical dance* (Champaign, IL: Human Kinetics).

Gumboot Dance

KNOWLEDGE QUEST

INFORMATION AND TEACHING TIPS
Video Clip Search
Category M: World (Subcategory: South Africa)
Category A: Social (Subcategory: Dances done in a line)
Name of Dance: Gumboot Dance

Rhythm is a language.

DIRECTIONS Give the students the job of researching clips of and about the Gumboot dance on the Internet. Many are available; have them choose one or two. They can do this in school if the Internet is available, at home, or at a library. Instruct them to take notes about the actual dancing so that they can complete the student worksheet.

BACKGROUND INFORMATION Before students view the video clip, share the following information with them and give them the KQ worksheets to complete as a homework assignment.

- **Translation:** The gumboot is the name of the footwear that South African miners wore to protect them from flooding shafts. The bosses discovered that providing gumboots (Wellington boots) to the workers was cheaper than attempting to drain the mines.

- **Country or culture of origin:** The Gumboot dance developed from traditional African roots and now has become a part of urban South African working-class culture. The practice began with rural laborers who came to work at the gold mines of Witwatersrand in South Africa and brought with them strong traditions of rhythm, song, and dance.

- **Timeline:** Born in the gold mines of South Africa, which opened in the 1880s, Gumboot dancing was a way to survive the isolation workers felt as a result of the migrant labor system and oppressive pass laws.

- **Function or reason:** Workers facing oppression and hardship at the mines, including punishment if they talked to each other while working, were forced to adapt and create new forms of communication and entertainment. Inside the mines, the workers used their Gumboots to communicate with each other, by slapping their boots, stamping their feet, and rattling their ankle chains.

- **Who does this dance:** Gumboot dance is now a popular art form performed worldwide to entertain and pass on elements of South African history to new generations and other cultures. Like many folkloric art forms, it is adapted to the modern contexts in which it is performed.

- **Music and rhythms:** Workers adapted traditional dances and rhythms to the only instruments available, their boots and bodies. The songs that were sung to go with the frenetic movements dealt with working-class life: drinking, love, family, low wages, and mean bosses.

- **Traditional clothing or costume:** "The 'miners' uniform consisted of heavy black Wellington boots to protect the feet . . . jeans (or overalls), bare chests (temperatures underground can reach above 40° C [104° F]), and bandannas to absorb eye-stinging sweat (and hard hats)" (www.worldartswest.org/plm/guide/locator/southafrican.shtml).

- **Other information:** Working in the mines was long, hard, repetitive toil. Talking was forbidden. White foremen beat and kicked black workers. Hundreds

From H. Scheff, M. Sprague, and S. McGreevy-Nichols, 2010, *Exploring dance forms and styles: A guide to concert, world, social, and historical dance* (Champaign, IL: Human Kinetics).

of workers were (and continue to be) killed every year in accidents. Back on the surface and in their overcrowded living quarters, the bosses refused to allow the workers to wear their traditional dress while they were not working. The bosses made all workers of the same ethnic or tribal background live together in order to perpetuate divisions between different groups of African workers.

REFERENCES

www.worldartswest.org/plm/guide/locator/southafrican.shtml

www.gumbootsworldtour.com/english/history.html

http://home.telkomsa.net/milesmet/history.htm

TEACHING STRATEGIES
The video clip should be viewed at least three times (see chapter 1). In the case where students are searching and observing from home, they will need to list the exact Web site used so that teachers and other students can see the basis for their documentation.

Facilitate a class discussion using the discussion starters listed next. Have students use their recorded answers as a resource. Feel free to paraphrase and choose the questions that work best with your students.

Viewing: What Did You See?

Suggested discussion starters and questions: What are the main body parts used? What are the various ways that the dancers make sound to produce the rhythm? What do you notice about the way the feet are used? What do you notice about the way the hands are used?

Connecting: What Do You Know?

Suggested discussion starters and questions: How do the dancers interact with each other? How is the dance organized? What other kind of dance does this remind you of and why? How is it like that dance? How is it different?

Responding: What Do You Think? What Do You Wonder?

Suggested discussion starters and questions: How do you think the men were able to communicate with each other using this method? How do you think the sounds and rhythms translated into a form of language? Research message drums on the Internet. How is Gumboot similar?

What questions do you have about this dance? Write them down and continue your research. Some of these questions can be answered through movement.

Performing: What Can You Do?

Choose both Re-create and Create, choose one of these two activities, or make your own performing work that you think is most appropriate for your students.

Re-create As a homework assignment, watch a video of a Gumboot dance. Re-create an eight-count rhythm from the video. Teach your rhythm to two other people and learn theirs. Combine the three different rhythms to create a short Gumboot dance. Perform.

Create In small groups, create rhythms or movements that represent specific words. Provide a book that decodes the various movements. Supply it to another group and have fun sending secret messages to each other.

*If you need music and don't have it among your resources, use the video.

From H. Scheff, M. Sprague, and S. McGreevy-Nichols, 2010, *Exploring dance forms and styles: A guide to concert, world, social, and historical dance* (Champaign, IL: Human Kinetics).

Gumboot Dance

FUN FACTS   Some enlightened employers eventually allowed the best dancers to form troupes to represent the company, to entertain visitors, and for public relations. It was not unusual for these performers' songs to openly mock their bosses and criticize wages and conditions while the bosses were blissfully ignorant of the content, sung in Xhosa, Sotho, or Zulu (http://home.telkomsa.net/milesmet/history.htm).

WEB EXPLORATIONS   Key terms to search for include Gumboot dance, apartheid, South African dance, and pass laws.

RECOMMENDED CLIPS

- www.youtube.com/watch?v=iSgFAG0mtac
- www.youtube.com/watch?v=ce_2p9wQRS4
- www.youtube.com/watch?v=A5Nk-VdDuv8

From H. Scheff, M. Sprague, and S. McGreevy-Nichols, 2010, *Exploring dance forms and styles: A guide to concert, world, social, and historical dance* (Champaign, IL: Human Kinetics).

Name: _____ Class: _____ Date: _____

STUDENT KNOWLEDGE QUEST WORKSHEET

Gumboot Dance

Name of Dance: Gumboot Dance

1. Viewing: What did you see?
   Record your observations. Describe what you see. Be specific.

   _____

   _____

   _____

   _____

   _____

2. Connecting: What do you know?

   _____

   _____

   _____

   _____

   _____

3. Responding: What do you think? What do you wonder?

   _____

   _____

   _____

   _____

   _____

4. Performing: What can you do?

   _____

   _____

   _____

   _____

   _____

From H. Scheff, M. Sprague, and S. McGreevy-Nichols, 2010, *Exploring dance forms and styles: A guide to concert, world, social, and historical dance* (Champaign, IL: Human Kinetics).

Raks Assaya

KNOWLEDGE QUEST
INFORMATION AND TEACHING TIPS
Category M: World (Subcategory: North Africa)
Category A: Concert
Category A: Historical
Name of Dance: Raks Assaya (Egyptian Cane Dance)

Women "CANE" dance with a stick too.

BACKGROUND INFORMATION   Before students view the video clip, share the following information with them.

- **Translation:** The term *raks assaya* means cane dance.

- **Country or culture of origin:** The origin of this folkloric dance is Upper (southern) Egypt.

- **Timeline:** The male version, Tahtib, referring to a stick dance or martial art, is thought to have survived from the times of the pharaohs. Paintings on walls of monuments, tombs, and temples showed this dance so that soldiers could learn it. It is uncertain when the female version of this dance, Raks Assaya, came about.

- **Function or reason:** Raks Assaya is performed in Egypt at celebrations and festivals.

- **Who does this dance:** Women perform the lighter, more flirty version that has been adopted by the cabaret or Oriental dancers.

- **Music and rhythms:** Saidi rhythms are named for where they originated, Upper Egypt, between Gizeh and Edfu. The time signature is 4/4 and the Makloub rhythm could be heard as dom-tak, dom-dom-tak. Instrumentation includes traditional instruments such as the rababa (an ancestor of the violin), the mizmar (a horn), and dumbek and tabla beledi drums.

- **Traditional clothing or costume:** This dance is usually done wearing a caftan with some type of hip scarf along with a headdress or wrap. *Note:* The clothing worn in the video clip is not this traditional clothing.

- **Other information:** Handling the canes takes skill. The women's cane is smaller than the men's and has a hook on the end. Both men and women can wield either one or two canes at once. The female version in the video clip could be a parody of the men's stick dance, Tahtib. The use of the cane could represent this parody, the training of the horses, or livestock herding. Other research states that peasants working in the fields would dance with reeds from the banks of the Nile during their breaks.

REFERENCES

Richards, T., (ed.). 2000. *The belly dance book: Rediscovering the oldest dance.* Concord, CA: Backbeat Press.

www.bdancer.com/history/BDhist2b.html

www.middleeasterndance.com/canedance1.html

From H. Scheff, M. Sprague, and S. McGreevy-Nichols, 2010, *Exploring dance forms and styles: A guide to concert, world, social, and historical dance* (Champaign, IL: Human Kinetics).

www.hetisharif.com/article-canedance.html

www.bellydanceforums.net/video-clips-youtube/7410-ive-been-set-homework.html

TEACHING STRATEGIES   The video clip should be viewed at least three times (see chapter 1). After students record and discuss their observations and before the third viewing, use the discussion starters listed next to facilitate class discussion. Feel free to paraphrase and choose the questions that work best with your students.

Viewing: What Did You See?

Suggested discussion starters and questions: What kinds of movements did the women do with the canes? What parts of their bodies did they isolate? Describe the types of movements that the dancers did with their hips. Describe the way the dancers walked most of the time.

Connecting: What Do You Know?

Suggested discussion starters and questions: What other dances use a prop? Raks Assaya may have originated as a martial art dance for men. Do you know of any other dances that have a male and a female version?

Responding: What Do You Think? What Do You Wonder?

Suggested discussion starters and questions: Could this dance be done without the cane? Explain your answer. The use of the cane could represent a parody of the men's martial arts dance, the training of horses, or livestock herding. Other research states that peasants working in the fields would dance with reeds from the banks of the Nile during their breaks. Which of these theories makes the most sense to you? Support your answer with specific reasons.

What questions do you have about this dance? Write them down and continue your research. Some of these questions can be answered through movement.

Performing: What Can You Do?

Choose both Re-create and Create, choose one of these two activities, or make your own performing work that you think is most appropriate for your students.

Re-create   Using a dowel or a short stick, copy three or four of the movements the dancers did with the canes, being careful to stay far enough away from other dancers. Add the locomotor (traveling) or nonlocomotor movements done with those particular cane movements. Show this short dance phrase to a partner and watch his or hers. Helpful hint: Use the information you recorded on the Viewing question to help you design your dance phrase.

Create   Choose a prop and create four or five movements that cannot be done without the prop. Put these movements into an order that you like. Perform your prop dance phrase for another student and watch his or hers.

*If you need music and don't have it among your resources, use the video.

FUN FACTS   While the traditional version of the male Tahtib dance looks almost like sword play, modern versions include what looks like juggling and balancing act moves.

WEB EXPLORATIONS   Key terms to search for include Cane Dance, Raks Assaya, Tahtib, Tahteeb, and Saidi Stick Dance.

From H. Scheff, M. Sprague, and S. McGreevy-Nichols, 2010, *Exploring dance forms and styles: A guide to concert, world, social, and historical dance* (Champaign, IL: Human Kinetics).

Raks Assaya

Name: _____ Class: _____ Date: _____

STUDENT KNOWLEDGE QUEST WORKSHEET

Name of Dance: Raks Assaya (Egyptian Cane Dance)

1. Viewing: What did you see?
   Record your observations. Describe what you see. Be specific.

   _____

   _____

   _____

   _____

   _____

2. Connecting: What do you know?

   _____

   _____

   _____

   _____

   _____

3. Responding: What do you think? What do you wonder?

   _____

   _____

   _____

   _____

   _____

4. Performing: What can you do?

   _____

   _____

   _____

   _____

   _____

From H. Scheff, M. Sprague, and S. McGreevy-Nichols, 2010, *Exploring dance forms and styles: A guide to concert, world, social, and historical dance* (Champaign, IL: Human Kinetics).

KNOWLEDGE QUEST

INFORMATION AND TEACHING TIPS
Category M: World (Subcategory: Africa)
Category A: Social (Subcategory: Alone in a group)
Name of Dance: Tiriba

Tiriba

The sign reads, "Gone Fishing." What does one do after a fishing trip? Dance, of course!

BACKGROUND INFORMATION
Before students view the video clip, share the following information with them.

- **Translation:** One translation of the word *tiriba* is sorcery.

- **Country or culture of origin:** Tiriba is a dance from the Laduma people in the Boke and Boffa areas of West Guinea and specifically the Baga ethnic group, who live in the coastal region of Guinea.

- **Function or reason:** According to dance master Abdoulaye Camara, it is a welcoming dance of the Baga people of northwest Guinea that was often danced to welcome back a successful fishing party. Originally, the dance may have been named for a great dancer who gathered his own drummers and wore a particular costume.

- **Who does this dance:** At one time, mothers and daughters danced Tiriba together as a rite of passage when girls were initiated as women. Now it is a general welcoming and celebration dance.

- **Music and rhythms:** The rhythms are played during circumcisions and for important medicine men's ceremonies. Small drums made of deerskin were the traditional instruments, but now the rhythm is played on the larger drums called djembe and dunun. Tiriba rhythm is usually a 6/8 African rhythm. Also see Fun Facts.

- **Traditional clothing or costume:** When this dance is done at harvest time, the dancer wears a mask.

- **Other information:** Some research suggests that the specific dance of Tiriba is no longer performed, yet the drum rhythms are still used at ceremonies and celebrations where there is dancing.

REFERENCES
www.sound-scape.org.uk/shikotiriba.htm

www.paulnas.eu/wap/tiriba.html

http://tontinkan.net/en/rhythm6.htm

www.proprofs.com/flashcards/download.php
?title=West-African-Dance

www.filmbaby.com/films/453

TEACHING STRATEGIES
The video clip should be viewed at least three times (see chapter 1). After students record and discuss their observations and before the third viewing, use the discussion starters listed next to facilitate class discussion. Feel free to paraphrase and choose the questions that work best with your students.

From H. Scheff, M. Sprague, and S. McGreevy-Nichols, 2010, *Exploring dance forms and styles: A guide to concert, world, social, and historical dance* (Champaign, IL: Human Kinetics).

Tiriba

Viewing: What Did You See?

Suggested discussion starters and questions: What did you notice about the dancers' posture or alignment during this dance? (Helpful hint: The teacher could pause the DVD at two places in the dance that most clearly show this posture or alignment change.) How did the dancers know it was time to change to the next dance phrase? Describe an example of when the dancers moved more than one body part at the same time. (Helpful hint: Replay any one of the steps after the entrance step for the students. Most any of the phrases will show multiple isolations.)

Connecting: What Do You Know?

Suggested discussion starters and questions: Tiriba is danced at celebrations and welcoming ceremonies. In your culture, what are some events where dance or special movement is used in celebrations or ceremonies? In the United States, what do people do when they are to recite the Pledge of Allegiance or sing the national anthem? When have you seen or had to learn to walk in a special way?

Responding: What Do You Think? What Do You Wonder?

Suggested discussion starters and questions: Originally, the Tiriba may have been named for a great dancer who gathered his own drummers and wore a particular costume. Then in later times, mothers and daughters danced Tiriba together as a rite of passage when girls were initiated as women. Now it is a general welcoming and celebration dance.

When has an invention, work of art, object, or tradition meant to serve one purpose but, over time, been used for other purposes? An example is the men's necktie. It was originally a cloth tied around the neck to wipe dirt off of the horse carriage driver's face. It is now usually worn with suits. You may have to do some research to find appropriate answers.

Can you find any similarities among the dances from the Caribbean (Perico Ripiao, La Bomba, and Salsa) and this West African dance? Why do you think this so?

Performing: What Can You Do?

Choose both Re-create and Create, choose one of these two activities, or make your own performing work that you think is most appropriate for your students.

Re-create   Choose and learn a favorite movement from Tiriba. Teach this movement to a partner and learn his or hers. Join with another couple to teach and learn each other's movements, then put them into an order that works best for your group. Practice and then share this mini-dance with the class.

Create   Think of a time in your life that could call for a rite of passage ceremony (e.g., first tooth falling out, a graduation). Create an entrance step that would bring you into the space. Create some movement that represents how you were before the ceremony. Create some movement that represents how you will be after the ceremony. Create an exit step that takes you out of the space. Make sure to emphasize the difference between *before* the ceremony and *after* the ceremony.

*If you need music and don't have it among your resources, use the video.

From H. Scheff, M. Sprague, and S. McGreevy-Nichols, 2010, *Exploring dance forms and styles: A guide to concert, world, social, and historical dance* (Champaign, IL: Human Kinetics).

Tiriba

FUN FACTS   In most African dances, the drummers and not the dancers are in control of the dance. They are not only responsible for the speed or tempo but also when the dancers are to change their steps. In the Tiriba video clip, the students should listen for a repeated drum phrase called a **break** that occurs every time the dancers change the steps they are doing.

WEB EXPLORATIONS   Key terms to search for include cities of Boke and Boffa, Western Guinea, and coastal regions of northwestern Guinea.

Tiriba

Name: _____ Class: _____ Date: _____

STUDENT KNOWLEDGE QUEST WORKSHEET

Name of Dance: Tiriba

1. Viewing: What did you see?
   Record your observations. Describe what you see. Be specific.

   _____

   _____

   _____

   _____

   _____

   _____

2. Connecting: What do you know?

   _____

   _____

   _____

   _____

   _____

   _____

3. Responding: What do you think? What do you wonder?

   _____

   _____

   _____

   _____

   _____

4. Performing: What can you do?

   _____

   _____

   _____

   _____

   _____

From H. Scheff, M. Sprague, and S. McGreevy-Nichols, 2010, *Exploring dance forms and styles: A guide to concert, world, social, and historical dance* (Champaign, IL: Human Kinetics).

KNOWLEDGE QUEST

INFORMATION AND TEACHING TIPS
Category M: World (Subcategory: Oceania)
Name of Dance: Hula (Hawaiian Wedding Song)

Hula

"Traditional hula is very verbal. We tell stories when we dance."

Manu Boyd, kumu hula (dance master)
(www.encyclopedia.com/doc/1G1-72704345.html)

BACKGROUND INFORMATION   Before students view the video clip, share the following information with them.

- **Translation:** The word *hula* means dance in Hawaiian. Written by Charles King, the Hawaiian wedding song's Hawaiian name is "Ke Kali Nei Au," which means "Waiting Here for You."

- **Country or culture of origin:** This dance is from the Hawaiian Islands in the United States.

- **Timeline:** The Hula is an ancient indigenous dance that is still performed today.

- **Function or reason:** The Hula was originally a religious dance. The dancers would sit on their heels and pantomime the meaning of the mele (poetry or chant). The Kahiko (traditional or ancient Hula) is the closest style. It is still danced to chants. The topics are about the various gods of Hawaiian native religion, the chiefs, the kings and queens in their history, earth, seas, sky, nature, love, and everyday life. It is usually performed in a serious, reverent way. The Auana, a more recent dance style, is accompanied by stringed instruments such as the guitar and ukulele (both instruments were imported to the islands). This style is what non-Hawaiians are more used to seeing. The mele can be about anything, but love is the most popular topic.

- **Who does this dance:** Both men and women dance the ancient Hula, but usually not together.

- **Music and rhythms:** Chants are usually in 2/4 or 4/4 time signatures. The dancers' feet and hips represent the beat of the music and the arms and hands express the flow and meaning of the melody and lyrics.

- **Traditional clothing or costume:** Female's clothing for the Auana style can be the mu'umu'u (long dress, as seen in the video clip on the DVD). Also seen are ti-leaf skirts with camisole tops or wraps (Tahitian influence). The men wear black or white pants with a cummerbund. The dancers wear flowers in their hair, around their necks (leis), and sometimes on their wrists and ankles. In Kahiko, women wear pa'u skirts and camisole tops or Victorian-looking blouses. The men wear malos (a short wrap around their hips). Green leaves are worn instead of the flowers.

- **Other information:** The origins of the Hula are connected to legends. One legend says a pair of male and female gods came to the islands and both danced. When the male vanished, the female remained to dance alone. Her worshippers learned her dance, the Hula. Another legend says that two male gods invented and danced the Hula. Hi'iaka, the sister of Pele, the powerful fire goddess, learned the Hula

From H. Scheff, M. Sprague, and S. McGreevy-Nichols, 2010, *Exploring dance forms and styles: A guide to concert, world, social, and historical dance* (Champaign, IL: Human Kinetics).

Hula

from Laka, which opened the dance for women as well. Another legend says Laka was a goddess of the Hula and she traveled through the islands teaching all who wished to learn.

It has been said that each island has its own flavor for the Hula because of the different environments. Hawaii (the Big Island) is bigger and earthy. The Hula of Moloka'i is more spiritual and about animals and nature, because it was not very populated. The Hula of Kauai is gentler because of the mists.

REFERENCES

Chujoy, A., and P.W. Manchester. 1967. *The dance encyclopedia.* New York: Simon and Schuster.

www.ifccsa.org/hula.html

www.soc.hawaii.edu/hwhp/hula/KAUAI.html

www.mauihawaii.org/wedding-honeymoon/hawaiian-wedding-song.htm

TEACHING STRATEGIES The video clip should be viewed at least three times (see chapter 1). After students record and discuss their observations and before the third viewing, use the discussion starters listed next to facilitate class discussion. Feel free to paraphrase and choose the questions that work best with your students.

Viewing: What Did You See?

Suggested discussion starters and questions: Describe the basic footwork in this dance. What did you notice about the arm and hand movements? What other body part was important to the dance? Which body parts related to the melody or words of the song and which body parts moved according to the beat of the song?

Connecting: What Do You Know?

Suggested discussion starters and questions: What other cultures communicate with hand gestures? Compare the arm and hand movements of the hula with the Bharatanatyam video clip (India's storytelling dance) on the DVD. Many uninformed people think all Polynesian dances are the same. Describe the differences between the Hula and Tahitian dancing (see the video clip on the DVD).

Responding: What Do You Think? What Do You Wonder?

Suggested discussion starters and questions: The modern Auana style of Hula owes its existence to the introduction of stringed instruments. The guitar came to the islands with the Mexican cowboys, who came to teach the Hawaiians how to herd cattle. The ukulele arrived with the Portuguese sailors. How do you think these musical instruments influenced the original Hula? Do you think that the mixing of cultural aspects is beneficial to or harmful for a culture?

What questions do you have about this dance? Write them down and continue your research. Some of these questions can be answered through movement.

Performing: What Can You Do?

Choose both Re-create and Create, choose one of these two activities, or make your own performing work that you think is most appropriate for your students.

Re-create After watching the video, try to identify the gestures for the words *heart* and *bells ringing*. Then with your arms and hands say, "The bells are ringing in my heart." Practice the step-together-step-touch sideways step, as seen in the video, to the right side and the left side. Combine with the arm and hand movements.

Create Find a favorite poem or write or make up your own short mele (poem or chant). Create gestures that represent the ideas or concepts in the mele. Practice

From H. Scheff, M. Sprague, and S. McGreevy-Nichols, 2010, *Exploring dance forms and styles: A guide to concert, world, social, and historical dance* (Champaign, IL: Human Kinetics).

Hula

the step-together-step-touch sideways step, as seen in the video, to the right side and the left side. Combine with the arm and hand movements. Share your storytelling dance with the class.

*If you need music and don't have it among your resources, use the video.

FUN FACTS The English lyrics of the Hawaiian wedding song are not a direct translation of the 1926 Charles King song, "Ke Kali Nei Au," which means "Waiting Here for You." Al Hoffman and Dick Manning wrote the lyrics in 1958. These lyrics became famous in 1961 because Elvis Presley sang them in the movie *Blue Hawaii*.

WEB EXPLORATIONS Key terms to search for include Hawaiian Hula dance and Hawaiian wedding song.

From H. Scheff, M. Sprague, and S. McGreevy-Nichols, 2010, *Exploring dance forms and styles: A guide to concert, world, social, and historical dance* (Champaign, IL: Human Kinetics).

Hula

Name: _____ Class: _____ Date: _____

STUDENT KNOWLEDGE QUEST WORKSHEET

Name of Dance: Hula (Hawaiian Wedding Song)

1. Viewing: What did you see?
   Record your observations. Describe what you see. Be specific.

   _____

   _____

   _____

   _____

   _____

2. Connecting: What do you know?

   _____

   _____

   _____

   _____

   _____

3. Responding: What do you think? What do you wonder?

   _____

   _____

   _____

   _____

   _____

4. Performing: What can you do?

   _____

   _____

   _____

   _____

   _____

From H. Scheff, M. Sprague, and S. McGreevy-Nichols, 2010, *Exploring dance forms and styles: A guide to concert, world, social, and historical dance* (Champaign, IL: Human Kinetics).

KNOWLEDGE QUEST

INFORMATION AND TEACHING TIPS
Category M: World (Subcategory: Oceania)
Name of Dance: Tahitian Dance

Continuing a cultural tradition against all odds.

BACKGROUND INFORMATION   Before students view the video clip, share the following information with them.

- **Translation:** The true name of the Tahitian dance is *ori Tahiti*. Today, only the word *hura* is still used. This is sometimes known as the *hula* (Hawaii).

- **Country or culture of origin:** Around 4,000 BC, a great migration began from Southeast Asia across open ocean to settle the Pacific Islands and continued to colonize all the Tahitian islands. This area is now called the Polynesian Triangle and includes Hawaii to the north, Easter Island to the southeast, and New Zealand to the southwest.

- **Timeline:** From ancient times through today, dancing has been directly related to all parts of life in Tahiti.

- **Function or reason:** Dance in Tahiti was an integral part of daily culture; it was used in religious rituals and social events to signal peace or to celebrate life. Before explorers arrived, a heiva (festival) with dancing and feasting was an integral part of community celebrations. The dancers would make gestures, reenacting daily occupations of life.

- **Who does this dance:** Males and females of all ages perform Tahitian dance, however the dances they perform reflect different themes. For example, the men's themes might include warfare or sailing and they may use spears or paddles to reflect those themes. The themes for the women usually are more domestic or represent nature-based topics such as combing their hair, fishing, or the flight of a butterfly.

- **Music and rhythms:** Percussion instruments and chanting are used in this dance. Other instruments include more traditional instruments, as well as conch shells and nasal flutes.

- **Traditional clothing or costume:** The costume varies from one dance to another. Every aspect of the dancers' costumes is drawn from the earth. Dancers might wear a pareo, or cloth dress, or skirts called the *more,* made of plant fibers and decorated with natural materials such as seashells, mother of pearl, seeds, and rooster feathers. Each Tahitian female dancer sources these materials and makes her own costumes.

- **Other information:** Like many Polynesian forms, dancing was prohibited in Tahiti when the missionaries arrived

From H. Scheff, M. Sprague, and S. McGreevy-Nichols, 2010, *Exploring dance forms and styles: A guide to concert, world, social, and historical dance* (Champaign, IL: Human Kinetics).

Tahitian Dance

and it did not resurface until the late 19th century. Much of the traditional dance culture and movements were lost in these years, but at the beginning of the 20th century, dance in Tahiti made its comeback. Permission was given to celebrate the taking of the Bastille and dancing soon became a part of all official festivities. By then its function in society changed, leading to a change in form as well. More emphasis was placed on swift hip movements done to powerful, polyrhythmic drumming.

REFERENCES

www.pinoybro.com/?p=1345

www.tahiti.com/english-version/about-tahiti/gen-resources/dance.html

www.worldartswest.org/edf/dancers/tahitian_KaUaTuahine.html

TEACHING STRATEGIES
The video clip should be viewed at least three times (see chapter 1). After students record and discuss their observations and before the third viewing, use the discussion starters listed next to facilitate class discussion. Feel free to paraphrase and choose the questions that work best with your students.

Viewing: What Did You See?

Suggested discussion starters and questions: What are the main body parts used? What are some key movements used? What do you notice about the way the feet are used? What do you notice about the way the hands are used in this dance? How do the dancers work with rhythm?

Connecting: What Do You Know?

Suggested discussion starters and questions: What is it about this dance that demonstrates how Tahitian dance has changed over time? When have you ever seen dance like this? Which of the movements could you easily demonstrate?

Responding: What Do You Think? What Do You Wonder?

Suggested discussion starters and questions: How do you think the dancers know when to change to a different movement? What do you think would be the hardest thing to learn in this dance? How could you represent certain everyday actions through dance? Give an example. What process could you do to learn this dance?

What questions do you have about this dance? Write them down and continue your research. Some of these questions can be answered through movement.

Performing: What Can You Do?

Choose both Re-create and Create, choose one of these two activities, or make your own performing work that you think is most appropriate for your students.

Re-create Choose three key movements to re-create. Arrange them in a sequence and repeat the sequence four times. *Note:* Use ideas from recorded observations from question 1 (What did you see?).

Create As an individual or with a small group, choose a topic or theme and create movements that represent aspects of that idea. Put the movements together to create your own version of Tahitian hura.

*If you need music and don't have it among your resources, use the video.

From H. Scheff, M. Sprague, and S. McGreevy-Nichols, 2010, *Exploring dance forms and styles: A guide to concert, world, social, and historical dance* (Champaign, IL: Human Kinetics).

Tahitian Dance

FUN FACTS   Tahitian dance is sometimes used to tell stories and share history. Each gesture has a meaning. Hand motions can mean many things, including animals, plants, or events such as war.

WEB EXPLORATIONS   Key terms to search for include Tahitian dance and Polynesian dance.

From H. Scheff, M. Sprague, and S. McGreevy-Nichols, 2010, *Exploring dance forms and styles: A guide to concert, world, social, and historical dance* (Champaign, IL: Human Kinetics).

**Tahitian
Dance**

Name: _____ Class: _____ Date: _____

STUDENT KNOWLEDGE QUEST WORKSHEET

Name of Dance: Tahitian Dance

1. Viewing: What did you see?
   Record your observations. Describe what you see. Be specific.

   _____

   _____

   _____

   _____

   _____

2. Connecting: What do you know?

   _____

   _____

   _____

   _____

   _____

3. Responding: What do you think? What do you wonder?

   _____

   _____

   _____

   _____

   _____

4. Performing: What can you do?

   _____

   _____

   _____

   _____

   _____

From H. Scheff, M. Sprague, and S. McGreevy-Nichols, 2010, *Exploring dance forms and styles: A guide to concert, world, social, and historical dance* (Champaign, IL: Human Kinetics).

KNOWLEDGE QUEST

INFORMATION AND TEACHING TIPS
Video Clip Search
Category M: World (Subcategory: Oceania)
Name of Dance: Maori Haka Dance

Maori Haka Dance

A dance of intimidation

DIRECTIONS Give the students the job of researching clips of and about the dance on the Internet. Many are available; have them choose one or two. They can do this in school if the Internet is available, at home, or at a library. Instruct them to take notes about the actual dancing so that they can complete the student worksheet.

BACKGROUND INFORMATION Before students view the video clip, share the following information with them and give them the KQ worksheets to complete as a homework assignment.

- **Translation:** Haka is the generic name for all Maori dance. Today, Haka is defined as that part of the Maori dance repertoire where the men dance in front and the women lend vocal support behind them.

- **Country or culture of origin:** A Haka is the traditional dance form of the Maori of New Zealand. Maori have used chants, song, and dance to record their history, to convey feelings, to express ideas, to tell stories, to celebrate important events, and to protest and persuade. Kapa haka, which combines movement, song, and chant, forms an integral part of Maori culture and ways of life.

- **Timeline:** Dance has always been a part of the Maori culture. The Maori probably arrived in southwestern Polynesia in several waves at some time before 1300. The Maori settled the islands and developed a distinct culture.

- **Function or reason:** Haka were originally performed by warriors before battle and were meant to intimidate the opposition. Today, Haka are performed for various reasons, including official welcome ceremonies for distinguished visitors or dignitaries.

- **Who does this dance:** Both men and women perform Haka, however they have gender-specific roles and movements such as the protruding of the tongue (performed by men) and the closing of the eyes at different points in the dance (performed by women).

- **Music and rhythms:** Sounds are created using a wide variety of vigorous body actions such as slapping the hands against the body and stamping of the feet. As well as chanted words, a variety of cries and grunts are used.

- **Traditional clothing or costume:** Performing dance groups (kapa haka) made up of men, women, and children have worn the piupiu skirt, crafted using flax plant leaves, as a standard in dress when performing. Costumes also include other items such as taniko (hand-woven) headbands and bodices, rapaki (men's malo), feathers, earrings, and bone and greenstone (pounamu) adornments.

- **Other information:** "If the Haka was not performed in total unison, this was regarded as a bad omen for the battle. Various actions are employed in the course of a performance, including facial contortions such as showing the whites of the eyes and the poking out of the tongue. The hands, arms, legs, feet, voice, eyes, tongue and the body as a whole combine to express courage, annoyance, joy or other feelings relevant to the purpose of the occasion. Unlike other indigenous

From H. Scheff, M. Sprague, and S. McGreevy-Nichols, 2010, *Exploring dance forms and styles: A guide to concert, world, social, and historical dance* (Champaign, IL: Human Kinetics).

Maori Haka Dance

dance forms, Kapa Haka is unique in the fact that the performers must sing, dance, and have expression as well as movement all combined into each item. Kapa haka could be seen as sign language, as each action has a meaning, which ties in with the words. For example, if the hand is by the ear, this would probably tie in with the word whakarongo which means to listen."

From http://www.statemaster.com/encyclopedia/Haka.

REFERENCES

http://en.wikipedia.org/wiki/Haka

www.haka.co.nz/haka.php

www.maori.org.nz

www.tki.org.nz/r/arts/dance/discover_dance/maori_e.php

TEACHING STRATEGIES

The video clip should be viewed at least three times (see chapter 1). In the case where students are searching and observing from home, they will need to list the exact Web site so that teachers and other students can see the basis for the documentation.

Facilitate a class discussion using the discussion starters listed next. Have students use their recorded answers as a resource. Feel free to paraphrase and choose the questions that work best with your students.

Viewing: What Did You See?

Suggested discussion starters and questions: How is sound used in this dance? What do you notice about the way the feet are used? What do you notice about the way the hands are used in this dance? What do you notice about the facial expressions?

Connecting: What Do You Know?

Suggested discussion starters and questions: When have you ever seen a dance like this performed? How was it like this dance? How was it different?

Responding: What Do You Think? What Do You Wonder?

Suggested discussion starters and questions: Kapa Haka could be seen as sign language; each action has a meaning, which ties in with the words. For example, if the hand is by the ear, this would probably tie in with the word *whakarongo,* which means to listen. View the video again, identify some specific movements, and project what word you think the movement is expressing.

What questions do you have about this dance? Write them down and continue your research. Some of these questions can be answered through movement.

Performing: What Can You Do?

Choose both Re-create and Create, choose one of these two activities, or make your own performing work that you think is most appropriate for your students.

Re-create   The Maori people have had much concern in regard to individuals and groups using their dance in irreverent ways. Because of this we are suggesting that you *do not re-create this dance.* In fact in February, 2009 they won a court battle that prompted the New Zealand government to assign intellectual property rights in the traditional Maori Haka, the Ka Mate, to Ngati Toa, a North Island tribal group. The new agreement is largely symbolic, but it is considered immensely significant by Maori leaders. "Ngati Toa's primary objective is to prevent the misappropriation and culturally inappropriate use of the Ka Mate Haka," the official settlement letter read. The tribe has been battling for a decade to stop commercial exploitation of

From H. Scheff, M. Sprague, and S. McGreevy-Nichols, 2010, *Exploring dance forms and styles: A guide to concert, world, social, and historical dance* (Champaign, IL: Human Kinetics).

the haka, saying its use in film and television has been culturally insensitive and has undermined its traditional significance. New Zealand's prime minister said he did not believe the New Zealand national rugby team All Blacks would be considered as commercially exploiting the Haka. (See Fun Facts section for more information on this topic.)

From http://www.guardian.co.uk/world/2009/feb/12/new-zealand-haka-maoris.

Create Maori war dances incorporate traditional movements that are meant to intimidate their enemies. Some examples are the following:

- Slapping the hands against the thighs and chest
- Stamping their feet
- Creating a fierce appearance by enlarging the whites of the eyes
- Making aggressive moves toward the opponents

In small groups, create an original movement sequence that might be intimidating to an enemy. Create an original chant that accompanies the dance. Perform this in unison.

FUN FACTS The New Zealand national rugby team All Blacks is famous for opening games using the Haka. See www.youtube.com/watch?v=kd0kDxP04eI. Because All Blacks is the official rugby team of New Zealand, their performance of the Haka is not considered irreverent. For more information on the All Blacks rugby performing the Haka, go to www.youtube.com/watch?v=tdMCAV6Yd0Y.

WEB EXPLORATIONS Key terms to search for include Haka, Maori dance, and New Zealand aboriginal dance.

RECOMMENDED CLIPS

- www.youtube.com/watch?v=c-lrE2JcO44
- http://video.google.com/videoplay?docid=8138785310000038075
- www.youtube.com/watch?v=5ar-gYlGjvc&feature=related

From H. Scheff, M. Sprague, and S. McGreevy-Nichols, 2010, *Exploring dance forms and styles: A guide to concert, world, social, and historical dance* (Champaign, IL: Human Kinetics).

191

**Maori Haka
Dance**

Name: _____ Class: _____ Date: _____

STUDENT KNOWLEDGE QUEST WORKSHEET

Name of Dance: Maori Haka Dance

1. Viewing: What did you see?
   Record your observations. Describe what you see. Be specific.

   _____

   _____

   _____

   _____

   _____

2. Connecting: What do you know?

   _____

   _____

   _____

   _____

   _____

3. Responding: What do you think? What do you wonder?

   _____

   _____

   _____

   _____

   _____

4. Performing: What can you do?

   _____

   _____

   _____

   _____

   _____

From H. Scheff, M. Sprague, and S. McGreevy-Nichols, 2010, *Exploring dance forms and styles: A guide to concert, world, social, and historical dance* (Champaign, IL: Human Kinetics).

CHAPTER 7

Social Dance

Social dance is dance in which the primary focus is interaction with others. Folk dances are social dances in the context of their time and place. Historically, vernacular dances were most common to the working class and the young.

Characteristics

Social dance is part of every era and every community worldwide. One of the characteristics of social dance is that it is nearly always accompanied by music. A few exceptions exist in areas where people were not permitted to make noise. For example, slaves in all times and locations danced in their quarters where no singing or music were allowed. The dancers used stomping rhythms and hand clapping to keep a beat; this helped to keep the dancers together rhythmically. The beaten sounds increased the power and excitement of the dance.

Another characteristic of social dance is that the dances reflect the current issues of the time in which they were created. The East Coast Swing and all the allied dances gained popularity during and after World War II when people wanted to have fun and danced for the pure joy of movement. The music of the time influenced the dances but the dancers also had an impact on the music making. Social dance and music have a real partnership.

Categories

In this book the social dance form is divided into the following four subcategories based on typical groupings of dancers:

- *Alone in a group* describes when many dancers are on the dance floor but one doesn't relate to another (similar to the Alley Cat or the Twist). One example would be the Tahitian.

- *Partners* describes when the dancers are connected by holding hands, using traditional ballroom stance, facing each other, or otherwise physically relating to each other as in most ballroom dances. These dances usually have leaders and followers. Examples include the Waltz, the East Coast Swing, the Polka, and Salsa dance.

- *Dances done in a line or line dances* describes a choreographed dance where the steps or movement patterns repeat in some sequence. Dances done in a line and line dances are not the same thing. In line dancing, dancers are not in physical contact with each other. Some historical dances have the lines facing each other as in one set of the Quadrille. Dancers may follow a leader around the dance floor. They can hold the hands of the dancers beside them, or they can travel on their own, such as in the Dabkee. For dancing in a line or line dances it doesn't matter whether they are all males, all females, or a mixture. The dancers can be young or old. The prescribed steps are executed in unison.

- *Dances done in a circle* describes a different form of dance. Sometimes a leader starts forming the circle. Sometimes the circle opens to let others join or to bring people to the middle of the circle where they might do steps that highlight different abilities, such as in the Freilach. The circle serves to engage dancers as a social community because they can all see each other as they dance, such as in the Freilach or contra dance. You can find these dances on the DVD or you can search the Web for others.

Role

Social dance is a way to create a sense of community. Throughout time, people have danced at celebratory functions and rites of passage such as cotillion and debutante parties, quinceañera (sweet 15 in the Latina tradition when a girl becomes a woman), weddings, and even funerals. Sometimes social dance crosses over into concert dance, such as in ballroom dance exhibitions. A new type of social dance is club dancing, also called freestyle, which is in the subcategory of alone in a group. You can search the Internet to view the many online clips in this style.

History and Culture

From early cultures, through the courts of Europe, and into the 21st century, we can trace a place and time for social dance. We explore some older social dance forms in chapter 8, Historical Dance and we address forms that cross categories here, too. The Waltz is is both a historical and a social dance. It started in the courts of the 17th century, became a popular dance in the 18th century, and is still popular on the dance floors of the 21st century. Both the standard ballroom Waltz and the historical Viennese Waltz are partner dances. The Waltz was the first partner dance in which the couple faced each other. In the Viennese Waltz, the couples spun while making a circular floor pattern. When you look at films of the Viennese Waltz where couples are in formal clothes, it appears that they are spinning like tops because of the speed and number of rotations. In the standard ballroom Waltz, the couples turn under arms and sway while they open away from each other and back to face each other. They do not necessarily travel in a circular floor pattern.

©Bruce Davis

Social dance has sets of etiquette from the past that are still practiced today.

Social dance is part of many cultures. Each culture has its own social dances, but some have influenced others. For example, the North American social dance scene has been influenced by Latin social dances such as Tango, Salsa, Rhumba, Cha-cha, Mambo, and Argentine Tango. Social dances of the past are kept alive by dedicated groups of dancers of all ages and nationalities who continue to practice, perform, and perfect these dances. Dance groups who focus on a particular of style of dance often participate in competitions. These events call attention to the particular dance, bringing pride to the culture and the dancers.

Etiquette

The social dance scene has always had an understood etiquette, certain do's and don'ts. This is not only true for social dances of today but for many dances of the past. It is interesting to note expectations from different areas of the world. In the Jewish tradition, males and females cannot hold hands if they are not related. Therefore a handkerchief is held between the two. In traditional Middle Eastern cultures women only dance in front of other women or male relatives. In social dance classes, students need to learn proper manners and then carry them out on the dance floor. For more information about social dance etiquette, see the video clips and their accompanying narration.

Summary

Social dances have become part of the ballroom culture with demonstrations, performances, competitions, and leisure activities. Rules and regulations govern the competitions with protocol for dress. Social dances are signs of the times in which they originated and it is also a way to look at a culture within the traditions of a society. Regardless of time or culture, bringing people together is the focus of social dance.

The following pages contain the Knowledge Quest worksheets for the following dances, unless otherwise noted. Those with a DVD icon next to them have video clips that appear on the DVD.

Dances Done Alone in a Group

- **•DVD** La Bomba (see KQ worksheet in chapter 6)
- **•DVD** Tiriba (see KQ worksheet in chapter 6)
- • Irish dancing (see KQ worksheet in chapter 6)
- **•DVD** Tahitian (see KQ worksheet in chapter 6)
- **•DVD** Break dancing
- **•DVD** Native American (see KQ worksheet in chapter 6)

Dances Done With a Partner

- • Cakewalk (see KQ worksheet in chapter 8)
- **•DVD** Waltz (also a historical dance)
- **•DVD** East Coast Swing
- **•DVD** Salsa
- **•DVD** Fox-trot
- **•DVD** Hustle
- • Minuet (see KQ worksheet in chapter 8)
- • Quadrille (see KQ worksheet in chapter 8)
- **•DVD** Cha-cha
- **•DVD** Polka
- **•DVD** Two-step (Texas Two-step)
- **•DVD** Der Unterwestner (see KQ worksheet in chapter 6)

Dances Done in a Line

- • Contra dance
- **•DVD** Dabkee (see KQ worksheet in chapter 6)
- • Gavotte (see KQ worksheet in chapter 8)
- • Gumboot (see KQ worksheet in chapter 6)
- **•DVD** Virginia Reel (see KQ worksheet in chapter 6)
- **•DVD** Farandole (see KQ worksheet in chapter 8)

Dances Done in a Circle

- • Washerwoman's Branle (see KQ worksheet in chapter 8)
- **•DVD** Freilach (see KQ worksheet in chapter 6)

KNOWLEDGE QUEST

INFORMATION AND TEACHING TIPS
Category M: Social Dance (Subcategory: Alone in a group)
Category A: Concert (Subcategory: Crossover)
Category A: World (Subcategory: North America)
Name of Dance: Break Dancing

Break Dancing

*"The winner was the one who could bust out moves
that hadn't been witnessed before;
who could do something the other guy couldn't match."*

Mandalit del Barco
(www.npr.org/programs/morning/features/patc/breakdancing)

BACKGROUND INFORMATION   Before students view the video clip, share the following information with them.

- **Translation:** Break dancing was introduced and promoted by superstar James Brown, with his big hit "Get on the Good Foot." The dance called Good Foot was soon called B-boy; shortly afterward it was called break dancing, or breaking.

- **Timeline:** Break dancing first came about in the late 1960s.

- **Function or reason:** What began as a way for rival street gangs to solve turf disputes, soon became a dance phenomenon. "As the 70's evolved, much emphasis was placed on groundwork involving stylized leg movements (so-called Floor Rock or Down Rock)." Soon spectacular moves were invented and were added to the mix. "Still, the basic form of both rocking and breakdance 'cutting' contests remained the same until the 'Rock Steady Crew' and the 'Electronic Boogaloo Lockers' (later renamed the 'Electric Boogaloos') literally hit the streets of New York with the spectacular hand-gliding, back-spinning, windmilling, and head-spinning ground moves that have since become synonymous with the word breakdance. The dance gained in worldwide popularity during the '80s and '90s with break-dance moves being incorporated into movies and musical theater productions and European and Asian aficionados adding their own exuberant spins and whirls to the mix." Today breakdancing is as popular and exciting as ever and combines with other street dance such as locking, popping, and krumping.
From http://www.centralhome.com/breakdance.htm.

- **Who does this dance:** Boys, girls, men, and women do this dance.

- **Music and rhythms:** Break dancing is usually done to hip-hop music.

- **Traditional clothing or costume:** Hip-hop fashion is a must. Hooded sweatshirts, ball caps, headbands, bandanas, baggy pants, and big brand-name basketball shoes are favorites.

- **Other information:** Four types of movements make up break dancing:

  - *Toprock* refers to any series of steps performed from a standing position. It is usually the first display of style and it serves as a warm-up for transitions into more athletic maneuvers.

  - *Downrock* includes all footwork performed on the floor such as a six step. Normally performed with the hands and feet on the floor, downrock displays the break dancer's foot speed and control and transitions into power moves.

  - *Power moves* are actions that require momentum and physical power to execute. In power moves, the break dancer relies more on upper body strength and is usually on his or her hands during moves. Power moves include the windmill, swipe, and flare.

From H. Scheff, M. Sprague, and S. McGreevy-Nichols, 2010, *Exploring dance forms and styles: A guide to concert, world, social, and historical dance* (Champaign, IL: Human Kinetics).

Break Dancing

- *Freezes* usually end the routine and halt all motion in a stylish pose. The more difficult freezes require the breakdancer to suspend himself or herself off the ground, using upper body strength, in poses such as the handstand or pike.

REFERENCES

http://en.wikipedia.org/wiki/Breakdance

www.globaldarkness.com/articles/history%20of%20breaking.htm

www.centralhome.com/breakdance.htm

TEACHING STRATEGIES

The video clip should be viewed at least three times (see chapter 1). After students record and discuss their observations and before the third viewing, use the discussion starters listed next to facilitate class discussion. Feel free to paraphrase and choose the questions that work best with your students.

Viewing: What Did You See?

Suggested discussion starters and questions: What is the first thing that strikes you about this dance? How would you describe this dance in three words? What body parts are used the most?

Connecting: What Do You Know?

Suggested discussion starters and questions: When have you ever seen a dance like this performed? How was it like this dance? How was it different?

Responding: What Do You Think? What Do You Wonder?

Suggested discussion starters and questions: Some experts think that break dancing is linked to Capoeira, a Brazilian dance invented by African slaves. Do an Internet search for a video of Capoeira. Compare and contrast it to break dancing.

What questions do you have about this dance? Write them down and continue your research. Some of these questions can be answered through movement.

Performing: What Can You Do?

Choose both Re-create and Create, one of these two activities, or make your own performing work that you think is most appropriate for your students.

Re-create Choose three movements that you can perform safely from the video to re-create. *Note:* Use ideas from recorded observations from question 1 (What did you see?).

Break Dancing

Create   There are four basic elements that form the foundation of break dance. They are toprock, downrock, power moves, and freezes. Create one movement that represents the big idea of each element and perform your routine.

*If you need music and don't have it among your resources, use the video.

FUN FACTS   A break dancer, breaker, B-boy or B-girl refers to a person who practices break dancing. Groups of break dancers are called crews.

WEB EXPLORATIONS   Key terms to search for include break dancing, hip-hop, vernacular dance, and street dance.

From H. Scheff, M. Sprague, and S. McGreevy-Nichols, 2010, *Exploring dance forms and styles: A guide to concert, world, social, and historical dance* (Champaign, IL: Human Kinetics).

Break Dancing

Name: _____ Class: _____ Date: _____

STUDENT KNOWLEDGE QUEST WORKSHEET

Name of Dance: Break Dancing

1. Viewing: What did you see?
   Record your observations. Describe what you see. Be specific.

   _____

   _____

   _____

   _____

   _____

2. Connecting: What do you know?

   _____

   _____

   _____

   _____

   _____

3. Responding: What do you think? What do you wonder?

   _____

   _____

   _____

   _____

   _____

4. Performing: What can you do?

   _____

   _____

   _____

   _____

   _____

From H. Scheff, M. Sprague, and S. McGreevy-Nichols, 2010, *Exploring dance forms and styles: A guide to concert, world, social, and historical dance* (Champaign, IL: Human Kinetics).

KNOWLEDGE QUEST

INFORMATION AND TEACHING TIPS
Category M: Social (Subcategory: Partner)
Category A: Historical (Subcategory: 18th and 19th Century)
Name of Dance: Waltz

Waltz

and one, two, three

BACKGROUND INFORMATION   Before students view the video clip, share the following information with them.

- **Translation:** Waltz comes from the German word *waltzen,* which means to turn.

- **Country or culture of origin:** The Waltz itself is Viennese, and it evolved in Austria and Bavaria under such names as the *Dreher*, the *Laendler,* and the *Deutscher.* The Waltz was created as a peasant dance and involved vigorous moves and lots of space. Many times partners were hurled into the air, which occasionally led to injury. Eventually it became popular in Viennese dance halls in the late 18th century, and the less refined aspects began to change.

- **Timeline:** The Waltz is the oldest of the ballroom dances, dating from the middle of the 18th century. In 1787, it was brought to the operatic stage, and invited huge controversy. Mozart was a fan of the Waltz, and in one of his operas, *Don Giovanni,* he included three in one scene! The dance could not be stopped. By the 1800s, Paris had fallen in love with the Waltz. It did not arrive in England until later, where it was first rejected, and eventually allowed to reach the popularity that it still has today.

- **Function or reason:** It was performed as part of the opera and later used as a social dance.

- **Who does this dance:** Men and women do it as a partner dance.

- **Music and rhythms:** The Waltz is best performed to a piece of music in triple meter, or 3/4 time; notable instruments used to play it were the piano, the violin, and the bass.

- **Traditional clothing or costume:** Even though there are no set outfits, dancers usually dress up, or wear formal attire.

- **Other information:** The basic movement is a three-step sequence that consists of a step forward or backward, a step to the side, and then a step to close the feet together. The timing is the same for all steps, and the timing can be called out as "Quick, quick, quick," or using numbers such as "1,2,3."

REFERENCES
http://en.wikipedia.org/wiki/Waltz

http://en.wikipedia.org/wiki/Waltz_(music)

www.centralhome.com/ballroomcountry/waltz.htmwww.essortment.com/all/historyofthew_rklu.htm

www.thedancestoreonline.com/ballroom-dance-instruction/waltz-free-lessons.htm

TEACHING STRATEGIES   The video clip should be viewed at least three times (see chapter 1). After students record and discuss their observations and before the third viewing, use the discussion starters listed next to facilitate class discussion. Feel free to paraphrase and choose the questions that work best with your students.

From H. Scheff, M. Sprague, and S. McGreevy-Nichols, 2010, *Exploring dance forms and styles: A guide to concert, world, social, and historical dance* (Champaign, IL: Human Kinetics).

Waltz

Viewing: What Did You See?

Suggested discussion starters and questions: What are the basic movements in this dance? What are the feet doing in the dance? How are the dancers connected to each other? What body parts do most of the work? What are the key movements in the Waltz?

Connecting: What Do You Know?

Suggested discussion starters and questions: How do the dancers relate to one another? What do you notice about the floor pattern? What do you notice about the rhythm of the movement? How do the dancers create the rise and fall action of the dance?

Responding: What Do You Think? What Do You Wonder?

Suggested discussion starters and questions: From a historical perspective, why do you think the man leads in the waltz? Many times verbal cues can help us learn a dance. For example, when performing a leap with a preparation movement you might cue it like this: "step, step, leap." What verbal cues would you use to help someone learn the Waltz?

What questions do you have about this dance? Write them down and continue your research. Some of these questions can be answered through movement.

Performing: What Can You Do?

Choose both Re-create and Create, choose one of these two activities, or make your own performing work that you think is most appropriate for your students.

Re-create   Without a partner, use your cue words to help you learn the foot pattern for the Waltz. *Note:* Review the notes from recorded observations for question 1 (What did you see?).

Face a partner and hold hands. Try to perform the movement pattern together. Eventually you can try it using a closed position (partners place one hand on male's shoulder and female's back or waist and the other hands are held.)

Create   Individually, draw a floor pattern on a piece of paper. Use the movements of the Waltz to travel around that pattern and add arm movements. Repeat while holding a partner's hand.

*If you need music and don't have it among your resources, use the video.

FUN FACTS   The Tango is thought to be the world's first forbidden dance. This is not so. The first dance to earn this notoriety was the Waltz. When it began to be danced in the Viennese dance halls, partners were allowed to touch! They faced each other with hands in ballroom position. Their bodies stood apart in the early days. Gradually, they were able to get closer. This was unheard of and led to the dance being criticized by many officials of the church and leaders of the Austrian community. However because it was a favored dance of the young, it continued to be danced.

WEB EXPLORATIONS   Key terms to search for include Waltz, ballroom dance, and Viennese Waltz.

From H. Scheff, M. Sprague, and S. McGreevy-Nichols, 2010, *Exploring dance forms and styles: A guide to concert, world, social, and historical dance* (Champaign, IL: Human Kinetics).

Name: _____ Class: _____ Date: _____

STUDENT KNOWLEDGE QUEST WORKSHEET

Name of Dance: Waltz

1. Viewing: What did you see?
   Record your observations. Describe what you see. Be specific.

   _____

   _____

   _____

   _____

   _____

2. Connecting: What do you know?

   _____

   _____

   _____

   _____

   _____

3. Responding: What do you think? What do you wonder?

   _____

   _____

   _____

   _____

   _____

4. Performing: What can you do?

   _____

   _____

   _____

   _____

   _____

From H. Scheff, M. Sprague, and S. McGreevy-Nichols, 2010, *Exploring dance forms and styles: A guide to concert, world, social, and historical dance* (Champaign, IL: Human Kinetics).

East Coast Swing

KNOWLEDGE QUEST

INFORMATION AND TEACHING TIPS
Category M: Social (Subcategory: Partner)
Name of Dance: East Coast Swing

"It don't mean a thing if it ain't got that swing."

Irving Mills

BACKGROUND INFORMATION   Before students view the video clip, share the following information with them.

- **Translation:** We did not have a term *East Coast Swing* until there was a *West Coast Swing*.
- **Country or culture of origin:** This dance originated in the United States.
- **Timeline:** This dance originated in the 1940s.
- **Function or reason:** The East Coast Swing (ECS) is a form of social partner dance that is also known as the Jitterbug, Lindy, and Lindy Hop. The ECS is not a street dance, rather a ballroom studio adaptation, derived from various street swing dancing patterns and styles, particularly the Lindy Hop, at the height of the swing era.
- **Who does this dance:** Men, women, and children dance this dance.
- **Music and rhythms:** East Coast Swing can be danced to jump blues or to country swing songs. The music is diverse and includes oldies (Elvis and Chuck Berry), jump blues, country, big band, and top 40. With a wide range of music to choose from you can swing to almost anything. Swing music is written in 4/4 time with a tempo of 145 to 170 beats per minute.
- **Traditional clothing or costume:** No specific dress is required.
- **Other information:** East Coast Swing is a swing dance that has many wraps, tunnels, and turns. The basic step is as follows: triple step, triple step, rock step. The swing is a fast dance. To maintain balance, a firm hand grip is essential. Beginners should try using the two-hand position, in which the man extends his arms forward with palms up and the woman then places her hands palms down in her partner's hands. Think of your fingers as a hook, cupping each other's fingers and maintaining a firm hold.

REFERENCES
http://en.wikipedia.org/wiki/East_Coast_Swing

www.streetswing.com/histmain/z3ecs1.htm

www.ballroomdancers.com/dances/dance_overview.asp?Dance=ECSwww.dancetv.com/tutorial/
  swing/sintro.html

TEACHING STRATEGIES   The video clip should be viewed at least three times (see chapter 1). After students record and discuss their observations and before the third viewing, use the discussion starters listed next to facilitate class discussion. Feel free to paraphrase and choose the questions that work best with your students.

Viewing: What Did You See?

Suggested discussion starters and questions: What is the first thing that strikes you about this dance? How would you describe this dance in three words? What are the main body parts that are used? How do the dancers relate to one another? How do the dancers move around the floor?

From H. Scheff, M. Sprague, and S. McGreevy-Nichols, 2010, *Exploring dance forms and styles: A guide to concert, world, social, and historical dance* (Champaign, IL: Human Kinetics).

East Coast Swing

Connecting: What Do You Know?

Suggested discussion starters and questions: When have you ever seen a dance like this performed? How was it like this dance? How was it different?

Responding: What Do You Think? What Do You Wonder?

Suggested discussion starters and questions: Among early swing dancers, improvisation and demonstrations of specialized skills such as jumps, spins, turns, and throw-outs were common. Why do you think ballroom dance studios like Arthur Murray wanted to codify (standardize and notate) this dance? What do you think the dance gained or lost by this action?

What questions do you have about this dance? Write them down and continue your research. Some of these questions can be answered through movement.

Performing: What Can You Do?

Choose both Re-create and Create, choose one of these two activities, or make your own performing work that you think is most appropriate for your students.

Re-create Read the following text and then look at the clip again and see how they perform the sequence of steps described.

1. To begin, stand in an upright position facing your partner. You will be assuming a two-hand hold in open swing position. This is a quick dance, so steps should be small and light. The knees should be relaxed and slightly flexed.

2. Triple step. The triple step consists of a series of three small steps. Let's try it. Stand in place with your feet together. Stomp your feet in place: 1-2-3, 1-2-3, LRL, RLR. Keep doing this, accenting count 1 and count 3. That's the basic rhythm. Now travel with this movement. The triple step moves freely around the floor; it is not stepped in place, nor is it a line-of-direction dance.

3. Back rock. A back rock follows a triple step. The man, who always begins his sequence on the left foot, will always rock back on the left foot as well. The woman will begin and rock back on the right foot.

Create Using the concept of swing as an inspiration, create a short dance that uses three variations of body parts that express swinging. Connect the three variations with movements that travel.

*If you need music and don't have it among your resources, use the video.

FUN FACTS   When you hear about swing dancing to the music of Elvis Presley and Chuck Berry back in the 1950s, this is the dance they were doing. The East Coast Swing is the official sock hop swing dance.

WEB EXPLORATIONS   Key terms to search for include East Coast Swing, Jitterbug, and Lindy Hop.

From H. Scheff, M. Sprague, and S. McGreevy-Nichols, 2010, *Exploring dance forms and styles: A guide to concert, world, social, and historical dance* (Champaign, IL: Human Kinetics).

East Coast Swing

Name: _____ Class: _____ Date: _____

STUDENT KNOWLEDGE QUEST WORKSHEET

Name of Dance: East Coast Swing

1. Viewing: What did you see?
   Record your observations. Describe what you see. Be specific.

   _____

   _____

   _____

   _____

   _____

2. Connecting: What do you know?

   _____

   _____

   _____

   _____

   _____

3. Responding: What do you think? What do you wonder?

   _____

   _____

   _____

   _____

   _____

4. Performing: What can you do?

   _____

   _____

   _____

   _____

   _____

From H. Scheff, M. Sprague, and S. McGreevy-Nichols, 2010, *Exploring dance forms and styles: A guide to concert, world, social, and historical dance* (Champaign, IL: Human Kinetics).

KNOWLEDGE QUEST

INFORMATION AND TEACHING TIPS
Category M: Social (Subcategory: Partner)
Category A: World (Subcategory: North America)
Name of Dance: Salsa

Salsa

Viva la Salsa!

BACKGROUND INFORMATION Before students view the video clip, share the following information with them.

- **Translation:** The word *salsa* means sauce. It is a saucy combination of Latin dances (which are mostly Cuban) including Són, Mambo, Cuban Rumba, and Guaguancó.

- **Country or culture of origin:** Salsa is a dance for Salsa music created by Spanish-speaking people from the Caribbean and their immigrant communities in the United States.

- **Timeline:** During the 20th century, specifically during the 1930s when the term *salsa* was coined.

- **Function or reason:** Salsa is a social partner dance.

- **Who does this dance:** Men, women, and children dance this dance.

- **Music and rhythms:** The key instrument that provides the core groove of a Salsa song is the conga drum. Every instrument in a Salsa band is either playing with the clave (congas, timbales, piano, tres guitar, bongos, claves [instrument], and strings) or playing independent of the clave rhythm (bass, maracas, güiro, cowbell).

- **Traditional clothing or costume:** Although casual clothing is always acceptable, women can dress things up by wearing a Salsa dress that flows with the hip movement. Salsa dance shoes with a suede bottom complete the outfit. Anything goes for men, but should match the formality (or lack of) of the woman's outfit.

- **Other information:** Salsa is not easily defined. Who invented Salsa? The Cubans, Puerto Ricans? Salsa is a distillation of many Latin and Afro-Caribbean dances. Each played a large part in its evolution. It is not only Cuban; nevertheless, we must give credit to Cuba for its origin. It is here where contra-danze (country dance) of England and France and later called danzón, which was brought by the French who fled from Haiti, began to mix itself with rumbas of African origin (Guaguancó, Colombia, Yambú). Add Són of the Cuban people, which was a mixture of the Spanish troubadour (sonero) and the African drumbeats, and flavora, and a partner dance grew to the beat of the clave. Salsa is played throughout the Hispanic world and has received influences of many places within it. Salsa is similar to Mambo in that both have a pattern of six steps danced over eight counts of music. The dances share many of the same moves. In Salsa, turns have become an important feature, so the overall look and feel are quite different form those of Mambo. Mambo moves generally forward and backward, whereas Salsa has more of a side-to-side feel.

REFERENCES

http://centralhome.com/ballroomcountry/salsa.htm

http://en.wikipedia.org/wiki/Salsa_(dance)

www.geocities.com/sd_au/mambo/sdssalsa.htm

From H. Scheff, M. Sprague, and S. McGreevy-Nichols, 2010, *Exploring dance forms and styles: A guide to concert, world, social, and historical dance* (Champaign, IL: Human Kinetics).

Salsa

TEACHING STRATEGIES   The video clip should be viewed at least three times (see chapter 1). After students record and discuss their observations and before the third viewing, use the discussion starters listed next to facilitate class discussion. Feel free to paraphrase and choose the questions that work best with your students.

Viewing: What Did You See?

Suggested discussion starters and questions: What are the feet doing in the dance? How are the dancers connected to each other? What are the key movements in the Salsa? How do the dancers work with rhythm and music?

Connecting: What Do You Know?

Suggested discussion starters and questions: When have you ever seen a dance like this performed? How is it like this dance? How is it different?

Responding: What Do You Think? What Do You Wonder?

Suggested discussion starters and questions: Salsa is considered a Latin dance. Where in the movement do you see evidence of Latin cultures? Cite specific examples. What do you think would be the hardest thing to learn in this dance? What process would you use to teach yourself this dance? What movements would you learn first, second, and third?

What questions do you have about this dance? Write them down and continue your research. Some of these questions can be answered through movement.

Performing: What Can You Do?

Choose both Re-create and Create, choose one of these two activities, or make your own performing work that you think is most appropriate for your students.

Re-create   Read the following description of the Salsa steps. View the clip again and notice where you see the movements performed. Without a partner, re-create the steps as described next.

The most universal basic steps for Salsa start with a tap left on the first beat, a step forward on the same foot, a rock back onto the right foot; the sequence is finished by stepping back left to close. This is the forward basic movement, which is followed by the back basic movement. Tap right, step back right, rock forward left, and close right.

Create   Working with a partner, create a new Latin partner dance, including the following:

- Turn
- Eight-count pattern that travels and repeats
- Stop with two focus changes or poses
- Latin flavor

*If you need music and don't have it among your resources, use the video.

FUN FACTS   There is no doubt that dancing is great aerobic exercise. You can burn between 264 and 528 calories per hour doing the Salsa.

WEB EXPLORATIONS   Key terms to search for include Salsa dance, Mambo, and Salsa music.

From H. Scheff, M. Sprague, and S. McGreevy-Nichols, 2010, *Exploring dance forms and styles: A guide to concert, world, social, and historical dance* (Champaign, IL: Human Kinetics).

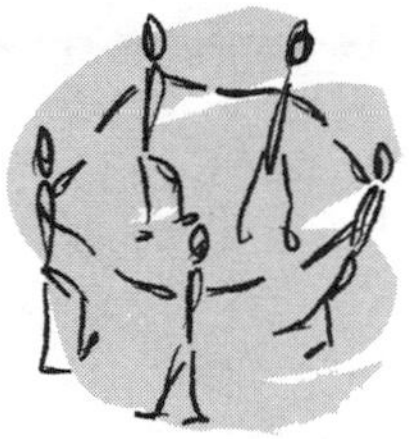

Name: _____ Class: _____ Date: _____

STUDENT KNOWLEDGE QUEST WORKSHEET

Salsa

Name of Dance: Salsa

1. Viewing: What did you see?
   Record your observations. Describe what you see. Be specific.

   _____

   _____

   _____

   _____

   _____

2. Connecting: What do you know?

   _____

   _____

   _____

   _____

   _____

3. Responding: What do you think? What do you wonder?

   _____

   _____

   _____

   _____

   _____

4. Performing: What can you do?

   _____

   _____

   _____

   _____

   _____

From H. Scheff, M. Sprague, and S. McGreevy-Nichols, 2010, *Exploring dance forms and styles: A guide to concert, world, social, and historical dance* (Champaign, IL: Human Kinetics).

Fox-Trot

KNOWLEDGE QUEST

INFORMATION AND TEACHING TIPS
Category M: Social (Subcategory: Partner)
Category A: Historical (Subcategory: Early 20th Century)
Name of Dance: Fox-Trot

"Ginger Rogers did everything Fred Astaire did, only backwards and in high heels."

Unknown

BACKGROUND INFORMATION
Before students view the video clip, share the following information with them.

- **Translation:** The Fox-trot (also *Fox trot, foxtrot, fox trot*) takes its name from its inventor, the Vaudeville actor Harry Fox.

- **Country or culture of origin:** This dance comes from New York City.

- **Timeline:** The dance premiered in 1914, quickly catching the eye of the talented husband and wife duo Vernon and Irene Castle, who lent the dance its signature grace and style.

- **Function or reason:** It is a ballroom dance. According to legend, Harry Fox was unable to find single female dancers capable of performing the more difficult two-step. As a result, he added stagger steps (two trots), creating the basic Fox-trot rhythm of slow-slow-quick-quick.

- **Who does this dance:** Men and women dance this dance.

- **Music and rhythms:** The Fox-trot was originally danced to ragtime music. Today, the dance is accompanied by the same big band music to which swing is also danced. Since it can be danced to music with a wide range of styles and tempo, it is very versatile.

- **Traditional clothing or costume:** No specific clothing is required.

- **Other information:** On October 23, 1915 the *Oakland Tribune* had an article based on how mathematics are changing dance and listed the Fox-trot and Waltz as being officially changed by the dance masters of the day. The Fox-trot was the dance that changed the dancing world. Without the Fox-trot, the music and dances that followed might be totally different today. The fast Fox-trot (originally a one-step) is called the Quickstep today.

REFERENCES
www.streetswing.com/histmain/z3foxtrt.htm

http://en.wikipedia.org/wiki/Foxtrot

www.ballroomdancers.com/Dances/dance_overview.asp?Dance=AFX

TEACHING STRATEGIES
The video clip should be viewed at least three times (see chapter 1). After students record and discuss their observations and before the third viewing, use the discussion starters listed next to facilitate class discussion. Feel free to paraphrase and choose the questions that work best with your students.

Viewing: What Did You See?

Suggested discussion starters and questions: What is the first thing that strikes you about this dance? How would you describe this dance in three words? What are the main body parts that are used? How do the dancers relate to one another? How do the dancers move around the floor?

From H. Scheff, M. Sprague, and S. McGreevy-Nichols, 2010, *Exploring dance forms and styles: A guide to concert, world, social, and historical dance* (Champaign, IL: Human Kinetics).

Fox-Trot

Connecting: What Do You Know?

Suggested discussion starters and questions: When have you ever seen a dance like this performed? How was it like this dance? How was it different?

Responding: What Do You Think? What Do You Wonder?

Suggested discussion starters and questions: Look at the video clip of the Waltz. How is the Waltz different from the Fox-trot? How is it same? Why do you think they have like qualities?

What questions do you have about this dance? Write them down and continue your research. Some of these questions can be answered through movement.

Performing: What Can You Do?

Choose both Re-create and Create, choose one of these two activities, or make your own performing work that you think is most appropriate for your students.

Re-create   Read the following description of the Fox-trot steps. View the video clip again and notice where you see the movements performed. Re-create the steps as described.

1. Forward step with left foot (slow).
2. Forward step with right foot (slow).
3. Step to left (quick).
4. Close right foot to left (quick).
5. Back step with right foot (slow).
6. Back step with left foot (slow).
7. Step to right (quick).
8. Close left foot to right (quick).
9. Back step with left foot (slow).
10. Back step with right foot (slow).
11. Step to left (quick).
12. Close right foot to left (quick).
13. Forward step with right foot (slow).
14. Forward step with left foot (slow).
15. Step to right (quick).
16. Close left foot to right (quick).

Create   Working with a partner, create a new partner dance including the following:

- A turn
- An eight-count pattern that travels and repeats
- A stop with two focus changes

*If you need music and don't have it among your resources, use the video.

FUN FACTS   Famously, Decca Records initially labeled its rock-and-roll releases as what they called "Fox trots," most notably "Rock Around the Clock" by Bill Haley and His Comets. Since then that recording, by some estimates, went on to sell more than 25 million copies, making "Rock Around the Clock" technically the biggest-selling "Fox trot" of all time.

WEB EXPLORATIONS   Key terms to search for include Fox-trot, ballroom dancing, and Harry Fox.

From H. Scheff, M. Sprague, and S. McGreevy-Nichols, 2010, *Exploring dance forms and styles: A guide to concert, world, social, and historical dance* (Champaign, IL: Human Kinetics).

Fox-Trot

Name: _____   Class: _____   Date: _____

STUDENT KNOWLEDGE QUEST WORKSHEET

Name of Dance: Fox-Trot

1. Viewing: What did you see?
   Record your observations. Describe what you see. Be specific.

   _____

   _____

   _____

   _____

   _____

2. Connecting: What do you know?

   _____

   _____

   _____

   _____

   _____

3. Responding: What do you think? What do you wonder?

   _____

   _____

   _____

   _____

   _____

4. Performing: What can you do?

   _____

   _____

   _____

   _____

   _____

From H. Scheff, M. Sprague, and S. McGreevy-Nichols, 2010, *Exploring dance forms and styles: A guide to concert, world, social, and historical dance* (Champaign, IL: Human Kinetics).

KNOWLEDGE QUEST
INFORMATION AND TEACHING TIPS
Category M: Social (Subcategory: Partner)
Name of Dance: Hustle

Hustle

Hustle to the beat.

BACKGROUND INFORMATION   Before students view the video clip, share the following information with them.

- **Country or culture of origin:** It comes from the United States but has become popular worldwide. Although it started as a line dance it is now a partner dance. The couples version of the Hustle is said to have come from Florida with the influx of Cubans. It was a mix of Salsa, swing dance, and the new disco beat. It made its way north to the eastern states such as New York.

- **Timeline:** Hustle gained prominence in 1968 as a freeform style of dance in discos; it had simple footwork and a simple count. It bears similarity to West Coast Swing and Texas Two-step.

- **Function or reason:** This is a fun social dance. It is done at ballroom dance clubs and celebration functions.

- **Who does this dance:** Men and women dance this dance in couples. As the dance form got more strenuous, it was no longer done as a plain couples' dance; instead, different people who had tricks to show would come to the center and solo.

- **Music and rhythms:** Hustle music has every beat accented. It sounds like a bass drum on every beat. In the heyday of the Hustle, the disco beat was heavily used.

- **Traditional clothing or costume:** People would dress in fancy clothing. John Travolta, who made the disco Hustle famous in the movie *Saturday Night Fever,* wore a white suit. Many men of that time would try to look like him. Woman would wear really high heels and skirts that would allow for leg action.

- **Other information:** John Travolta made this dance really famous in *Saturday Night Fever.* His movement with one arm reaching out and pulling back in while his hips swayed was synonymous with what people thought of as the Hustle and still do today.

REFERENCES

www.ballroomdanceacademy.com/the-dances/descriptions-of-dances/hustle/

www.streetswing.com/histmain/z3hustl1.htm

TEACHING STRATEGIES   The video clip should be viewed at least three times (see chapter 1). After students record and discuss their observations and before the third viewing, use the discussion starters listed next to facilitate class discussion. Feel free to paraphrase and choose the questions that work best with your students.

Viewing: What Did You See?

Suggested discussion starters and questions: What do you see as the main body parts used in this dance? How do the dancers connect to each other? What are the main positions of the dancers?

Connecting: What Do You Know?

Suggested discussion starters and questions: When have you seen a dance like this performed? How was it like this dance? How was it different?

From H. Scheff, M. Sprague, and S. McGreevy-Nichols, 2010, *Exploring dance forms and styles: A guide to concert, world, social, and historical dance* (Champaign, IL: Human Kinetics).

Hustle

Responding: What Do You Think? What Do You Wonder?

Suggested discussion starters and questions: Why do you think the man leads in this partnering dance? Compare this with a line dance version. Compare this competition dance from the video clip with what might happen on the dance club floor.

What questions do you have about this dance? Write them down and continue your research. Some of these questions can be answered through movement.

Performing: What Can You Do?

Choose both Re-create and Create, choose one of these two activities, or make your own performing work that you think is most appropriate for your students.

Re-create Looking at the basic step on the video, re-create the step and two floor patterns to re-create a portion of the dance.

Basic step: Step out on count 1, step out with other foot on count 2, step out with first foot on count 3, and ball change on count & 4. Don't forget the hip sway.

Create Using the short dance from the re-create section, create different kinds of partnered turns holding hands and going under each other's arms.

*If you need music and don't have it among your resources, use the video.

FUN FACTS When the dancers would get out on the floor in a ballroom setting, there would be a mirror ball hanging from the ceiling. There would be many different colored lights focused on the rotating ball. It created all sorts of images on the floor and on the dancers, lending additional excitement to the dance.

WEB EXPLORATIONS Key terms to search for include Hustle, ballroom, John Travolta, Saturday Night Fever, and disco.

From H. Scheff, M. Sprague, and S. McGreevy-Nichols, 2010, *Exploring dance forms and styles: A guide to concert, world, social, and historical dance* (Champaign, IL: Human Kinetics).

Name: _____ Class: _____ Date: _____

Hustle

STUDENT KNOWLEDGE QUEST WORKSHEET

Name of Dance: Hustle

1. Viewing: What did you see?
   Record your observations. Describe what you see. Be specific.

   _____

   _____

   _____

   _____

   _____

2. Connecting: What do you know?

   _____

   _____

   _____

   _____

   _____

3. Responding: What do you think? What do you wonder?

   _____

   _____

   _____

   _____

   _____

4. Performing: What can you do?

   _____

   _____

   _____

   _____

   _____

From H. Scheff, M. Sprague, and S. McGreevy-Nichols, 2010, *Exploring dance forms and styles: A guide to concert, world, social, and historical dance* (Champaign, IL: Human Kinetics).

Cha-Cha

KNOWLEDGE QUEST

INFORMATION AND TEACHING TIPS
Category M: Social (Subcategory: Partner)
Name of Dance: Cha-Cha

One! Two! One-Two-Three! That's the beat it has to be.

BACKGROUND INFORMATION Before students view the video clip, share the following information with them.

- **Translation:** The words *cha-cha* hail from certain plants, producing seedpods in the West Indies called cha-cha (in Spanish means nursemaid.) These seedpods are used to make a small rattle called a cha-cha (maracas).

- **Country or culture of origin:** Originally called the Cha-cha-cha, it is one of the five dances of the Latin American program of international ballroom competitions. It was brought to the United States from Cuba in the mid-1950s. It was created by Cuban violinist and orchestra director Enrique Jorrín in 1948 as a result of his experimentation with melody and rhythm. Of all Latin dances, it is the most recently incorporated into the Latin family. The dance may have been introduced to the world by a British dance teacher, Pierre Lavelle, who noticed that the Rumba was occasionally danced with a couple of extra steps. He brought the idea back with him to Europe around 1952.

- **Timeline:** Though it first appeared in Cuba in 1948, it hit the big cities in the United States in the 1950s and quickly became the ballroom rage.

- **Function or reason:** In this video clip we see the country-western style of the competition Cha-cha. In a nightclub, there would be many more people freestyling on the dance floor which would create a different energy.

- **Who does this dance:** Men, women, boys, and girls do this dance.

- **Music and rhythms:** The Cha-cha, or Triple Mambo, is basically a triple-rhythm Mambo. It is an in-between dance—not too fast and not too slow—which makes it an easy rhythm and speed for everybody, as opposed to the Mambo, where the music is faster and the rhythm more complex (three-step rhythm to two beats of music). Usually a slower form of Mambo music done in 4/4 time, around 126 beats per minute, is used.

- **Traditional clothing or costume:** In competition, the women wear some kind of ruffle or fringe that shows off hip action. The men wear close-fitting trousers and shirts.

- **Other information:** The Mambo probably started in Haiti and was introduced to the West in 1948. The word *Mambo* is the name of a voodoo priestess in a West African religion. Following this line of thinking, one could say that the Cha-cha had its origins in the ritual dances in West Africa. The video clip is of the country-western style of Cha-cha. Within one dance form, many styles exist.

REFERENCES
http://en.wikipedia.org/wiki/Cha-cha-cha_(dance)
www.salsa-in-cuba.com/eng/dance_chachacha.html
www.streetswing.com/histmain/z3cha.htm

TEACHING STRATEGIES The video clip should be viewed at least three times (see chapter 1). After students record and discuss their observations and before the third viewing, use the discussion starters listed next to facilitate class discussion. Feel free to paraphrase and choose the questions that work best with your students.

From H. Scheff, M. Sprague, and S. McGreevy-Nichols, 2010, *Exploring dance forms and styles: A guide to concert, world, social, and historical dance* (Champaign, IL: Human Kinetics).

Cha-Cha

Viewing: What Did You See?

Suggested discussion starters and questions: What are the main body parts that are used? What do you notice about the way the feet are used? How do the dancers work with rhythm?

Connecting: What Do You Know?

Suggested discussion starters and questions: What do you know about the difference between the country-western style of the dance and the style you might see in a nightclub? How do the dancers relate to each other and stay within the style?

Responding: What Do You Think? What Do You Wonder?

Suggested discussion starters and questions: Compare the rhythm and beat of the Mambo with the Cha-cha. The musical origins of the Cha-cha came from a composer. How did that impact the steps of the dance?

What questions do you have about this dance? Write them down and continue your research. Some of these questions can be answered through movement.

Performing: What Can You Do?

Choose both Re-create and Create, choose one of these two activities, or make your own performing work that you think is most appropriate for your students.

Re-create Establish the beat of the dance by clapping it out. Put the rhythm of the clapping into your feet to re-create eight measures of the dance. Use different facings. *Note:* Use ideas from recorded observations from question 1 (What did you see?).

Create Working with a partner, create your version of the dance with multiple facings and partnering hand clasps.

*If you need music and don't have it among your resources, use the video.

FUN FACTS Some people think that the term *cha-cha* is derived from the sound and rhythm that the feet make: cha, cha, cha-cha-cha (step 1, step 2, step 3-4-5).

WEB EXPLORATIONS Key terms to search for include Cha-cha, Latin rhythms, Mambo, Rumba, Rhumba, Rumba ballroom competitions, and country-western ballroom dance.

From H. Scheff, M. Sprague, and S. McGreevy-Nichols, 2010, *Exploring dance forms and styles: A guide to concert, world, social, and historical dance* (Champaign, IL: Human Kinetics).

Cha-Cha

Name: _____ Class: _____ Date: _____

STUDENT KNOWLEDGE QUEST WORKSHEET

Name of Dance: Cha-Cha

1. Viewing: What did you see?
   Record your observations. Describe what you see. Be specific.

   _____

   _____

   _____

   _____

   _____

2. Connecting: What do you know?

   _____

   _____

   _____

   _____

   _____

3. Responding: What do you think? What do you wonder?

   _____

   _____

   _____

   _____

   _____

4. Performing: What can you do?

   _____

   _____

   _____

   _____

   _____

From H. Scheff, M. Sprague, and S. McGreevy-Nichols, 2010, *Exploring dance forms and styles: A guide to concert, world, social, and historical dance* (Champaign, IL: Human Kinetics).

KNOWLEDGE QUEST

INFORMATION AND TEACHING TIPS
Category M: Social (Subcategory: Partner)
Category A: Historical (Subcategory: 18th and 19th Century)
Category A: World (Subcategory: Europe)
Name of Dance: Polka

Polka

Back in history, into the ballroom and out in the barn—a Polka is a Polka.

BACKGROUND INFORMATION   Before students view the video clip, share the following information with them.

- **Translation:** The name of the dance comes from a Czech word for half-step, *pulka*, which refers to the rapid shift from one foot to the other.

- **Country or culture of origin:** The Polka was originally a Czech peasant dance, developed in Eastern Bohemia (now part of Czechoslovakia).

- **Timeline:** The dance was first introduced into the ballrooms of Prague in 1835. In 1840, Raab, a dancing teacher of Prague, danced the Polka at the Odéon Theatre in Paris, where it was a tremendous success. The Polka was introduced in England by the middle of the 19th century. By this time, it had also reached the United States.

- **Function or reason:** Bohemian historians believe that the Polka was invented by a peasant girl (Anna Slezak, in Labska Tynice in 1834) one Sunday for her amusement. It was composed to a folk song "Strycek Nimra Koupil Simla" ("Uncle Nimra brought a White Horse"). Anna called the step "madera" because of its quickness and liveliness.

- **Who does this dance:** Men and women, boys and girls, young and old, novice and expert dancers dance it.

- **Music and rhythms:** The Polka is a vivacious couples' dance of Bohemian origin. It is done in duple meter, or 2/4 time, with a basic pattern of hop step close step. Instruments include the accordion, guitars, and sometimes clarinets.

- **Traditional clothing or costume:** When performed in Europe the people dancing wore their best regular dress. Women wore blouses with embroidery, vests with embroidery, and full skirts with petticoats. For the ballroom version, the woman would wear a plain ballroom gown as for most ballroom dances and for country-western dance or she would wear a blouse with a longish skirt and cowboy boots. The men would wear their regular shoes for the older versions, along with puffed out breeches and a good shirt. Some might wear a vest. For ballroom the man might wear a tuxedo or nice shirt and dancing shoes. For country-western dance they wore boots, jeans, and a cowboy-style shirt. Sometimes suspenders were worn and always a cowboy hat!

- **Other information:** Of all the dances originating in the 19th century, the only one that has survived is the Polka. After the initial enthusiasm, the Polka gradually declined in popularity and reached a low point with the introduction of ragtime, jazz, and the newer dances of the early 20th century. After World War II, however, Polish immigrants to the United States adopted the Polka as their "national" dance. It is also extremely popular with many other North Americans who have succumbed to the Polka craze popularized by Lawrence Welk and other postwar bands. Polka is a popular dance in the country and western sector. Polka and Schottische are competitive country-western dances.

REFERENCES

www.centralhome.com/ballroomcountry/polka.htm

www.pbs.org/riverofsong/music/e1-polka.html

From H. Scheff, M. Sprague, and S. McGreevy-Nichols, 2010, *Exploring dance forms and styles: A guide to concert, world, social, and historical dance* (Champaign, IL: Human Kinetics).

Polka

TEACHING STRATEGIES The video clip should be viewed at least three times (see chapter 1). In the case where students are searching and observing from home, they will need to list the exact Web site used so that teachers and other students can see the basis for their documentation.

Facilitate a class discussion using the discussion starters listed next. Have students use their recorded answers as a resource. Feel free to paraphrase and choose the questions that work best with your students.

Viewing: What Did You See?

Suggested discussion starters and questions: What are the main body parts that are used? What are some key movements that are used? What do you notice about the way the feet are used? What do you notice about the way the hands are used?

Connecting: What Do You Know?

Suggested discussion starters and questions: What are the basic movements in this dance? What are the dancers doing with their arms and hands? What kind of floor space did they use?

Responding: What Do You Think? What Do You Wonder?

Suggested discussion starters and questions: Go online and view the clips at the following address: www.youtube.com/watch?v=ajxfQk_zbjM&feature=related or others resulting from an Internet search for Polka.

What do the ladies' costumes used in the two different videos have in common? How are they not alike? Compare the two styles of dancing.

What questions do you have about this dance? Write them down and continue your research. Some of these questions can be answered through movement.

Performing: What Can You Do?

Choose both Re-create and Create, one of these two activities, or make your own performing work that you think is most appropriate for your students.

Re-create The basic step is hop, step out with raised leg, close the other foot in to a together position, and then step out with the other foot. Then reverse. When re-creating this step, do it in a circle, twirling your partner around, forward, and backward, being vivacious (bright and cheery) for 32 counts.

Create Using the basic Polka step, create a variation of the beginning step by doing a short jump with both feet. Then shift to the step-together-step. Be sure to use alternating sides even though you are starting with both feet on the ground.

*If you need music and don't have it among your resources, use the video.

FUN FACTS Polka became very popular. Dance academies were swamped and in desperation recruited ballet girls from the Paris Opéra as dancing partners to help teach the Polka. This naturally attracted many young men who were interested in things other than dancing, and manners and morals in the dance pavilions deteriorated. Dancing developed a bad name and many parents forbade their daughters dancing with anyone but close friends of the family.

WEB EXPLORATIONS Key terms to search for include Polka and country-and-western Polka.

From H. Scheff, M. Sprague, and S. McGreevy-Nichols, 2010, *Exploring dance forms and styles: A guide to concert, world, social, and historical dance* (Champaign, IL: Human Kinetics).

Name: _____   Class: _____   Date: _____

STUDENT KNOWLEDGE QUEST WORKSHEET

Polka

Name of Dance: Polka

1. Viewing: What did you see?
   Record your observations. Describe what you see. Be specific.

   _____

   _____

   _____

   _____

   _____

2. Connecting: What do you know?

   _____

   _____

   _____

   _____

   _____

3. Responding: What do you think? What do you wonder?

   _____

   _____

   _____

   _____

   _____

4. Performing: What can you do?

   _____

   _____

   _____

   _____

   _____

From H. Scheff, M. Sprague, and S. McGreevy-Nichols, 2010, *Exploring dance forms and styles: A guide to concert, world, social, and historical dance* (Champaign, IL: Human Kinetics).

Two-Step

KNOWLEDGE QUEST

INFORMATION AND TEACHING TIPS
Category M: Social (Subcategory: Partner)
Name of Dance: Two-Step (Texas Two-Step)

A truly American ballroom dance form with different styles.

BACKGROUND INFORMATION   Before students view the video clip, share the following information with them.

- **Translation:** The country-western Two-step, often called the Texas Two-step or simply the Two-step, is a country-western dance usually danced to country music in 4/4 time. It is a progressive dance that proceeds counterclockwise around the floor.

- **Country or culture of origin:** The Texas Two-step is the most widely known and performed country dance in North America. There are really two histories of what is called "two step dance," because the name jumped from one type of dance that is no longer done to another that is done, called the Texas Two-step or collegiate Fox-trot. The original Two-step was a simple dance that caught on with the public when John Philip Sousa came out with the "Washington Post March" in 1891. The old Quadrilles, Glides, and Reels were cast aside in favor of dances such as the Two-step.

- **Timeline:** The traditional Two-step is a dance with roots in European and Mexican dance history and appeared in Germany and Hungary in the 1800s. Similar steps danced at Mexican fandangos were also an influence.

- **Function or reason:** This ballroom or social dance in both forms is part of the ballroom competition scene as well as a vehicle for socializing with the community.

- **Who does this dance:** The Two-step is a partner dance with a leader (traditionally a man) and a follower (traditionally a woman). The leader determines the movements and patterns of the pair as they move around the dance floor.

- **Music and rhythms:** Texas Two-step is usually danced to country music in 4/4 time. It is danced 4 steps to 6 beats of music.

- **Traditional clothing and costume:** When danced in the Southwest, men and women wear cowboy boots. Men wear jeans and usually a cowboy hat. His shirt can be plaid or embellished with designs. Sometimes women wear a shirt that matches her partner's and usually a skirt that allows for movement.

- **Other information:** Texas Two-step is a progressive dance that goes counterclockwise around the floor. Many believe John Philip Sousa's music to be the historical parent to the Two-step dance. With time people lost its roots and began calling it the Texas Two or country Fox-trot. As these dancers got older it became a stable dance for all to do in the square dance community, which later became the country-western dance community as well. The Texas Two-step (slow, slow, quick-quick version) has nothing to do with Sousa's original dance. It also enjoys a place in country-western ballroom competition circles.

REFERENCES
http://en.wikipedia.org/wiki/Texas_Two-Step
http://dance.lovetoknow.com/Two_Step_Dance
www.streetswing.com/histmain/z3tworg.htm

TEACHING STRATEGIES   The video clip should be viewed at least three times (see chapter 1). After students record and discuss their observations and before

the third viewing, use the discussion starters listed next to facilitate class discussion. Feel free to paraphrase and choose the questions that work best with your students.

Viewing: What Did You See?

Suggested discussion starters and questions: How did the dancers move across the floor? Did you notice the basic floor pattern? Did you notice the space between the partners?

Connecting: What Do You Know?

Suggested discussion starters and questions: What did you see as the starting position of the partners? What do you notice about the dance step pattern in relation to the rhythmic pattern? How did the costumes represent the country-western feel of the dance?

Responding: What Do You Think? What Do You Wonder?

Suggested discussion starters and questions: What are some of the ways the dancers transitioned from one position to another while keeping the tempo and rhythm? Why do you think the intricate spins and hand holds make for a more interesting dance?

What questions do you have about this dance? Write them down and continue your research. Some of these questions can be answered through movement.

Performing: What Can You Do?

Choose both Re-create and Create, choose one of these two activities, or make your own performing work that you think is most appropriate for your students.

Re-create   With a partner, practice the Texas Two-step dance steps from the video until you are comfortable doing them. Re-create a 16-count sequence using two of the arm or hand exchanges. *Note:* Use ideas from recorded observations from question 1 (What did you see?).

Create   With a partner, create two different dance phrases that:

1. Use the basic dance steps where you reverse the slow and the fast patterns.
2. Have no changes in facings and stay in the original starting position.

*If you need music and don't have it among your resources, use the video.

FUN FACTS   The Two-step is a dance for two. In 1891, famous composer John Philip Sousa composed the *Washington Post March,* which was a big hit of the day. Even though he was not born in the United States, he was very patriotic. About the same time, people were dancing dances such as the Virginia Reel and the Quadrille. The music for these dances was very different from Sousa's *Washington Post March*. With this song came a dance based on the French Waltz in double time. That dance consisted of several chassé steps done in sequence. Just to make it more confusing, one chassé is also called a triple-step, but since two of them are done in the basic form, the entire dance came to be called the Two-step. Another interesting fact is that people dance this triple-step dance to music that is in 4/4 time.

WEB EXPLORATIONS   Key terms to search for include country-western dance, Texas dance, country music, Two-step, Texas Two-step, and collegiate Fox-trot.

From H. Scheff, M. Sprague, and S. McGreevy-Nichols, 2010, *Exploring dance forms and styles: A guide to concert, world, social, and historical dance* (Champaign, IL: Human Kinetics).

Two-Step

Name: _____ Class: _____ Date: _____

STUDENT KNOWLEDGE QUEST WORKSHEET

Name of Dance: Two-Step

1. Viewing: What did you see?
    Record your observations. Describe what you see. Be specific.

    _____

    _____

    _____

    _____

    _____

    _____

2. Connecting: What do you know?

    _____

    _____

    _____

    _____

    _____

    _____

3. Responding: What do you think? What do you wonder?

    _____

    _____

    _____

    _____

    _____

4. Performing: What can you do?

    _____

    _____

    _____

    _____

    _____

From H. Scheff, M. Sprague, and S. McGreevy-Nichols, 2010, *Exploring dance forms and styles: A guide to concert, world, social, and historical dance* (Champaign, IL: Human Kinetics).

KNOWLEDGE QUEST

INFORMATION AND TEACHING TIPS
Video Clip Search
Category M: Social (Subcategory: Dances done in a line)
Category A: World (Subcategory: Europe)
Name of Dance: Contra Dance

Contra Dance

When is a line a square?

DIRECTIONS Give the students the job of researching clips of and about the dance on the Internet. Many are available; have them choose one or two. They can do this in school if the Internet is available, at home, or at a library. Instruct them to take notes about the actual dancing so that they can complete the student worksheet.

BACKGROUND INFORMATION Before students view the video clip, share the following information with them and give them the KQ worksheets to complete as a homework assignment.

- **Translation:** One theory held by James Hutson in his article "A Capsule Chronicle of Contradancing, Part One," from the Fall 1994 issue of *Contra Corners*, the newsletter of the California Dance Co-Operative is as follows: "The French, who thought that they invented country dancing (as well as anything else culturally significant), and who were miffed at the notion that the English should receive credit for anything, converted the name 'country dance' to French *contredans* (which conveniently translates as 'opposites dance'), then turned around and claimed that the English term was a corruption of the French!"

- **Country or culture of origin:** Contra dancing is a traditional dance form that originated in Scotland, Ireland, and in England. The French had a turn at adding to the dance form, which is now popular world wide. Contra dancing is also known as square dancing in the United States.

- **Timeline:** Toward the end of the 17th century, English country dances were taken up by French dancers. It has been noted that different steps existed to this dance form that were taken from Baroque French court dance and used in English country dances. The French called these dances *'contra-dance,'* or *'contredanse.'* Over time, the English country dances became known and were done throughout the Western world. Eventually this form became part of North American folk dance tradition, especially in New England.

- **Function or reason:** These contra dances, in their many forms, are for social occasions and are enjoyed at large and small gatherings. Since the dancers change partners often, it is a good way to meet new people.

- **Who does this dance:** Both men and women do this dance in groups. Partners do not have to be men and women and, as they change partners, it might be that men dance with men and women with women.

- **Music and rhythms:** Some contra dance musicians play a variety of instruments. Most of the contra dance music comes from Anglo-Celtic tradition. The music consists of tunes and songs that come from Ireland and Scotland and music from French Canada. Old, simple country tunes are common, and klezmer tunes have also been used. Tunes used for a contra dance tend to be 64-beat tunes, which allows dancers to go through the dance pattern twice.

- **Traditional clothing or costume:** Women wear full skirts but the clothes worn by everyone are comfortable so that the dancing can continue for hours. Broken-in,

From H. Scheff, M. Sprague, and S. McGreevy-Nichols, 2010, *Exploring dance forms and styles: A guide to concert, world, social, and historical dance* (Champaign, IL: Human Kinetics).

Contra Dance

soft-soled shoes such as dance shoes, sneakers, or sandals that won't mark up the floors of the dance hall are sometimes required. Occassionally, the dancers don't wear any shoes.

- **Other information:** There are contra dance groups all over the United States that meet regularly in community centers, schools, and social lodges. Usually an hour before the actual dance starts is devoted to instruction where several of the dances are taught. This hour is for all those who care to attend. There are usually live musicians. Contra dances are set up in long lines where the people face each other. This is called a *set*. The *bottom* of the line is usually farthest away from the musicians and caller. The *top* or *head* of the set is the end closest to the band and caller. The *square* part comes from the fact that two adjacent couples work together in the dance. The most common locomotor (traveling) movement is a smooth walking step.

REFERENCES

www.sbcds.org/contradance/whatis/

www.tcdancers.org/aboutcontra.html

www.tftm.org/contradancing/Dance%20moves

TEACHING STRATEGIES

The video clip should be viewed at least three times (see chapter 1). In the case where students are searching and observing from home, they will need to list the exact Web site used so that teachers and other students can see the basis for their documentation.

Facilitate a class discussion using the discussion starters listed next. Have students use their recorded answers as a resource. Feel free to paraphrase and choose the questions that work best with your students.

Viewing: What Did You See?

Suggested discussion starters and questions: Describe the basic formation of the dancers. What are the most common moves in the dance you chose to observe?

Connecting: What Do You Know?

Suggested discussion starters and questions: Who dances contra dances? What are the names of some of the moves and figures that make up a contra dance? How do the dancers know what to do next?

Responding: What Do You Think? What Do You Wonder?

Suggested discussion starters and questions: What do you think is easier to do? Would it be ballroom dancing like the Waltz or Cha-cha, or doing a contra dance? Why do you think so? What would be the trickiest part of doing contra dances? Why?

What questions do you have about this dance? Write them down and continue your research. Some of these questions can be answered through movement.

Performing: What Can You Do?

Choose both Re-create and Create, choose one of these two activities, or make your own performing work that you think is most appropriate for your students.

Re-create View the videos you chose. Carefully view one full pattern and stop. Review the same pattern several times. With your classmates replicate what you saw on the video clip. Keep time with the music.

From H. Scheff, M. Sprague, and S. McGreevy-Nichols, 2010, *Exploring dance forms and styles: A guide to concert, world, social, and historical dance* (Champaign, IL: Human Kinetics).

Contra Dance

Create Make a set of dancers. Work out some dance moves that you can do as sets. Refer to the Web site www.tftm.org/contradancing/Dance%20moves for the steps and how to do them.

*If you need music and don't have it among your resources, use the video.

FUN FACTS Since any person of any gender, any age, any size, and any ability can take their place on the dance floor, the look of the dancers can be amusing where a man over 6 feet tall can dance with a tiny fourth grader. Just imagine some of the steps you see on the video done by such a match.

WEB EXPLORATIONS Key terms to search for include Jig, Reel, left-hand star, caller, fiddler, ladies chain, barn dances, contra dance, New England county dances, and English country dances.

RECOMMENDED CLIPS

- www.youtube.com/watch?v=j9L0dz3qmsc
- www.youtube.com/watch?v=qTtEOaruqr4
- www.youtube.com/watch?v=N1o7tdtHZyE&feature=related

From H. Scheff, M. Sprague, and S. McGreevy-Nichols, 2010, *Exploring dance forms and styles: A guide to concert, world, social, and historical dance* (Champaign, IL: Human Kinetics).

Contra Dance

Name: _____ Class: _____ Date: _____

STUDENT KNOWLEDGE QUEST WORKSHEET

Name of Dance: Contra Dance

1. Viewing: What did you see?
   Record your observations. Describe what you see. Be specific.

   _____

   _____

   _____

   _____

   _____

2. Connecting: What do you know?

   _____

   _____

   _____

   _____

   _____

3. Responding: What do you think? What do you wonder?

   _____

   _____

   _____

   _____

   _____

4. Performing: What can you do?

   _____

   _____

   _____

   _____

   _____

From H. Scheff, M. Sprague, and S. McGreevy-Nichols, 2010, *Exploring dance forms and styles: A guide to concert, world, social, and historical dance* (Champaign, IL: Human Kinetics).

CHAPTER 8

Historical Dance

"Dance has existed since the beginning of time—
as ritual, as recreation, as spectacle."

Nancy Reynolds (The Dance Notebook 1984)

Historical dance is sometimes referred to as early dance. It actually covers an expansive variety of dance forms and styles from the past. From notations in early literature, dance scholars have been able to come up with ideas and facts about the dances from the past. Some of these earlier dances have been reconstructed from evidence such as surviving notations and instruction manuals. Friezes, tapestries, etchings, and lithographs show and support evidence that dance was an integral part of the European medieval period. Early paintings show dancers in lines and circles. Other documentation is found in illustrations in literature, in poetry books, and in music scores. You can even discern dramatic expressions on the faces in the paintings and illustrations. All of the various sources are like pieces of a jigsaw puzzle. When put together, these pieces of information give a more complete picture of historical dance forms and styles.

In the field of culture preservation, people reenact historical dances. Dance has been part of rituals, ceremonies, and prayer. Historical dance reflects what was happening at the time and place of origin. One example is the Washerwoman's Branle. The name of the dance reflects the never-ending work of women in the Middle Ages. The fact that it is a circle dance indicates that community was valued.

Interest in Historical Dance

Historical dances are not currently in use by the general populace except by certain special interest groups that preserve the dances through learning about, dancing, and performing them. Historical dance is different from the study of

dance history. The study of dance history is an academic quest. For the people who belong to historical dance clubs, their passion is to research and preserve dance forms from the past. In the United States and in Europe, historical dance clubs exist for just this reason (www.streetswing.com/; this Web site has links to over 600 dance clubs and ballrooms and each link tells you of the special interest of each club). The members of these groups look for hints about the decorum and manners of the dances and dancers. They look at the costumes in the old paintings and illustrations and they imagine how the people would have had to stand and move while in those costumes. **Dance historians** and members of historical dance clubs have found manuals describing the dances, and information on the required etiquette and manners (www.ushistoricalarchive.com/cds/dance2.html; this Web site has professional dancers emulating the historical dances. Some of the dances are only one half minute long, but it is long enough for one to see the actual steps and learn from them.).

The members of the early dance groups also listen carefully to the music to which the dances were done. They study the rhythms and phrasing to help them to re-create the dances. At times, different people act as the choreographer and invent new ways of using the traditional steps.

Clothing in Historical Dance

Many of the outfits seen in books and on Web sites are the everyday and formal clothes worn during different historical periods. People wore clothing that suited their occupations and stations in life. Wealthy people could afford more layers of clothing. Most people wore a chemise (tunic-like undergarment worn by both males and females) under their outer clothing. Ladies frequently wore petticoats, underskirts, and overskirts. Because of the weight and bulk, jumps were left to the gentlemen, who had their legs free. They were able to leap, jump, and make cabrioles (beats of the legs) and flourishes (circles with the lower legs). Traditionally the nobles wore clothes that appeared to be heavier, more cumbersome, and limiting than the peasant class. This clothing might have dictated how they executed steps. During the Renaissance period, the noblemen wore boots or shoes with higher heels. This was thought to make the men's calves look more developed, which appealed to the ladies. Well-developed calf muscles indicated the strength and power needed to fight, dance, and protect. Highly skilled male dancers would be granted higher positions in the hierarchy of the courts and might even be deeded land by the kings and queens.

Examples of period clothing.

Summary

Historical dance, or early dance, crosses over to other categories of dance. Historical dances were the social dances of their time and they currently may be performed as concert dance. Therefore, a basic knowledge of all categories of dance is helpful when studying historical dance. You can learn so much about people, their time in history, and their culture through observing historical dance.

The following pages contain the Knowledge Quest Worksheets for the following dances in the noted subcategories of historical dance, unless otherwise noted. Those with a DVD icon next to them have video clips that appear on the bound-in DVD.

Middle Ages

- •DVD Farandole
- Washerwoman's Branle (Branle des Lavandières)

Renaissance

- Pavane
- Gavotte

Baroque

- Minuet (or Menuet)
- •DVD Virginia Reel (see KQ worksheet in chapter 6)
- •DVD La Bomba (see KQ worksheet in chapter 6)

18th and 19th century

- Quadrille
- Cakewalk
- •DVD Polka (see KQ worksheet in chapter 7)
- •DVD Waltz (see KQ worksheet in chapter 7)
- Capoeira (see KQ worksheet in chapter 6)

Early 20th Century

- •DVD Fox-trot (see KQ worksheet in chapter 7)
- •DVD Brahms Waltz (see KQ worksheet in chapter 5)

Farandole

KNOWLEDGE QUEST
INFORMATION AND TEACHING TIPS
Category M: Historical (Subcategory: Middle Ages)
Category A: Social (Subcategory: Dances done in a line)
Name of Dance: Farandole

Some dances are meant to be done outdoors, with teamwork and no superstars.

BACKGROUND INFORMATION   Before students view the video clip, share the following information with them.

- **Translation:** Different cultures use different words to describe this chain dance (line of dancers holding hands). It is called *farandole* in France, *choros* in Greece, and *kolo* in Serbia and Croatia. It is still the national dance of Provence.

- **Country or culture of origin:** The dance was popular throughout Europe, but it is thought to have originally come from Greece.

- **Timeline:** This dance was most popular during the early Middle Ages (12th and 13th centuries).

- **Function or reason:** This was a social dance. According to history, it was used to say goodbye to winter and to welcome spring, and also to protect water wells. Because houses and castles were usually dark and smoky, most such social events happened outdoors.

- **Who does this dance:** Both social classes, peasants and courtiers or nobles, did this dance, but mostly the classes didn't mix. The dance could be done by all males, all females, or in mixed couples.

- **Music and rhythms:** Usually the music for this dance was a song (carole). Dancers usually sang the chorus and the leader sang the verse.

- **Other information:** Speculation has it that during the 15th century the figures with arches disappeared from the Farandole done by nobility because of women's fashion. The women's hats were tall, pointed dunce-cap shaped or had the configuration of horns. One can imagine how the headdresses and the arches would not fit with each other. By the beginning of the 16th century, figures with arches only appeared in peasant dances.

REFERENCES

Kassing, G. 2007. *History of dance: An interactive arts approach*. Champaign, IL: Human Kinetics.

Quirey, B. 1976. *May I have the pleasure?: The story of popular dancing*. London: Dance Books.

TEACHING STRATEGIES   The video clip should be viewed at least three times (see chapter 1). After students record and discuss their observations and before the third viewing, use the discussion starters listed next to facilitate class discussion. Feel free to paraphrase and choose the questions that work best with your students.

Viewing: What Did You See?

Suggested discussion starters and questions: What is the difference between the two versions of the Farandole as shown on this video clip? Describe how the leaders changed.

From H. Scheff, M. Sprague, and S. McGreevy-Nichols, 2010, *Exploring dance forms and styles: A guide to concert, world, social, and historical dance* (Champaign, IL: Human Kinetics).

Farandole

Connecting: What Do You Know?

Suggested discussion starters and questions: With what you know about nobility and peasants, which socioeconomic group do you think would have preferred the walking version and which would have preferred the skipping and running version? Why do you think so? (Helpful hint: To help students answer this question, show illustrations of the aristocracy and peasants of the Middle Ages, e.g., Pieter Bruegel's "The Wedding Dance," 1566).

What would happen to this dance if one or two people (when they weren't the leaders) decided not to cooperate with the rest of the line? Support your answer with any experience you may have had working with a team or group. The Farandole does not use a front and back spatial awareness. Later court dances are done with an unchanging front. If court dances were held in the throne or common rooms of the castles, why do you think this was so?

Responding: What Do You Think? What Do You Wonder?

Suggested discussion starters and questions: The patterns shown in the dance clip (also called figures) are called labyrinth, snail, arches, and thread the needle. Identify and match the names with the figures in the video clip and, using lines and stick figures, draw diagrams of them. (Helpful hint: You can draw a diagram of one of the figures shown on the video clip to model for the students how to diagram the figures. See the illustrations on the answer sheet for the student Knowledge Quest worksheet.)

What questions do you have about this dance? Write them down and continue your research. Some of these questions can be answered through movement.

Performing: What Can You Do?

Choose both Re-create and Create, choose one of these two activities, or make your own performing work that you think is most appropriate for your students.

Re-create   After watching, copying, and trying each of the figures, you and your classmates take turns leading a Farandole line. Remember that the thread the needle is used to change the leader.

Create

1. Using locomotor steps such as walk, run, leap, hop, slide, assemblé (an elevation step that goes from standing on one foot to landing on two feet), and sissonne (an elevation step that goes from standing on two feet to landing on one foot), create a traveling phrase that can be repeated.

2. Choose an order for the Farandole figures. Do your traveling phrase in your chosen order of the Farandole figures.

*If you need music and don't have it among your resources, use the video.

FUN FACTS   The Farandole was a true social dance; the leaders of the line kept changing and the dancers had no front to face. Eventually both the circle and serpentine dances were replaced with dances that faced the throne of the king and the first dance was often led by the ruler.

WEB EXPLORATIONS   Key terms to search for include carole, 14th century, Guillaume de Machaut, Remède de Fortune, Pieter Bruegel 1566, and "The Wedding Dance."

From H. Scheff, M. Sprague, and S. McGreevy-Nichols, 2010, *Exploring dance forms and styles: A guide to concert, world, social, and historical dance* (Champaign, IL: Human Kinetics).

Farandole

Name: _____ Class: _____ Date: _____

STUDENT KNOWLEDGE QUEST WORKSHEET

Name of Dance: Farandole

1. Viewing: What did you see?
   Record your observations. Describe what you see. Be specific.

   _____
   _____
   _____
   _____
   _____

2. Connecting: What do you know?

   _____
   _____
   _____
   _____
   _____

3. Responding: What do you think? What do you wonder?

   _____
   _____
   _____
   _____
   _____

4. Performing: What can you do?

   _____
   _____
   _____
   _____
   _____

From H. Scheff, M. Sprague, and S. McGreevy-Nichols, 2010, *Exploring dance forms and styles: A guide to concert, world, social, and historical dance* (Champaign, IL: Human Kinetics).

KNOWLEDGE QUEST
INFORMATION AND TEACHING TIPS
Video Clip Search
Category M: Historical (Subcategory: Middle Ages)
Category A: Social (Subcategory: Dances done in a line)
Name of Dance: Washerwoman's Branle (Branle des Lavandières)

Washerwoman's Branle

A woman's work is never done.

DIRECTIONS   Give the students the job of researching clips of and about the dance from the Internet. Many are available; have them choose one or two. They can do this in school if the Internet is available, at home, or at a library. Instruct them to take notes about the actual dancing so that they can complete the student worksheet.

BACKGROUND INFORMATION   Before students view the video clip, share the following information with them and give them the KQ worksheets to complete as a homework assignment.

- **Translation:** The word *branle*— pronounced BRAHN-lee—sometimes refers to a brawl. Many different Branle exist. It is also named for its characteristic side-to-side movement (the French word *branler* means to sway).

- **Country or culture of origin:** This dance comes from France.

- **Timeline:** Approximately between 1450 and 1650 European aristocrats, especially in France and England, adopted the 12th-century French chain dance.

- **Function or reason:** The Branle des Lavandières is a dance that mimics the hard life of washerwomen during the Middle Ages.

- **Who does this dance:** The aristocracy did some of the Branle variations while the townspeople did others.

- **Music and rhythms:** Branles were danced with walking, running, gliding, or skipping steps depending on the speed of the music, which was composed in 4/4 time.

- **Traditional clothing or costume:** When the aristocracy performed dances, they wore clothes that represented their status in society. Both men and women wore heavy brocades. When the townspeople danced, they wore their simple clothes, which still meant many layers of skirts for the women and tunics for the men.

- **Other information:** Some of the Branle dances were performed by a chain of dancers who alternated large sideways steps to the left (frequently four) with an equal number of smaller steps to the right. Thus the chain, usually of couples, intertwining arms or holding hands, progressed to the left in a circle or serpentine figure.

REFERENCES
www.vjw.biz/ebook/wash.htm

http://dictionary.reference.com/browse/branle?qsrc=2446of

www.streetswing.com/histmain/z3branl1.htm

TEACHING STRATEGIES   The video clip should be viewed at least three times (see chapter 1). In the case where students are searching and observing from home, they will need to list the exact Web site they used so that teachers and other students can see the basis for the documentation.

From H. Scheff, M. Sprague, and S. McGreevy-Nichols, 2010, *Exploring dance forms and styles: A guide to concert, world, social, and historical dance* (Champaign, IL: Human Kinetics).

Washerwoman's Branle

Facilitate a class discussion using the discussion starters listed next. Have students use their recorded answers as a resource. Feel free to paraphrase and choose the questions that work best with your students.

Viewing: What Did You See?

Suggested discussion starters and questions: What did you first notice about the dancers? If they were in period costume, what impressed you about them? If they were in practice clothes, what did you notice about their stature?

Connecting: What Do You Know?

Suggested discussion starters and questions: What do you know about how the dancers relate to one another? What do you notice about the use of rhythm?

Responding: What Do You Think? What Do You Wonder?

Suggested discussion starters and questions: Look at two different Branles. Compare and contrast the styles and steps. Why do you think that the dance form lasted for so many years?

What questions do you have about this dance? Write them down and continue your research. Some of these questions can be answered through movement.

Performing: What Can You Do?

Choose both Re-create and Create, choose one of these two activities, or make your own performing work that you feel is most appropriate for your students.

Re-create   To re-create any one of the Branles, study a specific video clip, observing the exact steps. Explain to the other dancers how the steps are done. Make this dance into a 32-count phrase.

Create   Using two different video clips found through an Internet video search, create a dance phrase that intermingles several steps and formations. Double the counts to 64. Find a percussion instrument to play the 64 counts.

*If you need music and don't have it among your resources, use the video.

FUN FACTS   The Branle was the washerwomen's way of showing the hard work they did and why you wouldn't want to mess with them. People didn't mess around with washerwomen. How strong would you be if you lifted wet clothing all day?

WEB EXPLORATIONS   Key terms to search for include Branle, Washerwoman's Branle, and court dances.

RECOMMENDED CLIPS

- www.vjw.biz/ebook/wash.htm
- www.youtube.com/watch?v=FBnlfigRQlw
- http://lcweb2.loc.gov/ammem/dihtml/divideos.html (video clip no. 46)

Name: _____   Class: _____   Date: _____

STUDENT KNOWLEDGE QUEST WORKSHEET

Washerwoman's Branle

Name of Dance: Washerwoman's Branle
(Branle des Lavandières)

1. Viewing: What did you see?
   Record your observations. Describe what you see. Be specific.

   _____

   _____

   _____

   _____

   _____

2. Connecting: What do you know?

   _____

   _____

   _____

   _____

   _____

3. Responding: What do you think? What do you wonder?

   _____

   _____

   _____

   _____

   _____

4. Performing: What can you do?

   _____

   _____

   _____

   _____

   _____

From H. Scheff, M. Sprague, and S. McGreevy-Nichols, 2010, *Exploring dance forms and styles: A guide to concert, world, social, and historical dance* (Champaign, IL: Human Kinetics).

Pavane

KNOWLEDGE QUEST

INFORMATION AND TEACHING TIPS
Video Clip Search
Category M: Historical (Subcategory: Renaissance)
Name of Dance: Pavane

Stately Renaissance dances allow for social engagement and a bit of gossip.

DIRECTIONS   Give the students the job of researching clips of and about the Pavane on the Internet. Many are available; have them choose one or two. They can do this in school if the Internet is available, at home, or at a library. Instruct them to take notes about the actual dancing so that they can complete the student worksheet.

BACKGROUND INFORMATION   Before students view the video clip, share the following information with them and give them the KQ worksheets to complete as a homework assignment.

- **Translation:** The word *pavane* means peacock's strut.

- **Country or culture of origin:** It was originally a solemn ceremonial court dance from Italy.

- **Timeline:** The Pavane has been documented back to 1508 in Italy (by the names *Pavana* or *Padovana-Italian*). It was called the "le Grand Bal" because it was used on state occasions. However, it is best known as a Renaissance court dance.

- **Function or reason:** The Pavane was danced at functions of the court both in the ballrooms and in pageant parades. It served as a chance for the people of the court to socialize as they danced.

- **Who does this dance:** The men and women of the court, either married or not, would participate. The upper class and nobility favored these dances at the time and was most popular in Italy, Spain, and France. It was much danced during the reign of Louis XIV (1638-1715,) and afterward seems to have disappeared.

- **Music and rhythms:** It is done to a 2/4 time signature. It is danced very slowly and sedately. Instruments that often went with the music were solo hand bells with flute, with clarinet and guitar (or harp or pizzicato cello), or with piano.

- **Traditional clothing or costume:** "The clothes were of silks, satins, and rich brocade. The men wore feathered hats, close fitting tunics, puffed breeches, and shoulder capes, with swords at their sides, as the courtiers of Queen Elizabeth's (1553-1603) Courts. The women would wear velvet or satin trains from the shoulders attached beneath ruffs, over brocaded or satin gowns with the distinct front breadth of lace or jeweled embroidery, hoops, long pointed bodices with jeweled bodices, and sleeves puffed from shoulder to wrist."
From S. Watson. Available: http://www.streetswing.com/histmain/z3pavane.htm.

- **Other information:** The Pavane was a very solemn dance done by couples using long, gliding, walking steps in procession. The dance also included curtsies, retreats, and advances. The lady placed her hand on the back of the man's hand. According to some sources, the Minuet comes from the Pavane. In an evening of dancing, the Minuet or Galliard followed the Pavane. The Pavane was replaced by the Courante by Louis XIV.
From S. Watson. Available: http://www.streetswing.com/histmain/z3pavane.htm.

From H. Scheff, M. Sprague, and S. McGreevy-Nichols, 2010, *Exploring dance forms and styles: A guide to concert, world, social, and historical dance* (Champaign, IL: Human Kinetics).

Pavane

REFERENCES

www.streetswing.com/histmain/z3pavane.htm

www.thegoldendance.com/Music/TGD1010-Pavane.htm

http://en.wikipedia.org/wiki/Pavane

TEACHING STRATEGIES

The video clip should be viewed at least three times (see chapter 1). In the case where students are searching and observing from home, they will need to list the exact Web site so that teachers and other students can see the basis for their documentation.

Facilitate a class discussion using the discussion starters listed next. Have students use their recorded answers as a resource. Feel free to paraphrase and choose the questions that work best with your students.

Viewing: What Did You See?

Suggested discussion starters and questions: What was your first impression of the dance? Did you notice the distinct steps? How did the facings change?

Connecting: What Do You Know?

Suggested discussion starters and questions: Did you notice how the hands of the dancers are positioned? What floor pattern did they use? Describe. How would this set of steps translate into a processional dance?

Responding: What Do You Think? What Do You Wonder?

Suggested discussion starters and questions: What were the costumes and dress of the day? How do you think those clothes impact the dancers' movements? From viewing the suggested video, compare and contrast what the man does in the dance with what the woman does.

What questions do you have about this dance? Write them down and continue your research. Some of these questions can be answered through movement.

Performing: What Can You Do?

Choose both Re-create and Create, choose one of these two activities, or make your own performing work that you think is most appropriate for your students.

Re-create Study the video to learn the steps. Put the steps into the floor pattern. Be sure that the hands are properly placed.

Create Use the basic step. Get other students to work with you to create a processional dance that travels forward and then reverses without turning around (move backward).

*If you need music and don't have it among your resources, use the video.

FUN FACTS

Since the dance steps are so simple and are repeated, the dancers did not need to concentrate very hard. Therefore they had time to discuss whatever came to mind and comment on the other dancers and their attire.

WEB EXPLORATIONS

Key terms to search for include: Renaissance dances, Pavane dance, Pavane music, and court dances.

RECOMMENDED CLIPS

- www.library.ucsb.edu/subjects/dance/dance.html. Go to Renaissance and then to number 39.
- http://lcweb2.loc.gov/ammem/dihtml/divideos.html

From H. Scheff, M. Sprague, and S. McGreevy-Nichols, 2010, *Exploring dance forms and styles: A guide to concert, world, social, and historical dance* (Champaign, IL: Human Kinetics).

Pavane

Name: _____ Class: _____ Date: _____

STUDENT KNOWLEDGE QUEST WORKSHEET

Name of Dance: Pavane

1. Viewing: What did you see?
   Record your observations. Describe what you see. Be specific.

   _____

   _____

   _____

   _____

   _____

2. Connecting: What do you know?

   _____

   _____

   _____

   _____

   _____

3. Responding: What do you think? What do you wonder?

   _____

   _____

   _____

   _____

   _____

4. Performing: What can you do?

   _____

   _____

   _____

   _____

   _____

From H. Scheff, M. Sprague, and S. McGreevy-Nichols, 2010, *Exploring dance forms and styles: A guide to concert, world, social, and historical dance* (Champaign, IL: Human Kinetics).

KNOWLEDGE QUEST

INFORMATION AND TEACHING TIPS
Video Clip Search
Category M: Historical (Subcategory: 14th Century Through Renaissance and Baroque)
Category A: Social (Subcategory: Dances done in a line)
Name of Dance: Gavotte

Gavotte

A dance that includes showing off and kissing, what could be better?

DIRECTIONS   Give the students the job of researching clips of and about the Gavotte on the Internet. Many are available; have them choose one or two. They can do this in school if the Internet is available, at home, or at a library. Instruct them to take notes about the actual dancing so that they can complete the student worksheet.

BACKGROUND INFORMATION   Before students view the video clip, share the following information with them and give them the KQ worksheets to complete as a homework assignment.

- **Translation:** The Gavotte is said to have taken its name from the Gavot people from the Pays de Gap region of France.

- **Country or culture of origin:** The Pays de Gap region is in southeast France in the province of Dauphiné.

- **Timeline:** Versions of the Gavotte span from the 14th-century peasant dances to the Renaissance and through the Baroque era (17th and 18th centuries). It seems the dance is still done today; many clips of it are available on YouTube.

- **Function or reason:** The famous author of *Orchesography,* Thoinot Arbeau, wrote that some hostesses of the parties used the dance to choose (by giving flowers) the host of the next party. The hosts were responsible for paying the musicians. It was also an opportunity for partners to take turns dancing for all the others in the center place. When they were done, the couple circulated around the room, the male dancer kissing all the females and the female dancer kissing all the males. Later, as the dance became more formalized, flowers were substituted for the kisses.

- **Who does this dance:** Males and females have always danced this dance together, sometimes in lines, circles, or with partners in formal dance figures (sections of dances done in specific formations).

- **Music and rhythms:** The music for the Gavotte is in 2/2 or 4/4 time. The tempo is usually about medium speed. The phrase usually starts in the middle or the third quarter note in the measure. Instruments and accompaniment vary by the geographic and time period; accompaniment includes singing with a soloist and groups, violins, drums, and even bagpipes.

- **Traditional clothing or costume:** This dance spanned various historical eras, so the clothing could be peasant garb or the fashion popular in a Renaissance or Baroque court.

- **Other information:** The Gavotte is similar to the Branle in that it uses sideways steps. However, the feet do not come together on the double steps; rather, one

From H. Scheff, M. Sprague, and S. McGreevy-Nichols, 2010, *Exploring dance forms and styles: A guide to concert, world, social, and historical dance* (Champaign, IL: Human Kinetics).

Gavotte

crosses behind the first stepping foot and hops and some Galliard (another hopping dance) steps can be inserted. The line dance version of the Gavotte is as follows:

- Count 1: (Moving to the left) Step left.
- Count 2: Step right, crossing back.
- Counts 3 & 4: Quickly step left-right-together-step left.
- Count 5: Step right, crossing back.
- Count 6: Step left.
- Counts 7&8: Step right with a hop.

REFERENCES

http://en.wikipedia.org/wiki/Gavotte

www.kickery.com/2008/07/more-promiscuou.html

Arbeau, T. 1967. *Orchesography.* New York: Dover Publications, Inc.

Chujoy, A. and P.W. Manchester. 1967. *The dance encyclopedia.* New York: Simon and Schuster.

TEACHING STRATEGIES

The video clip should be viewed at least three times (see chapter 1). In the case where students are searching and observing from home, they will need to list the exact Web site they used so that teachers and other students can see the basis for the documentation.

Facilitate a class discussion using the discussion starters listed next. Have students use their recorded answers as a resource. Feel free to paraphrase and choose the questions that work best with your students.

Viewing: What Did You See?

Suggested discussion starters and questions: In which direction did the dancers move most of the time? Which body parts did they use the most? For you, what is the most interesting aspect about this dance?

Connecting: What Do You Know?

Suggested discussion starters and questions: What other dance seems similar to this dance? What steps or aspects do they share? If you can access video clips of the different versions of the Gavotte, compare the line, circle, and partner versions of this dance.

Responding: What Do You Think? What Do You Wonder?

Suggested discussion starters and questions: Versions of the Gavotte have been danced from the 14th century through the 18th century and are still danced today. Why do you think this dance has been danced for so long?

The Gavotte gave an opportunity for partners to take the center place and dance for all the other dancers. When they were done, the couple circulated around the room, the male dancer kissing all the females and the female dancer kissing all the males. In later years, as the dance became more formalized, flowers were substituted for the kisses. How does this substitution of the giving of flowers instead of kisses show how the society's values changed?

What questions do you have about this dance? Write them down and continue your research. Some of these questions can be answered through movement.

Performing: What Can You Do?

Choose both Re-create and Create, choose one of these two activities, or make your own performing work that you think is most appropriate for your students.

Gavotte

Re-create   Using the following directions, learn the simple line dance version of the Gavotte:

- Count 1: (Moving to the left) Step left.
- Count 2: Step right, crossing back.
- Counts 3 & 4: Quickly step left-right-together-step left.
- Count 5: Step right, crossing back.
- Count 6: Step left.
- Counts 7 & 8: Step right with a hop.
- Repeat.

Create   Create a partner dance that uses the steps in the re-create section. Make sure that your partner is facing you and matches your direction of travel.

*If you need music and don't have it among your resources, use the video.

FUN FACTS   An interesting fact is that Marie Antoinette made this dance popular in her court before she met her end.

WEB EXPLORATIONS   Key terms to search for include Gavotte dance video and Gavotte dance.

RECOMMENDED CLIPS

- www.youtube.com/watch?v=Aiaq_dFpviM&NR=1

  The dance is titled "Rond: Branles d'Escosse, Gavotte." It includes couples dancing in the center and kisses at the end of their turn. One can compare the Gavotte to its forerunner the Branles. (Video clip posted by MichalMedVed.)

- www.youtube.com/watch?v=J8SXvHj5J9k&feature=related

  This dance is danced in lines with partners, four couples changing partners, with the hey (walking in a circle while giving each person you pass your right and left hands alternating) and other figures.

- www.youtube.com/watch?v=oRUu394AP6o&NR=1

  Gavotte Renaissance shows a solo by a male dancer.

- www.youtube.com/watch?v=SM0Uv7-SdXs&feature=related

  The simple folk dance version. Dancers step in a circle. The men take turns performing an interesting side bell kick on the last hop. (Video clip posted by evepompom.)

- www.youtube.com/watch?v=zEvhTDXIllo&feature=related

  Keep watching. After a while the clip shows the Gavotte in a line dance where you can copy the simple Gavotte step. (Video clip posted by Lanost.)

- www.youtube.com/watch?v=QXQUIqvCxl4&NR=1.

  A duet that shows Gavotte partner work in costume. (Video posted by Lady-Elana.)

- www.youtube.com/watch?v=u9b6ldKKqu0&NR=1

  "Baroque Dance: Gavotte from Atys" is a performance video of this dance.

- www.youtube.com/watch?v=7pqdPIn430E&NR=1

  "Renaissance Dance—Gavotte" shows a circle dance with many complicated hops and weight changes.

From H. Scheff, M. Sprague, and S. McGreevy-Nichols, 2010, *Exploring dance forms and styles: A guide to concert, world, social, and historical dance* (Champaign, IL: Human Kinetics).

Gavotte

Name: _____ Class: _____ Date: _____

STUDENT KNOWLEDGE QUEST WORKSHEET

Name of Dance: Gavotte

1. Viewing: What did you see?
   Record your observations. Describe what you see. Be specific.

   _____

   _____

   _____

   _____

   _____

2. Connecting: What do you know?

   _____

   _____

   _____

   _____

   _____

3. Responding: What do you think? What do you wonder?

   _____

   _____

   _____

   _____

   _____

4. Performing: What can you do?

   _____

   _____

   _____

   _____

   _____

From H. Scheff, M. Sprague, and S. McGreevy-Nichols, 2010, *Exploring dance forms and styles: A guide to concert, world, social, and historical dance* (Champaign, IL: Human Kinetics).

KNOWLEDGE QUEST
INFORMATION AND TEACHING TIPS
Video Clip Search
Category M: Historical (Subcategory: Baroque)
Category A: Social (Subcategory: Dances done in a line)
Name of Dance: Minuet or Menuet

Minuet

"The dances most frequently performed in 18th-century America were the country dance, the cotillion, the minuet and the reel."

The Colonial Music Institute
(www.colonialmusic.org/Resource/howtoCD.htm)

DIRECTIONS   Give the students the job of researching clips of and about the Minuet on the Internet. Many are available; have them choose one or two. They can do this in school if the Internet is available, at home, or at a library. Instruct them to take notes about the actual dancing so that they can complete the student worksheet.

BACKGROUND INFORMATION   Before students view the video clip, share the following information with them and give them the KQ worksheets to complete as a homework assignment.

- **Translation:** The name *minuet* comes from the small steps *(menu = small)* that are taken during the dance. The Minuet is an open-position couple's dance.

- **Country or culture of origin:** The Minuet or Menuet was originally derived from the Branle of Poitou, France.

- **Timeline:** The Minuet appeared during the 17th century. It remained part of the culture of every king and queen and their court for over 150 years.

- **Function or reason:** Kings and queens often led this dance around the ball-room floor. They made different shapes, such as serpents, and the members of their court would follow them. In later days the dance slowed down considerably so that the dancers had time for social conversations.

- **Who does this dance:** Men and women were partners. They were not alone, but part of a large group of people.

- **Music and rhythms:** The music is in a 3/4 waltz or march time signature and the tempo is rather slow. The music is very majestic and courtly in manner. The dance terms for the dance are the same as those used in ballet (e.g., jeté, pas, en avant).

- **Traditional clothing or costume:** Men would dance with swords attached to the waist and danced in their awkward boots. Brawls and duels were frequent and the heavy clanking of armor on the dance floor was annoying. Women would sometimes wear riding habits, but the master of ceremonies at Bath (an English resort) would change all this and add what is known as the Code of Etiquette at Bath (rules for conduct). Included in these codes was the banishment of all swords, along with the banishment of the exuberant country dances, while the French dances would become the only known dances in these so-called "polite society's" programs. These rules were the start of the proper dance etiquette we still use somewhat today.

- **Other information:** The Minuet has been spelled differently at different times as well as in different parts of the world. This happened with most dances of the time. The English called it *the Minuet*, the Italians called it *il Minuetto,* and the Germans called it *die Menuett*. The Quadrille usually followed the Minuet. Originally

From H. Scheff, M. Sprague, and S. McGreevy-Nichols, 2010, *Exploring dance forms and styles: A guide to concert, world, social, and historical dance* (Champaign, IL: Human Kinetics).

Minuet

there were only four Minuets: 1) the Queen's Minuet or le Menuet de la Reine, 2) le Menuet de Dauphin, 3) le Menuet d'Exaudet, and 4) le Menuet de la Cour (still popular today in certain circles).

REFERENCES

www.streetswing.com/histmain/z3minuet.htm

www.britannica.com/EBchecked/topic/384631/minuet

www.colonialmusic.org/Resource/howtoCD.htm

TEACHING STRATEGIES   The video clip should be viewed at least three times (see chapter 1). In the case where students are searching and observing from home, they will need to list the exact Web site so that teachers and other students can see the basis for their documentation.

Facilitate a class discussion using the discussion starters listed next. Have students use their recorded answers as a resource. Feel free to paraphrase and choose the questions that work best with your students.

Viewing: What Did You See?

Suggested discussion starters and questions: What is the first thing that strikes you about this dance? How would you describe this dance in three words? What are the main body parts that are used? How do the dancers relate to one another? How do the dancers move around the floor?

Connecting: What Do You Know?

Suggested discussion starters and questions: What did you notice about the rhythm? Have you ever seen a dance like this before? Where and when? How was it the same? How was it different?

Responding: What Do You Think? What Do You Wonder?

Suggested discussion starters and questions: View a clip of the woman in the costume of the time. What is the impact on the viewer seeing the dance done in costume? How does it impact the dancer? This dance seems to be more complicated than the Middle Ages dances and the Renaissance dances. Compare and contrast the steps.

What questions do you have about this dance? Write them down and continue your research. Some of these questions can be answered through movement.

Performing: What Can You Do?

Choose both Re-create and Create, choose one of these two activities, or make your own performing work that you think is most appropriate for your students.

Re-create   After viewing a few different videos, re-create a solo dance using the footwork you get from the video. Be sure to include the little hops and sideways movement. Have someone check to see if you accomplished the re-creation of some of the steps.

Create   With the help of fellow students, create a dance with many couples doing the Minuet. Have the leaders (king and queen) take the line of couples around the room. End in your starting positions.

*If you need music and don't have it among your resources, use the video.

FUN FACTS   George Washington's (1732-1799) favorite dance was the Minuet. Washington would dance with Betsy Hamilton (wife of the secretary of treasury),

From H. Scheff, M. Sprague, and S. McGreevy-Nichols, 2010, *Exploring dance forms and styles: A guide to concert, world, social, and historical dance* (Champaign, IL: Human Kinetics).

Minuet

who was said to be his favorite dance partner. Seven motions are used in the Minuet, named as follows: pas marché, pas balancé, pas grave, pas menuet, pas bourré, pas sissoné, and pas de basque pirouette.

WEB EXPLORATIONS   Key terms to search for include Minuet, Menuet, court dances, and ceremonies.

RECOMMENDED CLIPS

- http://memory.loc.gov/ammem/dihtml.html. Click on Baroque, then on clip 26 and clip 27.
- http://music.case.edu/duffin/dance/default.html. Click on Baroque and then on Minuet – done as a solo and in costume.

From H. Scheff, M. Sprague, and S. McGreevy-Nichols, 2010, *Exploring dance forms and styles: A guide to concert, world, social, and historical dance* (Champaign, IL: Human Kinetics).

247

Minuet

Name: _____ Class: _____ Date: _____

STUDENT KNOWLEDGE QUEST WORKSHEET

Name of Dance: Minuet

1. Viewing: What did you see?
   Record your observations. Describe what you see. Be specific.

   _____
   _____
   _____
   _____
   _____

2. Connecting: What do you know?

   _____
   _____
   _____
   _____
   _____

3. Responding: What do you think? What do you wonder?

   _____
   _____
   _____
   _____
   _____

4. Performing: What can you do?

   _____
   _____
   _____
   _____
   _____

From H. Scheff, M. Sprague, and S. McGreevy-Nichols, 2010, *Exploring dance forms and styles: A guide to concert, world, social, and historical dance* (Champaign, IL: Human Kinetics).

KNOWLEDGE QUEST

INFORMATION AND TEACHING TIPS
Video Clip Search
Category M: Historical (Subcategory: 18th and 19th Century)
Category A: Social (Subcategory: Partner)
Name of Dance: Quadrille

Quadrille

Shifting partners to maintain a balance of power

DIRECTIONS   Give the students the job of researching clips of and about the Quadrille on the Internet. Many are available; have them choose one or two. They can do this in school if the Internet is available, at home, or at a library. Instruct them to take notes about the actual dancing so that they can complete the student worksheet.

BACKGROUND INFORMATION   Before students view the video clip, share the following information with them and give them the KQ worksheets to complete as a homework assignment.

- **Translation:** The word *quadrille* is probably derived from the Spanish word *cuadrillo* (diminutive Spanish, meaning four; in French *quadrille de contredanses*) and from the Latin word *quadratus* (meaning square).

- **Country or culture of origin:** It originally came from France and later appeared in England.

- **Timeline:** In the 18th century the Quadrille evolved from the Cotillion, a patterned social dance. It was introduced in France around 1760, and later in England around 1808. It was introduced to the Duke of Devonshire and became fashionable by 1813.

- **Function or reason:** It was a social dance for the upper classes. The dance requires a constant shifting of partners, which led it to be compared to the European political system in the 18th century; countries were constantly changing their alliances in order to maintain the balance of power in Europe.

- **Who does this dance:** Men and women dance.

- **Music and rhythms:** Where the music was new with every Quadrille composed, the names of the five parts (or figures) remained the same. The parts were called the following:
  - Le pantalon (a pair of trousers)
  - L'été (summer)
  - La poule (hen)
  - La pastourelle (shepherd girl)
  - Finale

All the parts were popular dances and songs from that time (19th century).

- **Traditional clothing or costume:** The ladies wore big hoop skirts made with many yards of fabric. The gentlemen wore long, tight trousers, shirts with ruffles, and fancy waistcoats.

- **Other information:** Structurally, the Quadrille involves four couples, arranged in the shape of a square; each couple faces the center of that square. One pair was called the head couple, the other pairs the side couples. A dance figure was often performed first by the head couple and then repeated by the side couples.

From H. Scheff, M. Sprague, and S. McGreevy-Nichols, 2010, *Exploring dance forms and styles: A guide to concert, world, social, and historical dance* (Champaign, IL: Human Kinetics).

Quadrille

In the original French version only two couples were used, but two more couples were eventually added to form the sides of a square. The couples in each corner of the square took turns in performing the dance; one couple danced while the other couples rested. Terms used in the Quadrille are mostly the same as those in ballet. Dance figures have names such as jeté, chassé, croisé, plié, arabesque, and so on.

REFERENCES

www.eaasdc.de/history/shequadr.htm

www.streetswing.com/histmain/z3quad1.htm

http://worldfordance.blogspot.com/2007/10/quadrille.html

http://en.wikipedia.org/wiki/Quadrille

TEACHING STRATEGIES

The video clip should be viewed at least three times (see chapter 1). In the case where students are searching and observing from home, they will need to list the exact Web site used so that teachers and other students can see the basis for their documentation.

Facilitate a class discussion using the discussion starters listed next. Have students use their recorded answers as a resource. Feel free to paraphrase and choose the questions that work best with your students.

Viewing: What Did You See?

Suggested discussion starters and questions: How are the dancers connected to each other? What body parts do most of the work? What are the key movements? What patterns do you notice?

Connecting: What Do You Know?

Suggested discussion starters and questions: There is a strong connection between the Quadrille and the North American square (or contra) dances. What movements do you see that are common to both dances? How are they different?

Responding: What Do You Think? What Do You Wonder?

Suggested discussion starters and questions: Why do you think the Quadrille evolved into the square dance? What is the difference in the way it is presented and performed?

What questions do you have about this dance? Write them down and continue your research. Some of these questions can be answered through movement.

Performing: What Can You Do?

Choose both Re-create and Create, choose one of these two activities, or make your own performing work that you think is most appropriate for your students.

Re-create In a group of eight, re-create the dance exactly as you see it on the video.

Create In groups of eight (four couples), create a modern-day Quadrille performed to current music, using the structure and the style of the Quadrille. Each couple should create a movement series, give it a name, and teach it to the others in the group. The group should then decide on a sequence for all the movements and perform. For a challenge, try to put the sequences into five distinct sections, as in a traditional Quadrille.

*If you need music and don't have it among your resources, use the video.

From H. Scheff, M. Sprague, and S. McGreevy-Nichols, 2010, *Exploring dance forms and styles: A guide to concert, world, social, and historical dance* (Champaign, IL: Human Kinetics).

Quadrille

FUN FACTS   The term *quadrille* came to exist in the 17th century in military parades, in which four horsemen and their horses performed special square-shaped formations or figures.

WEB EXPLORATIONS   Key terms to search for include Quadrille, square dance, and 18th and 19th century dance.

RECOMMENDED CLIPS

- www.youtube.com/watch?v=3JPrMGiGJdo&feature=related
- www.youtube.com/watch?v=hh6cWrA2DKg
- www.youtube.com/watch?v=YzyzbnscaFE

From H. Scheff, M. Sprague, and S. McGreevy-Nichols, 2010, *Exploring dance forms and styles: A guide to concert, world, social, and historical dance* (Champaign, IL: Human Kinetics).

Quadrille

Name: _____ Class: _____ Date: _____

STUDENT KNOWLEDGE QUEST WORKSHEET

Name of Dance: Quadrille

1. Viewing: What did you see?
   Record your observations. Describe what you see. Be specific.

   _____

   _____

   _____

   _____

   _____

2. Connecting: What do you know?

   _____

   _____

   _____

   _____

   _____

3. Responding: What do you think? What do you wonder?

   _____

   _____

   _____

   _____

   _____

4. Performing: What can you do?

   _____

   _____

   _____

   _____

   _____

From H. Scheff, M. Sprague, and S. McGreevy-Nichols, 2010, *Exploring dance forms and styles: A guide to concert, world, social, and historical dance* (Champaign, IL: Human Kinetics).

KNOWLEDGE QUEST

INFORMATION AND TEACHING TIPS
Video Clip Search
Category M: Historical (Subcategory: 18th and 19th Century)
Category A: Social (Subcategory: Dances done in a line)
Category A: Concert
Name of Dance: Cakewalk

Cakewalk

"Imitation is the sincerest form of flattery."

Charles Caleb Colton

DIRECTIONS　Give the students the job of researching clips of and about the dance on the Internet. Many are available; have them choose one or two. They can do this in school if the Internet is available, at home, or at a library. Instruct them to take notes about the actual dancing so that they can complete the student worksheet.

BACKGROUND INFORMATION　Before students view the video clip, share the following information with them and give them the KQ worksheets to complete as a homework assignment.

- **Country or culture of origin:** The dance originated in Florida by the African American slaves who got the basic idea from the Seminole Indians. The Seminoles in Florida walked as couples with great dignity and in slow rhythm. The slaves who watched performances and ceremonies thought that they looked very much like the plantation owners and their wives when they did the grand walkaround at the beginning of festivities.

- **Timeline:** Around 1850 in the Southern plantations, this dance was known as the Chalk Line Walk. From 1895 to 1905 the Cakewalk became popular. It had another spurt of popularity with Vaudeville around 1915. Many of the special movements of the Cakewalk, such as the bending back of the body, the dropping of the hands at the wrists, and others, were a distinct feature in African dances.

- **Function or reason:** The idea of the Cakewalk was that of a couple promenading in a dignified manner, high stepping and kicking. Some of the more generous plantation owners would bake a special cake, called a hoecake, wrapped in cabbage leaf. On some Sundays and holidays they might invite their neighbors and they would stage a contest of the slaves doing the Cakewalk. Sometimes, different prizes were given but originally it was a hoecake for the males and molasses pulled candy (sort of like taffy) for the ladies. The winners would "take the cake," which is where that expression came from.

- **Who does this dance:** Originally, these so-called *walkers* would walk a straight line and balance buckets of water on their heads. After a while these slaves would mock the white plantation owners of the master's house and from their observations they developed the straight back and the leaning forth and back. Cakewalk was the sole organized—and even condoned—forum for servants to mock their masters.

- **Music or rhythms:** Some pieces of music made famous by the Cakewalk and its competition events are "Golliwog's Cakewalk" (composed by Debussy) and the "Grand Walkaround." Most Cakewalk music is notated in 2/4 time. Cakewalk music incorporated syncopation and a habanera-like rhythm into the regular march

From H. Scheff, M. Sprague, and S. McGreevy-Nichols, 2010, *Exploring dance forms and styles: A guide to concert, world, social, and historical dance* (Champaign, IL: Human Kinetics).

Cakewalk

rhythm. This kind of syncopation is also true of African music. The Cakewalk music eventually evolved into the birth of ragtime (around 1899).

- **Traditional clothing or costume:** The dancers wore their finest clothing. For the duration of the performance they were not slaves but the stars of the show. Slave owners would sometimes dress their slaves in exaggerated costumes suggested by the clothing worn by whites, then order the slaves to dance in a Cakewalk.

- **Other information:** Many theories and legends exist about the term *cakewalk*. Some hold true and others are just fun to think about:

  - The term *cakewalk* is often used to indicate something that is very easy or effortless, as in "That is a cakewalk" or "That is a piece of cake." Although the dance itself could be physically demanding, it was generally considered a fun, recreational pastime. The phrase *takes the cake* may come from the winner of the Cakewalk competition being awarded cake.

  - Another idea is that the slaves were never to eat the food during a plantation party. When the party was over and they were cleaning up, they went up and down the long tables eating the cakes that were left by the guests.

  - The Cakewalk would finish with a grand march mimicking the final parade of guests at the plantation banquets. They would form two straight lines and the walkers (slaves) would walk through the lines while eating cake.

REFERENCES:

www.absoluteastronomy.com/topics/Cakewalk

www.streetswing.com/histmain/z3cake1.htm

http://xroads.virginia.edu/~ug03/lucas/cake.html

www.economicexpert.com/a/Cakewalk.htm

TEACHING STRATEGIES

The video clip should be viewed at least three times (see chapter 1). In the case where students are searching and observing from home, they will need to list the exact Web site used so that teachers and other students can see the basis for the documentation.

Facilitate a class discussion using the discussion starters listed next. Have students use their recorded answers as a resource. Feel free to paraphrase and choose the questions that work best with your students.

Viewing: What Did You See?

Suggested discussion starters and questions: What sorts of steps do you see the dancers doing in the clips? What appears to be the mood or emotion of the dancers? Describe the formations.

Connecting: What Do You Know?

Suggested discussion starters and questions: When have you ever heard people say something is a "piece of cake"? What do they mean and how do you think it relates to the Cakewalk?

Responding: What Do You Think? What Do You Wonder?

Suggested discussion starters and questions: What idea or emotion do you think this dance is expressing? All the video clips are of performers at performances. What do you think was different when the dance was done on the plantations?

From H. Scheff, M. Sprague, and S. McGreevy-Nichols, 2010, *Exploring dance forms and styles: A guide to concert, world, social, and historical dance* (Champaign, IL: Human Kinetics).

Performing: What Can You Do?

Choose both Re-create and Create, choose one of these two activities, or make your own performing work that you feel is most appropriate for your students.

Re-create   Gather a great number of students to reproduce a Cakewalk competition. Couples can dance the way the couples on the video clips dance. There should be a judging team who awards a prize to the couple they deem the winners. (Make a list of the important parts of a Cakewalk to use as a guide for judging.)

Create   Watch as many video clips as you can find. Some are very old but you can see the same steps appear in many clips. Think about the step that looks like the dancers are prancing. Make some pathways of floor patterns using that prance step, which is also called an emboité.

*If you need music and don't have it among your resources, use the video.

FUN FACTS   As the dance form evolved it went from being a mimicking of slave owners at plantation parties to competitions with real prizes to stage acts first in minstrel shows and then to Vaudeville. The dancers usually performed in a clumsy way that made fun of the elaborate elegance of European dances that the rich and not-so-rich white houseguests would do.

WEB EXPLORATIONS   Key terms to search for include ragtime, Scott Joplin, U.S. slave entertainment, Cakewalk dance, history of Cakewalk, Southern plantations, and "Golliwog's Cakewalk" by Debussy.

RECOMMENDED CLIPS:

- www.youtube.com/watch?v=7sDnVIeSn_k
- www.mefeedia.com/tags/cakewalk
- www.youtube.com/watch?v=28iTvSOi5PM
- www.youtube.com/watch?v=gjVw0kNBM_A
- www.youtube.com/watch?v=Ksuz8AI_hRo

From H. Scheff, M. Sprague, and S. McGreevy-Nichols, 2010, *Exploring dance forms and styles: A guide to concert, world, social, and historical dance* (Champaign, IL: Human Kinetics).

Cakewalk

Name: _____ Class: _____ Date: _____

STUDENT KNOWLEDGE QUEST WORKSHEET

Name of Dance: Cakewalk

1. Viewing: What did you see?
   Record your observations. Describe what you see. Be specific.

   _____

   _____

   _____

   _____

   _____

2. Connecting: What do you know?

   _____

   _____

   _____

   _____

   _____

3. Responding: What do you think? What do you wonder?

   _____

   _____

   _____

   _____

   _____

4. Performing: What can you do?

   _____

   _____

   _____

   _____

   _____

PART III

Using Dance Forms: Looking at Dance Through Different Lenses

Part I introduces the process of looking at dances by viewing, connecting, responding, and performing. Part II provides information about different types of dances and their classifications. Part III allows a deeper level of investigation and is meant to support teachers as they deepen the students' learning experiences. Dance can illuminate such abstract ideas as universal themes, sociopolitical issues, aesthetic values, diversity, and the impact of globalization. The video clips and other support materials on the DVD can be combined with other ideas to broaden and deepen students' understanding of topics beyond specific dance content. The chapters in part III give information on how to use this dance content so that students can do even more rigorous work.

- *Chapter 9, Helping Students Develop Aesthetic Values*, equips students and teachers to use the dance video clips and supporting materials on the DVD to better understand other cultures' aesthetic values as well as to develop and expand what they themselves consider valid, beautiful, or worthwhile.

- *Chapter 10, Comparing Dance Forms and Dances*, uses the strategy of comparing and contrasting as a way of interacting with the dance forms and dances. Specific examples and graphic organizers are included. The act of comparing and contrasting not only hooks new information to past experiences, it also helps in analysis.

- *Chapter 11, Focusing on Universal Themes and Sociopolitical Issues*, is a way to use the video clips and materials in lessons about themes and issues. Because dance originates in a time and a place, it is a repository for cultural values, specific sociopolitical issues, and universal themes.

> "Students' sense of values surfaces when educators encourage students to view dances and reflect on the principles they identify in the work. Many aspects of dance are transmitted from one generation to the next. Consequently, dance is a repository of values and a telling imprint of civilization."
>
> *(Hanna 1999, p. 99)*

- *Chapter 12, Reflecting on Diversity and the Blending of Cultural Aspects,* contains a unit outline with lessons that celebrate both the diversity and the blending of cultures.

Each chapter gives ideas for lessons using video clips, Knowledge Quest worksheets, and other materials. The lessons are presented in a simple format. Also included is a blank lesson template on page 291 of the appendix and in the ancillary materials on the DVD. You can use this template to develop your own original lessons.

The lesson plans first describe student work. Next is a section in which to insert the local standards (see the standards table and the key words in part I). The third section of the lesson plan, Teaching Required, is about what the teacher does: (1) pulls up and assesses what the students already know about the topic; (2) helps the students learn the new information; and (3) has students reflect on and evaluate the quality of their work. The fourth section, Resources Needed, is a listing of the materials and resources used in the lesson. Be aware that in keeping with the goal of student as worker, the teacher prompts and the student does the work! For more information about lesson building, please refer to the book *Dance About Anything* (Sprague et al. 2006).

⊙DVD

Lesson for _____

Description of Student Work
Provide a description of the work students will do during this lesson.

Standards Met by Student Work
Use your completed standards table to find appropriate standards.

Teaching Required

Accessing and Assessing Prior Knowledge
Ask a lead-in question or do a short activity that will tell you what students already know about the topic.

Warm-up Activity
Have students do some warm-up movements as appropriate for the lesson content.

Exploring New Knowledge
Teach the content either through direct teaching or facilitation.

Reflection on Student Learning
Facilitate students' reflections and revisions as well as final reflections or self-evaluations.

Resources Needed
Gather the materials and equipment necessary for the teaching and learning in the lesson.

CHAPTER 9

Helping Students Develop Aesthetic Values

Aesthetics is defined as a particular theory or conception of what is artistically valid or beautiful. Tell your students that **aesthetic values** are personal; they are knowing what *you* like, what *you* consider valuable and worth *your* attention, and what *you* consider beautiful or pleasing. Education in the arts has always been a major factor in the development of aesthetic values in students. Students need exposure to new experiences and encounters with art works so that they can eventually make their own decisions about what they consider valid, beautiful, or worthwhile. Generally schools offer fewer dance classes than they do visual arts and music classes, so many students have little opportunity to develop aesthetic values in dance. This chapter helps you teach students how to develop their aesthetic values in dance.

Influences on Students' Dance Experiences

It is reasonable to expect that by expanding students' experiences, with various dance forms, an increase would occur in the range of dances that students consider valuable and worthwhile. It also makes sense that the more students interact with dance, the more they can engage with dance work at a higher developmental level. Michael J. Parsons (1987) proposed the existence of five developmental levels or stages of ability to maturely interact with art. The earlier stages have responses that generally relate the artwork to the viewer's personal experience. One response at an early stage could be, "I like that dance. It is my favorite." The later stages have responses that take into account the viewer's knowledge of techniques, styles, and traditions of the times. This type of response also takes into account how the viewers' own biases have an effect on what they see and in what they think about the work. An example of a response at these later stages could be, "Isadora's free-flowing costume reflected her preference of the natural and her resistance to the Industrial Revolution." These stages correspond to higher critical-thinking abilities. Each Knowledge Quest worksheet in this book asks students to progress through the levels of thinking by viewing, connecting to, responding to, and performing dance. As the thinking skills develop, so too will the ability to perceive, respond to, and perform dance. As the interaction with dance gets more complex and meaningful, students develop their aesthetic values.

In addition to experience, aesthetic values are also influenced by one's own culture. Such cultural experiences can include how and where one was raised and what kind of interaction one has had with other cultures and dances. These cultural experiences determine one's own cultural preferences and biases. Additional factors can affect cultural values. The type of community one currently lives in, whether in urban, rural, or specific ethnic neighborhoods, influences values. Peers influence values. Cultural fads, which are usually what one's peers consider cool, are valued for the moment. One should not underestimate the impact that media have on cultural values. Biases and preferences are not bad, but one should be aware of them while interacting with a dance. While viewing dances, students should be aware of these biases, especially during interpretation and evaluation activities.

Performance Competencies

The video clips on the DVD contain performances by both professionals and students. As they view and analyze the dances, viewers need to be conscious of these various levels of performance. The levels of performance are influenced by the dancers' performance competencies, which are defined as:

Using projection to communicate.

- projection—Confident presentation of one's body and energy to vividly communicate movement and meaning to an audience.

- awareness of space—To know the location of self and others on stage; the ability to dance while maintaining the formation or line dictated by the choreography.

- concentration—The ability to focus on choreography and technical accuracy throughout a dance.

- clarity—The ability to execute each step in a dance clearly and completely.

Maryland VSC Dance Glossary 2004, pp. 1-4.

The more highly trained dancer will deliver a clearer performance and make the dance elements and the intent of the dance more visible to the viewer. For this reason, dancers are always working to improve their performance competencies.

Viewing the Dances

Different teaching situations call for different levels of involvement with content. Different viewing procedures can be adapted for different levels of involvement. A lesson can stop at the first viewing reflection or extend into writing a dance critique or review. This book asks students to do more than just look at a dance. Rather, students are asked to interact with a dance in more than one way.

As mentioned in chapter 1, it is recommended that a student view the dance at least three times. On the first viewing, students should try to see the dance as a whole and then write a reflection about their immediate impressions and observations. Some suggested discussion starters and questions could be selected for the students to answer from Viewing: What did you see? on the Knowledge Quest: Information and Teaching Tips page of the KQ forms for each dance. Following are some examples:

1. After viewing this dance, what was your first impression? What impact did it make on you?

2. After this viewing, what part or movement of the dance stands out in your mind?

3. With what personal memory or experience does this dance connect?

4. Write any other thoughts that come to your mind.

The second viewing should be used to deconstruct the dance by selecting and recording the emphasized movements and qualities. In other words, students are asked to analyze the dance to answer the question "How does this dance "work?" Here are three different methods for this task:

- Students can write what they saw under question #1 on the Knowledge Quest Worksheet.

- They can use the 4-Square Level 1 (appropriate for students with limited dance experience) or the 4-Square Level 2 (appropriate for students with dance experience).

- They can answer questions 1 through 6 and 9 on the Viewing Guide (found in the appendix on page 295).

The third viewing is important for extending observations and knowledge and for seeing the dance again as a whole piece for interpretation and evaluation. In any critical evaluation in a classroom setting, students are asked to support their ideas and answers with evidence and details. The same concept applies here. Interpretations and evaluations must be supported by visual evidence from the dance. Students can also use the information from the second viewing as support data. Knowledge Quest Worksheet questions 2 through 4 can help students with this more intense thought process of interpretation and evaluation. Viewing Guide questions 7 through 11 also ask for these deeper insights or personal opinions. In the following example, notice that the students are asked to support these answers with evidence visible in the dance.

7. What do you think was communicated in this dance? What did you see in the dance that makes you think this?

8. What other thoughts or ideas did the dance give you as you watched it? Support your answer with observations visible in the dance.

9. Describe the traditional clothing or costumes and props. How were they important to the dance's main idea or quality?

10. What did you learn from viewing the clip? Support your answer with observations visible in the dance.

11. Did you like this dance? Why or why not? Support your answer with observations visible in the dance.

Table 9.1 is a summary of the viewing procedures for each of the three viewings of the video clips. The specific tool, the work the student should do, and a further extension of the student work are listed in this table. For example, the first viewing of the video clip uses the Viewing Questions on the Knowledge Quest: Information and Teaching Tips page as the tool. The student work is a recording of their first impressions, and the extension of the work is to have class discussions. A similar breakdown for the second and third viewings is in this table as well.

Table 9.1 Viewing Procedures

Viewing	Tool	Student work	Extensions of student work
1	KQ worksheet question 1	Record first impressions.	Have class discussions.
2	• 4-Square Level 1 (appropriate for students with limited dance experience) • 4-Square Level 2 (appropriate for students with dance experience) • Answer questions 1-6 and 9 on the Viewing Guide	Deconstruct the dance by selecting and recording the emphasized movements and qualities; analyze the dance.	• Compare with other dances. • Have discussions on dance content or linking with social, historical, or cultural topics. • Do warm-ups for movement activities. • Use this information as the basis for technique or composition classes.
3	• Viewing Guide questions 7-11 • KQ worksheet questions 2- 4	Interpret and evaluate.	• Re-create (replicate) sections of the dance or the whole dance. • Create (design) sections of a new dance. • Have in-depth discussions. • Write a critique or review.

A Sample Lesson Using the KQ Worksheets and Forms

The opening text for part III (page 257) included a general description and defense of a format for a lesson plan. The main focus is on what the students do (i.e., Description of Student Work) and which standards they are meeting by doing this work. The section called Teaching Required includes Accessing and Assessing Prior Knowledge, Warm-up Activity, Exploring New Knowledge, and Reflection on Student Learning. Finally, a list of resources needed for the lesson is provided.

Included on page 264 is a lesson plan that you can use to lead students through the process of viewing, analyzing, and evaluating any dance. It follows the viewing procedures for the three viewings and illustrates how to use the various materials in a lesson. Through your use of this book and DVD, your students can see enough different dances to broaden their exposure and to develop their own aesthetic values.

General Lesson for Viewing, Analyzing, and Evaluating a Dance

Description of Student Work

Students will view, analyze, and evaluate a dance, in writing or discussion, and either re-create a section of the dance or create a new dance based on the content of the dance.

Standards Met by Student Work

Use your completed standards table to find appropriate standards.

Teaching Required

Accessing and Assessing Prior Knowledge

You can ask a general question about the culture, time period, or dance form. Another option is to show the video clip for the first time and have the students either answer the viewing questions in the Knowledge Quest worksheet or just record their first observations.

Exploring New Knowledge

1. If you choose, use the Information and Teaching Tips page in the Knowledge Quest worksheets for the particular dance to give students background information.

2. If you haven't already done so, show the students the video clip and have them answer the viewing questions. Make sure the students write something under each question.

3. Have the students turn and talk to a partner, then facilitate a sharing of the reflection answers.

4. Show the video clip a second time. Have the students fill out question 1 on the Knowledge Quest worksheet, the appropriate 4-Square form (Level 1 or 2), or the Viewing Guide (questions 1-6 and 9).

5. Facilitate a discussion of this analysis.

6. Show the video clip a third time. Have the students complete either the Knowledge Quest worksheet (questions 2-4), the Viewing Guide (questions 7-11), or both.

7. In either a written document or a class discussion, have students interpret and evaluate the dance. Make sure that the students are able to support all statements with evidence or details visible in the dance.

Reflection on Student Learning

Have the students write a quick reflection on this question: How did the three viewings build your knowledge about the dance?

Resources Needed

- DVD video clip of dance
- Knowledge Quest worksheet
- Knowledge Quest—Information and Teaching Tips page
- 4-Square Level 1 and Level 2 forms
- Viewing Guide

From H. Scheff, M. Sprague, and S. McGreevy-Nichols, 2010, *Exploring dance forms and styles: A guide to concert, world, social, and historical dance* (Champaign, IL: Human Kinetics).

CHAPTER 10

Comparing Dance Forms and Dances

When students compare new dance forms and dances with more familiar dance forms and dances, they are able to connect the new learning to prior knowledge, thereby providing an anchor in their minds to hold new learning in their memory. When comparing new dances with others, students can recognize connections that cross the dance categories, subcategories, forms, styles, cultures, and historical periods. It is important to recognize both similarities and differences among dances. Comparing and contrasting can lead to a study of what factors cause differences. Some of these factors are cultural values, rebellion against what came before, gender, or even a change in government.

Compare and Contrast Graphic Organizers

Graphic organizers are good for all types of learners, especially for students with a visual learning preference. Teachers know that graphic organizers not only organize information, they also help motivate and engage students. Graphic organizers for comparing and contrasting align aspects and attributes and categorize them. This helps students to construct meaning. Without meaning and context, new learning will not be stored or learned. Following are the main types of graphic organizers useful for compare and contrast activities:

- T chart (see figure 10.1)
- Compare and contrast matrix (see figure 10.2)
- Venn diagram (2 interlocked circles; see figure 10.3)
- Extended Venn diagram (3 interlocked circles; see figure 10.4)

Any of these graphic organizers can be used to compare dances as well.

FIGURE 10.1 T chart.

	Subject 1	Subject 2
Characteristic 1		
Characteristic 2		
Characteristic 3		

FIGURE 10.2 Compare and contrast matrix.

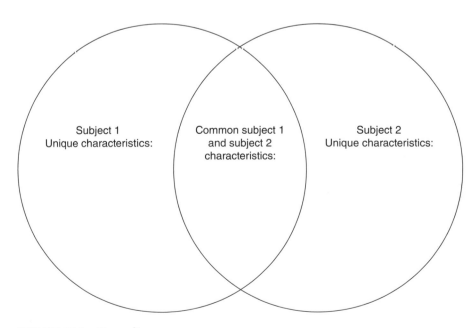

Subject 1
Unique characteristics:

Common subject 1
and subject 2
characteristics:

Subject 2
Unique characteristics:

FIGURE 10.3 Venn diagram.

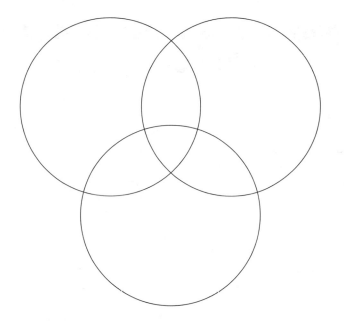

FIGURE 10.4   Extended Venn diagram.

Using the 4-Square Forms to Compare and Contrast Dances

The 4-Square forms in this book can aid in comparing and contrasting dances. Here is the process:

1. Use the 4-Square form as a template by printing it on an overhead transparency.
2. Select the dances to compare and contrast.
3. Place a blank transparency over the 4-Square form.
4. For one of the dances, use a colored transparency pen to record student answers.
5. When complete, remove the transparency from the 4-Square.
6. Place a new blank transparency over the 4-Square form.
7. For the next dance, choose a different-colored transparency pen to record student answers. (If comparing more than two dances, repeat steps 5, 6, and 7.)
8. Place all student answer transparencies over the 4-Square form.
9. Have students analyze the similarities and differences.

This method has been successful when comparing a West African dance with vintage jazz movement and a hip-hop dance. It was clear to the students that a movement lineage runs through these dances.

Comparing and Contrasting Dances Within Categories

Following are some ideas for comparing and contrasting the dances in the video clips that appear on the DVD. One could compare aspects of dances that are within the same category. For example, in the concert or theatrical dance category, the Soft Shoe shares many similarities with the tap dance, Shim Sham. Both dances originated in the United States with links to Vaudeville, both dances use syncopation and accented beats, and the sounds made by the feet are very important.

When analyzed in both levels of the 4-Square forms, the dance elements for the Soft Shoe and the Shim Sham are mostly similar. The legs, feet, and arms are used the most. Both dances are percussive, controlled, done at medium speed, and include repeated rhythmic patterns, and in both dances the dancers relate to an audience. The major difference is that while the Shim Sham uses movement qualities of *power* and *strength,* the soft shoe uses *little power* and *lightness.* As observed in the video clips this difference dictates the style and overall look and feel of the dances. Figure 10.5 is a Venn diagram comparing Shim Sham with the Soft Shoe.

An interesting comparison of two world dances could bring out cultural differences and influences. For example, compare the dance El Fon de la Negra (Mexican folkloric dance) with the Capoeira (from Brazil) to show the influences of the different blends of communities. In El Fon de la Negra, the percussive footwork and the skirt work of the girls indicate Spanish influences (a quick look at the Flamenco would show this connection). The body posture that sometimes twists and dips toward the ground hints at the Native American influence (see the Native American Narragansett clip). Capoeira, originating from slaves in Brazil, illustrates the West African movement and dance posture of the Yoruba people as well as the use of Portuguese rhythms taken from their masters.

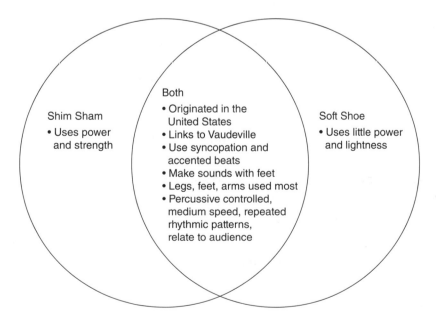

FIGURE 10.5 Venn Diagram comparing the Shim Sham and Soft Shoe.

Skirt work in a Mexican folkloric dance.

Comparing and Contrasting Dances in Different Categories

You can compare and contrast across categories, too. Many similarities stand out when comparing the Quadrille (a historical dance that originated in France) with the Virginia Reel (a world dance from the United States). Both dances use partners who change places in the formation and take turns leading the section of the dance (set). Also, during one of the sets in the Quadrille, the **formation,** or place where the dancers stand, is double lines of dancers facing each other. This formation is the same as the main formation in the Virginia Reel. There is an important difference between the two dances. The Virginia Reel is mostly made up of a short, repeated sequence of steps, which anyone could easily pick up at a community gathering. The Quadrille usually consists of five sets that contain different movements, **floor patterns,** (dancers' pathways on the floor as they move through space), and formations. The more intricate Quadrille dance requires much time to learn and practice. Also note that the Quadrille includes very formal bearing and polite acknowledgment of the other dancers. Even though partner etiquette is visible in the Virginia Reel, it has a more informal quality mostly because of the quick tempo and the skipping and sliding steps.

Other comparisons could be between dances that use hands to symbolize words and concepts (Bharatanatyam and Hula), dances that symbolize work (Raqs al Balas and Raks Assaya), and dances that emphasize percussive movements ("Rainbow Repertory Etude," Shim Sham, Native American, El Fon de la Negra, the Flamenco, Der Unterwestner, Gumboot, and Tahitian).

A Bharatanatyam dancer demonstrating mudras or double hand gesture.

Hula's hand gestures also represent words and concepts.

Comparing and contrasting is a simple way to interact with content in a deeper manner or to connect with other concepts or topics. Following is a lesson comparing Tiriba, a West African dance, with a U.S. hip-hop dance. The lesson uses the KQ worksheets and 4-Square forms to help students create small partner comparison dances.

Tiriba's use of low levels and strong weight can be compared with hip-hop dance.

Lesson Comparing a West African Dance With a U.S. Hip-Hop Dance

Description of Student Work

Students view and analyze two dances and then, with a partner, create and organize three dance sentences (phrases) to compose a comparison dance.

Standards Met by Student Work

Use your completed standards table to find appropriate standards.

Teaching Required

Accessing and Assessing Prior Knowledge

As an opening activity, ask students to write what they know about West African dance and about hip-hop dance. Have the students share what they know in a short discussion.

Exploring New Knowledge

1. Have students view the Tiriba dance video clip and a video from the Internet (search the term *hip-hop dance;* teachers suggest searching for *World Hip-Hop Championships*).

2. Ask students to use a Venn diagram to record aspects and movements that stand out for each of the two dances using the intersecting space for aspects and movements that are similar.

3. Facilitate as students compare, defend, and collate their answers.

4. Show the video clips again and, with partners, have students do the following:

   - Create a dance sentence (phrase), called C, from movements that are different.
   - Create a dance sentence (phrase), called B, from movements that are similar.
   - Create a dance sentence (phrase), called A, from their favorite movements from either dance.

5. Allow students to review the video clips as needed and facilitate the partner work.

6. Allow students to choose one of the following formats (choreographic structures) to organize their partner comparison dances:

   - Students use the choreographic structure ABACA, in which A = favorite movements from either dance, B = movements that are similar, and C = movements that are different.
   - Students create the order in which A, B, C are performed.

7. If you wish, students can add school-appropriate music. (Note: Some hip-hop music lyrics are not appropriate for some sites.)

Reflection on Student Learning

1. Have the students share and evaluate their partner comparison dances.

2. Use the accessing and assessing question as an exit reflection or create your own questions.

Resources Needed

- Tiriba video clip from the DVD
- A hip-hop video from the Internet
- KQ worksheets for Tiriba and the video search KQ for hip-hop
- Appropriate 4-Square forms
- Optional: CD player and music

From H. Scheff, M. Sprague, and S. McGreevy-Nichols, 2010, *Exploring dance forms and styles: A guide to concert, world, social, and historical dance* (Champaign, IL: Human Kinetics).

CHAPTER 11

Focusing on Universal Themes and Sociopolitical Issues

Dances are usually about something, **Universal themes** and **sociopolitical** issues are part of the human experience and can be the driving forces behind the content of many art forms. Dance is no exception.

Universal Themes

Universal themes are large concepts that can be useful in all disciplines and in cross-disciplinary work. Table 11.1 on page 274 shows how universal themes might play out in dance and how dance can be used to help students understand these concepts. It also points out where these themes might be illustrated in the dances included in the video clips.

Table 11.1 Universal Themes in Dance

Universal theme	Big idea	Examples of dance ideas	Examples seen in video clips
Change	Make different or transform	A dance about metamorphosis or evolution	Change is visible when comparing historical dances; also compare court dance to ballet.
Conflict	Clash between opposing positions or ideas	A dance about the struggle between good and evil	See page 277 for the lesson on conflict.
Exploration	Act of discovering new ideas	Exploring various movement ideas	Compare tap dance with the soft shoe. The removal of taps from the shoes changed the quality of the dance steps.
Force or influence	To control or move by physical or moral power	A dance in which one person demonstrates control over another person	Track the various cultures that interacted with the country in which dances originated. See chapter 10 and KQs for information on Brazil's Capoeira and the Mexican folkloric dance El Fon de la Negra.
Order versus chaos	Organization versus confusion	Use two groups of dancers. One group expresses the concept of organization and the other the concept of confusion.	View dances from various cultures to understand their preferences for organization.
Patterns	Recurring events or objects	A dance using A, B, and C movement phrases in patterns, e.g.: AA-BB-CC A-B-A-C-A ABCC-ABCC-A	See page 275 for the lesson on structure, which also contains work with recognition of patterns.
Power	Show of strength or force	A dance using elements of force and energy and space to demonstrate understanding of power	Compare the formations of Farandole and Pavane (changed from the circular formation with many leaders to presentational formations to face the king or person in power). Or, while watching various clips identify the following: Who leads? Who follows? Who dances particular dances?
Relationships	Specific connection between objects, entities, concepts, or people	Dances that involve connections between duets and trios of dancers	Watch any dance with more than one dancer and analyze the relationships between and among them as well as any use of an object (some suggested video clips are Salsa, Raks Assaya, Raqs al Balas, Farandole, Der Unterwestner, and Tahitian).
Structure	Organize or arrange; give form to	Use choreographic structures to organize movement patterns and phrases.	See page 275 for the lesson on structure.
Systems	Sets of interacting or interdependent entities	A machine dance, in which one dancer influences the next dancer in the manner of parts in a machine.	Find information on systems in the culture of the time in the background material of chapter 8 and in the Information and Teaching Tips form of the historical dances. Research for any influences on the culture of a particular dance.

Following are two sample lessons that explore the universal themes of structure and conflict.

Lesson on the Universal Theme of Structure

Description of Student Work

Students identify repeated movements and phrases and analyze how they are used to establish a structure. For each dance viewed, students design a diagram of the structure. Here is an example for a dance done to a popular song.

| Verse 1 | Chorus | Verse 2 | Chorus | Chorus |

Standards Met by Student Work

Use your completed standards table to find appropriate standards.

Teaching Required

Accessing and Assessing Prior Knowledge

- Brainstorm with the students' types of structures.
- From the generated lists, have students (in partners or small groups) make up their own definition of the word *structure*.
- Have the students report to the class.
- Facilitate a working definition made out of the partner or small group definitions.

Exploring New Knowledge

1. Teach the following information: A structure is made of separate parts connected in a specific way. The parts can interrelate in the following ways:
   - Parts of structures support and are supported by other parts.
   - Smaller structures may be combined to form a large structure.

2. Explain to the students that dances are organized through the use of structures. One example is a **canon** (round). The main movement is done exactly by two or three dancers or groups of dancers but at different intervals, as in "Row, Row, Row Your Boat."

3. Have the students view and analyze the following dances one at a time. They should look for (1) parts of the dance that repeat or form patterns and (2) where in the dance these repetitions are placed. Here are suggested answers:
   - Shim Sham: For the design of the structure, look for the **break.**
   - Virginia Reel: It has a repeat of the same set with new leaders.
   - Der Unterwestner: Look for repetition of the **plattling** (hand clapping and slapping) and the spinning circles.
   - Quadrille: See repetition in each set; each set has a different structure.

From H. Scheff, M. Sprague, and S. McGreevy-Nichols, 2010, *Exploring dance forms and styles: A guide to concert, world, social, and historical dance* (Champaign, IL: Human Kinetics).

4. Have the students create a drawing that represents the structure of each dance.

Reflection on Student Learning

Direct and help the students match the designs of the three dances with the two examples of structures listed under number 1 in Exploring New Knowledge. Here are suggested answers:

- Shim Sham: Parts of structures support and are supported by other parts.
- Virginia Reel: Smaller structures may be combined to form larger structures.
- Der Unterwestner: Smaller structures may be combined to form larger structures.
- Quadrille: Smaller structures may be combined to form larger structures.

Resources Needed

- DVD video clips of the Shim Sham, Virginia Reel, and Der Unterwestner
- Video search clip of the Quadrille
- Paper and drawing implements

From H. Scheff, M. Sprague, and S. McGreevy-Nichols, 2010, *Exploring dance forms and styles: A guide to concert, world, social, and historical dance* (Champaign, IL: Human Kinetics).

Lesson on the Universal Theme of Conflict

Description of Student Work
Students create a **dance study** demonstrating their understanding of the theme of conflict.

Standards Met by Student Work
Use your completed standards table to find appropriate standards.

Teaching Required

Accessing and Assessing Prior Knowledge
Have the students write a short reflection on a time in their lives when they faced a **conflict**. Ask for volunteers to share their reflections.

Exploring New Knowledge
1. Teach the following aspects of conflict:
   - Conflict is composed of opposing forces.
   - Conflict may be natural or human made.
   - Conflict may be intentional or unintentional.
   - Conflict may allow for synthesis and change.
2. Show the *Conflict* video clip. Have the students complete questions 1, 2, and 3 on the *Conflict* Knowledge Quest worksheet.
3. Give the students information from the Knowledge Quest Information and Teaching Tips form that relates to this dance.

From H. Scheff, M. Sprague, and S. McGreevy-Nichols, 2010, *Exploring dance forms and styles: A guide to concert, world, social, and historical dance* (Champaign, IL: Human Kinetics).

4. If possible, show these two scenes from the movie version of *Fiddler on the Roof:*

   • The men gathering to celebrate the wedding that shows the Jewish and Russian men sharing their dances

   • The Russian townspeople wrecking the oldest daughter's wedding

5. Have the students discuss the moments of conflict in both scenes and their resolution or consequences. *Note:* If this movie is unavailable to you, discuss other examples of conflicts, one that resolves peacefully and one that does not.

6. Show the video clip of *Conflict* again and have the students each pick out one favorite step.

7. Have the students create a group dance phrase using the method of dance building given here: "Find another person to teach your favorite movement to and learn theirs. Join the movements together. Continue to build the group dance phrase by adding more people and their movements. The groups will grow in this pattern: 1 person joins with 1 person, 2 people join with 2 other people, and 4 people with join 4 other people. Stop when you have a dance phrase that has 8 people and 8 movements. Practice the dance phrase until you feel confident that you can share it with the class." *Note:* Adapt the numbers to fit your class size.

8. Have these small groups work with another group and have them design a dance phrase that shows the moment of conflict. (It is suggested that students use stillness with poses, slow-motion movement, or far space between the two groups or between conflicting dancers.) Make sure the students use the aspects of conflict to create their dance study.

9. Have the students then design a dance phrase that shows the resolution or consequences of the conflict.

10. Have the students practice and revise their dance studies. *Note:* In all movement activities, make sure to move about the room asking students to show what they have completed, and ask probing questions to make sure students stay on task and that they understand the work.

Reflection on Student Learning

• Ask students to share their dances.

• Have the students who are watching them evaluate the dance study to see if it demonstrated an understanding of the aspects of conflict.

• As an exit reflection, have students write 3 to 5 statements on what they learned about conflict. (An extension of this lesson could be a reflective essay on this activity.)

Resources Needed

• Video clip of *Conflict* from the DVD

• Knowledge Quest worksheet

• Knowledge Quest Information and Teaching Tips form

• Copy of the film *Fiddler on the Roof* (Jewison, N. 2001. *Fiddler on the Roof.* Santa Monica, CA: MGM Home Entertainment.)

• DVD player and monitor

From H. Scheff, M. Sprague, and S. McGreevy-Nichols, 2010, *Exploring dance forms and styles: A guide to concert, world, social, and historical dance* (Champaign, IL: Human Kinetics).

Sociopolitical Issues

Dances are like time capsules. Encased in the movements, formations, floor patterns, and qualities of movement are reflections of earlier societies and their issues. These reflections can be central and blatantly visible in the dances or they may require some careful observation and unpacking in conjunction with extra research into the era.

Dances have been purposely choreographed to bring a social or political issue forward to public attention. Dances have illustrated such social issues as homelessness in Eve Gentry's *Tenant of the Street* (1938), lynching in Charles Weidman's *Lynch Town* (1936) and Pearl Primus' *Strange Fruit* (1943), and the state of people with terminal illness in Bill T. Jones' *Still/Here* (1994). War has been a topic of dances such as Kurt Jooss' *The Green Table* (1932), which is a satire on the architects of war and the destruction they design. Paul Taylor also dealt with World War II by contrasting lively dancing to music of the Andrews Sisters with shadows of war (literally, shadows of soldier figures) moving across the stage in the background.

The "Rainbow Repertory Etude," an American Dance Legacy Repertory Etude (see references for American Dance Legacy Institute), is based on Donald McKayle's *Rainbow 'Round My Shoulder* (1959). *Rainbow* was about the life of men on a prison chain gang. McKayle "focused on the degradation of human beings . . . the men in *Rainbow* find existence oppressive, and it is only through dreams... that they can escape. The modern dance classic is set to prison and blues songs" (McGhee and Sofras 2003, p. 10). A clip of this dance is found on the DVD with the accompanying KQ Answer Sheet, Information and Teaching Tips, and 4-Square forms. In addition, a lesson in this chapter is based on the "Rainbow Repertory Etude."

Some dances say as much about sociopolitical issues as the specifically choreographed dances but they may need more analysis to bring the commentary to the surface. For example, the formations and **facings** of the historical dances Branle, Farandole, and the Pavane clearly show the political change from dancing in a circle for and with other people of the same socioeconomic class

In Farandole, the dancers focus on each other.

Demonstrating a more democratic concept, the Virginia Reel allows each couple a chance to lead the dance.

(whether peasants were dancing in their villages or nobility dancing for themselves in social situations) to dancing facing a power higher than themselves, the king. In those days, dancing well often decided one's socioeconomic status. The North American Virginia Reel borrowed the figures' choreographic paths (Franko 2001) from the earlier court dance, but it demonstrated a more democratic approach by changing the leaders during each repeat of the set.

In the United States in the 1920s, a clear connection existed between dance and upward social mobility. During this time, industrialization gave rise to an increase in the size of the middle class, more leisure time for the working class, a rise of the consumer mentality, population migration from rural to urban areas, and a larger and freer role for women in society. If one compares the highly organized dances of the 19th century such as the Quadrille to the wilder Charleston of the early 20th century, these social changes become apparent. The smoother Fox-trot as demonstrated by Irene and Vernon Castle gave a sense of gentility and upper class manners. This type of social dance was marketed as a way to demonstrate one's worthiness to rise in socioeconomic class and to give grace, rhythm, and agility to females. The Fox-trot even affected women's fashion; looser bodices and shorter skirts aided in mobility (Malnig 2001).

The Fox-trot gave a sense of gentility and upper-class manners.

Who leads and who plays only a supporting role in dance forms can spotlight the more dominant gender. In court dance, the men played the dominant role with the fancier steps and lead the women through the often complex figures. As ballet developed, the role of the ballerina rose at times to dominance over the men, who often seemed to be on stage only to partner the female stars. It wasn't until after World War II that Native American women performed fancy dances, which include more percussive and rhythmically complex steps than the more traditional women's dances. The social dances in the United States in the late 1960s and 1970s feature dancers as equals, not even touching each other as they danced.

Dance exists in time and space and it is performed by human beings, so it naturally reflects its social and political surroundings. If a person feels strongly about something, these feelings are communicated either purposefully or unconsciously through the body. Dance is a discreet mode of non-verbal communication. As one becomes an observer of movement, one cannot help but learn about the human condition.

Lesson: Dance Study
Based on "Rainbow Repertory Etude"

Description of Student Work

Students create a dance study based on "Rainbow Repertory Etude."

Standards Met by Student Work

Use your completed standards table to find appropriate standards.

Teaching Required

Accessing and Assessing Prior Knowledge

Ask the students to reflect about a time when they may have felt controlled and helpless.

Exploring New Knowledge

1. Without giving the students any background about it, have students view the "Rainbow Repertory Etude" video clip for the first time.

2. Have the students complete the Viewing: What did you see? part of the KQ worksheet. Conduct a discussion.

3. Use the Information and Teaching Tips form to give students some background information.

4. With the second and third viewing, have the students analyze, interpret, and evaluate the dance, using the KQ and the appropriate level of the 4-Square form. *Note:* Have the class discuss and agree on the analysis.

5. Individually, have the students view the clip again to choose their favorite movements (at least two).

6. Individually, have the students create their own movements (at least two) that use the same dance elements found in the completed class 4-Square form.

7. In small groups, put the individual movements together in a dance study that communicates the dehumanization of individuals.

Reflection on Student Learning

1. Have the students share their group dances and get constructive suggestions for improvement. Give them time to make revisions.

2. Have the students share their revised dances with the group and reflect on their experiences during this lesson.

Resources Needed

- Video clip of "Rainbow Repertory Etude"
- Knowledge Quest Information and Teaching Tips form
- "Rainbow Repertory Etude" Knowledge Quest worksheet and answer sheet
- Appropriate 4-Square forms

From H. Scheff, M. Sprague, and S. McGreevy-Nichols, 2010, *Exploring dance forms and styles: A guide to concert, world, social, and historical dance* (Champaign, IL: Human Kinetics).

CHAPTER 12

Reflecting on Diversity and Blending of Cultural Aspects

The world is a big place filled with all sorts of wonders, not the least of these is the diversity of the human race. According to The American Dictionary of the English Language, **diversity** is "difference; variety or multiformity." When considering diversity, it is more than race or ethnicity. One should also think about gender, disability, body types, age, religion, socioeconomic status, politics, and cultural traditions and values. Each of these can find expression in dance.

When looking at these facets of diversity as expressed in and through dance, students can look at who leads and who follows, who the power people are (teacher, choreographer, star, patron), who does the dance and for whom, and for what purpose. Where and when the dance is done will give much information about the people whose dance it is and what values they hold dear. Some **cultures** only dance in specific places and times, while others have dance fully integrated in their daily lives. Who is included and who is excluded from a dancing event is also telling about the culture of the group. All individuals should have the opportunity to dance and express themselves through dance. There are many successful dance companies that employ dancers of all abilities. These companies embrace abilities of all types and have come up with a new innovative movement vocabulary.

Each culture has its own set of cultural values that run deep. What a people group believes and the traditions they develop, define and differentiate them from other groups. These cultural values not only affect religion, relationships, clothing, and language, but also dance. What a people group maintains of their own culture as they come in contact with others shows the strength of the culture. What a people group borrows from other cultures and incorporates into their own shows how resilient they are.

One cultural value shown in the Eastern European Jewish dances is that unrelated men and women were not permitted to hold hands.

Blending of Cultural Aspects

Today there is a blending of cultures caused by economic needs and opportunities, instantaneous communication, and faster transportation. When people move, they must make decisions as to which aspects of their culture they keep, which aspects they change in order to adapt to the new culture, and which aspects of the new culture that they totally adopt. The reverse is true for the culture that receives the migrants. Does it change because of this contact? Some people are worried about losing parts of their traditional cultures to this globalization. One has to wonder what traditional Kathak teachers think about the **fusion** dance form called **Bollywood.**

Cultural blending and globalization also offers opportunities. An American belly dancer uses Middle Eastern music that incorporates a reggaeton (reggae mixed with hip-hop) beat. Listening to the new musical form of **world beat** one often hears American hip-hop rhythms or instruments from multiple countries. Imagine a didgeridoo (Australian aboriginal wind instrument) in a piece of jazz music. On the Internet video sites, traditional dance forms are joined by fusion dances.

Exploring this **cultural blending** can help our students to become truly multicultural. To become more multicultural, a student is tooled to be aware of, understand, appreciate, and be able to interact successfully with different cultures. In dance, this can take the form of a dancer studying another culture's traditional form to perform it as purely as possible. Fusion of different dance forms is another answer.

Cultural blending is not new. The following unit maps the cross-pollenization of traditions and dance that occurred as the Gypsy people group, the Rom, traveled from Northern India, through the Middle East, and into North Africa and Europe (Spain and Romania).

Unit Outline for Culture: Adapt, Adopt, Maintain

Core Question: How does a culture's dance form(s) reflect its own traditions or adaptations from other cultures?

Introducing the Concepts
of Adapt, Adopt, and Maintain

Description of Student Work

Students find information about what traditions, values, and behaviors were **adapted** (changed), **adopted** (taken from the new cultures), or **maintained** during the African diaspora.

Standards Met By Student Work

Use your completed standards table to find appropriate standards.

Teaching Required

Accessing and Assessing Prior Knowledge

Have the students complete this reflection: Describe when you have had to adapt to a new environment or situation. What behaviors did you have to change?

Exploring New Knowledge

1. Model the cultural analysis worksheet using the video *Dancing: New Worlds, New Forms*. Students will find information about what traditions, values, and behaviors were adapted, adopted, or maintained during the African diaspora.

2. Make a cultural analysis worksheet by dividing a paper into four quarters and placing one of the following questions in each quarter.

   • Which traditions, values, and behaviors did the _____ people have to adapt?

   • Which traditions, values, and behaviors did the _____ people adopt?

   • Which traditions, values, and behaviors did the _____ people maintain?

   • What other important information was presented about the _____ people?

3. Teaching Tip: Stop the video at each important fact. Without speaking, rewind and replay that part of the video one or two more times so that the students can record the fact on their worksheets. In this way students will have to focus on the video.

Reflection on Student Learning

Ask the students to share their answers. Then ask them for their opinions on which fact or idea was most important.

Resources Required

   • A copy of the video *Dancing: New Worlds, New Forms* (Barnes, R.A. 1993. *Dancing: New Worlds, New Forms*. Thirteen, New York: WNET, Educational Resources Center.)

   • A teacher-created cultural analysis worksheet

From H. Scheff, M. Sprague, and S. McGreevy-Nichols, 2010, *Exploring dance forms and styles: A guide to concert, world, social, and historical dance* (Champaign, IL: Human Kinetics).

Comparing Three Dance Forms
(Kathak, Raqs al Balas, and Flamenco)

Description of Student Work

Students view and compare three dance forms.

Standards Met by Student Work

Use your completed standards table to find appropriate standards.

Teaching Required

Accessing and Assessing Prior Knowledge

Have the students write a prediction about what the traditional dance forms from India, the Middle East, and Spain have in common.

Exploring New Knowledge

1. Have the students view these video clips and complete a 4-Square form on each dance. Video clips of Kathak and Raqs al Balas are available on the DVD; the Flamenco is a video search clip.

2. Have the students share their answers and come to a teacher-guided consensus on what dance elements were emphasized in each dance form.

3. Use the transparency layering idea described in chapter 10 so that students in small groups can transfer appropriate information on an extended Venn diagram with three intersecting circles (figure 10.4 on page 267).

Reflection on Student Learning

Ask the students which dance form they preferred and have them support their answers with a description of the movement from the video. (This is a written exit reflection or discussion.)

Resources Required

- DVD video clips of Kathak and Raqs al Balas
- Video search clip of the Flamenco
- Appropriate 4-Square forms

From H. Scheff, M. Sprague, and S. McGreevy-Nichols, 2010, *Exploring dance forms and styles: A guide to concert, world, social, and historical dance* (Champaign, IL: Human Kinetics).

Adapt, Adopt, and Maintain: A Case Study of the Rom

Description of Student Work

1. Students view the video on the Rom people and fill in a cultural analysis worksheet.

2. Homework assignment: Students design an interview based on the concepts of adapt, adopt, and maintain.

Standards Met by Student Work

Use your completed standards table to find appropriate standards.

Teaching Required

Accessing and Assessing Prior Knowledge

Have the students write what they may know about the Gypsy (Rom) people.

Exploring New Knowledge

As a class, have the students view the film *Latcho Drom* and fill in a cultural analysis worksheet. *Note:* If this video is not available to you, design a research lesson on the migration of the Rom people.

Reflection on Student Learning

Have the students write a reflection that responds to their first reflection, Ask, "After viewing *Latcho Drom,* how accurate was the information about the Gypsy people that you wrote in your prior knowledge activity?"

Give the following homework assignment: Design an interview based on adapt, adopt, and maintain. Create at least four probing questions under each heading. Interview someone that has changed cultures. (Remember that a culture doesn't necessarily mean another country.) Record their answers on a cultural analysis worksheet that you have created yourself.

Resources Required

- Cultural analysis worksheet (teacher created)
- Video on the Rom people: *Latcho Drom* (Gatlif, T. 1996. *Latcho Drom.* New Yorker Video, New York: New Yorker Films Artwork.)

From H. Scheff, M. Sprague, and S. McGreevy-Nichols, 2010, *Exploring dance forms and styles: A guide to concert, world, social, and historical dance* (Champaign, IL: Human Kinetics).

Mirroring the Rom: Blending Movements to Make a New Dance Form

Description of Student Work

1. Students learn movements from Kathak, Raqs al Balas, and Flamenco.
2. Students will create their own dance phrase that blends and mixes the movements.

Standards Met by Student Work

Use your completed standards table to find appropriate standards.

Teaching Required

Accessing and Assessing Prior Knowledge

Have the students share their interview responses.

Exploring New Knowledge

1. Using the video clips, have the students learn movements from Kathak, Raqs al Balas, and Flamenco. Video clips of Kathak and Raqs al Balas are available on the DVD; Flamenco is a video search clip.
2. Have the students create their own dance phrase that blends and mixes the movements. (This work can be done individually, in partners, or small groups.)

Reflection on Student Learning

Have the students share their dance phrases with the class. The viewers should be ready to identify the different dance elements taken from each dance.

Using the appropriate 4-Square form or a Venn diagram, have the students compare their dances' phrases with the Rom dances to analyze the process of cultural blending.

Assign the following homework: Create a narrative product based on your interview. The narrative product should tell the interviewee's story (e.g., story book, comic book, journal, story cloth).

Resources Required

- DVD video clips of Kathak and Raqs al Balas
- Video search clip of Flamenco
- Appropriate 4-Square Level and a Venn diagram
- Video on the Rom people: *Latcho Drom* (Gatlif, T. 1996. *Latcho Drom*. New Yorker Video, New York: New Yorker Films Artwork.)

From H. Scheff, M. Sprague, and S. McGreevy-Nichols, 2010, *Exploring dance forms and styles: A guide to concert, world, social, and historical dance* (Champaign, IL: Human Kinetics).

289

APPENDIX

Lesson for _____

Description of Student Work

Provide a description of the work students will do during this lesson.

Standards Met by Student Work

Use your completed standards table to find appropriate standards.

Teaching Required

Accessing and Assessing Prior Knowledge

Ask a lead-in question or do a short activity that will tell you what students already know about the topic.

Warm-up Activity

Have students do some warm-up movements as appropriate for the lesson content.

Exploring New Knowledge

Teach the content either through direct teaching or facilitation.

Reflection on Student Learning

Facilitate students' reflections and revisions as well as final reflections or self-evaluations.

Resources Needed

Gather the materials and equipment necessary for the teaching and learning in the lesson.

From H. Scheff, M. Sprague, and S. McGreevy-Nichols, 2010, *Exploring dance forms and styles: A guide to concert, world, social, and historical dance* (Champaign, IL: Human Kinetics).

Depth of Knowledge (DOK) Levels

Level One Activities	Level Two Activities	Level Three Activities	Level Four Activities
Recall elements and details of story structure, such as sequence of events, character, plot and setting. Conduct basic mathematical calculations. Label locations on a map. Represent in words or diagrams a scientific concept or relationship. Perform routine procedures like measuring length or using punctuation marks correctly. Describe the features of a place or people.	Identify and summarize the major events in a narrative. Use context cues to identify the meaning of unfamiliar words. Solve routine multiple-step problems. Describe the cause/effect of a particular event. Identify patterns in events or behavior. Formulate a routine problem given data and conditions. Organize, represent and interpret data.	Support ideas with details and examples. Use voice appropriate to the purpose and audience. Identify research questions and design investigations for a scientific problem. Develop a scientific model for a complex situation. Determine the author's purpose and describe how it affects the interpretation of a reading selection. Apply a concept in other contexts.	Conduct a project that requires specifying a problem, designing and conducting an experiment, analyzing its data, and reporting results/solutions. Apply mathematical model to illuminate a problem or situation. Analyze and synthesize information from multiple sources. Describe and illustrate how common themes are found across texts from different cultures. Design a mathematical model to inform and solve a practical or abstract situation.

Webb, Norman L. and others. "Web Alignment Tool" 24 July 2005. Wisconsin Center of Educational Research. University of Wisconsin-Madison. 2 Feb. 2006. <http://www.wcer.wisc.edu/WAT/index.aspx>.

Reprinted, by permission, from N.L. Webb et al., "Web Alignment Tool" 24 July 2005. Wisconsin Center of Educational Research. University of Wisconsin-Madison, 2 Feb. 2006. Available: http://www.wcer.wisc.edu/WAT/index.aspx.

Studio Thinking Framework: Eight Habits of Mind

Develop Craft

- Technique: Learning to use tools (e.g., viewfinders, brushes) and materials (e.g., charcoal, paint). Learning artistic conventions (e.g., perspective, color mixing)
- Studio practice: Learning to care for tools, materials, and space

Engage and Persist

- Engage: Learning to embrace problems of relevance within the art world or of personal importance
- Persist: Learning to develop focus and other mental states conducive to working and persevering at art tasks

Envision

Learning to picture mentally what cannot be directly observed and imagine possible next steps in making a piece

Express

Learning to create works that convey an idea, a feeling, or a personal meaning

Observe

Learning to attend to visual contexts more closely than ordinary looking requires, thereby seeing things that otherwise might not be seen

Reflect

- Question and explain: Learning to think and talk with others about an aspect of one's work or working process
- Evaluate: Learning to judge one's own work and working process and the work of others in relation to standards of the field

Stretch and Explore

Learning to reach beyond one's capacities, to explore playfully without a preconceived plan, and to embrace the opportunity to learn from mistakes and accidents.

Understand Art World

- Domain: Learning about art history and current practice
- Communities: Learning to interact as an artist with other artists (i.e., in classrooms, in local arts organizations, and across the art field) and within the broader society

Based on R. Ritchart et al., 2006, *Thinking routines: Establishing patterns of thinking in the classroom.* Paper prepared for the AERA Conference.

I See, I Think, I Wonder:
A Routine for Exploring Works of Art and Other Interesting Things

- What do you see?
- What do you think about that?
- What does it make you wonder?

Why

Ask this question to help students make careful observations and thoughtful interpretations, stimulate curiosity, and set the stage for inquiry.

When

Use this routine when you want students to think carefully about why something looks the way it does or is the way it is.

How

Ask students to make an observation about the artwork or topic and follow up with what they think might be going on or what they think this observation might be. Encourage students to back up their interpretation with reasons. Ask the students to think about what this makes them wonder about the artwork or topic.

The routine works best when a student responds by using the three stems together at the same time (I see, I think, I wonder). However, you may find that students begin by using one stem at a time and that you need to scaffold each response with a follow-up question for the next stem.

The routine works well in a group discussion but in some cases you may want to have students carry out the routine individually on paper or in their heads before sharing them out as a class. Student responses to the routine can be written down and recorded so that a class chart of observations, interpretations, and wonderings are listed for all to see and return to during the course of study.

Based on R. Ritchart et al., 2006, *Thinking routines: Establishing patterns of thinking in the classroom*. Paper prepared for the AERA Conference.

VIEWING GUIDE

Name: _____ Class: _____ Date: _____

1. What was the name of the dance? What was the era or country of origin? If appropriate, name the choreographer.

2. What category of dance did you see? Check the appropriate box.
   ❏ concert or theatrical   ❏ social   ❏ historical   ❏ world
   a. If the category was concert or theatrical, what was its subcategory?
      ❏ ballet   ❏ tap   ❏ jazz   ❏ musical theater   ❏ modern
      ❏ crossover
   b. If the category was social, what was its subcategory?
      ❏ alone in a group   ❏ partners   ❏ dances done in a line
      ❏ dances done in a circle
   c. If the category was historical, what was its subcategory?
      ❏ Middle Ages   ❏ Renaissance   ❏ Baroque
      ❏ 18tth and 19th century   ❏ Ragtime or 1920s
   d. If the category was world dance, what was its subcategory?
      ❏ North America   ❏ South and Central America   ❏ Europe
      ❏ Asia   ❏ Africa   ❏ Oceania

3. How did the dancers use the space?

4. Describe some of the ways that the dancers moved.

5. What were the dancers' relationships to other dancers?

6. Describe the types of movements that were emphasized or repeated.

7. What do you think was communicated in this dance? What did you see in the dance that influenced your thoughts?

8. What other thoughts or ideas did the dance give you as you watched it? Support your answer with observations from the dance.

9. Describe the traditional clothing or costumes and props. How were they important to the dance's main idea or quality?

10. What did you learn from viewing the clip? Support your answer with observations visible in the dance.

11. Did you like this dance? Why or why not? Support your answer with observations visible in the dance.

From H. Scheff, M. Sprague, and S. McGreevy-Nichols, 2010, *Exploring dance forms and styles: A guide to concert, world, social, and historical dance* (Champaign, IL: Human Kinetics).

KNOWLEDGE QUEST
INFORMATION AND TEACHING TIPS

Video Clip Search

Category M: (Subcategory:)

Category A: (Subcategory:)

Name of Dance:

DIRECTIONS   Give students the job of researching clips of and about the dance on the Internet. Many clips are available; have them choose one or two. They can do this in school if the Internet is available, at home, or at a library. Instruct them to take notes about the actual dancing so that they can complete the student worksheet.

BACKGROUND INFORMATION   Before students view the video clip, share the following information with them and give them the KQ worksheets to complete as a homework assignment.

- **Translation:**
- **Country or culture of origin:**
- **Timeline:**
- **Function or reason:**
- **Who does this dance:**
- **Music and rhythms:**
- **Traditional clothing or costume:**
- **Other information:**

REFERENCES

TEACHING STRATEGIES   The video clip should be viewed at least three times (see chapter 1). In the case where students are searching and observing from home, they will need to list the exact Web site so that teachers and other students can see the basis for the documentation.

Facilitate a class discussion using the discussion starters listed next. Have students use their recorded answers as a resource. Feel free to paraphrase and choose the questions that work best with your students.

Viewing: What Did You See?

Suggested discussion starters and questions:

Connecting: What Do You Know?

Suggested discussion starters and questions:

Responding: What Do You Think? What Do You Wonder?

Suggested discussion starters and questions:

What questions do you have about this dance? Write them down and continue your research. Some of these questions can be answered through movement.

From H. Scheff, M. Sprague, and S. McGreevy-Nichols, 2010, *Exploring dance forms and styles: A guide to concert, world, social, and historical dance* (Champaign, IL: Human Kinetics).

Performing: What Can You Do?

Choose both Re-create and Create, choose one of these two activities, or make your own performing work that you think is most appropriate for your students.

Re-create

Create
*If you need music and don't have it among your resources, use the video.

FUN FACTS

WEB EXPLORATIONS   Key terms to search for include

RECOMMENDED CLIPS

From H. Scheff, M. Sprague, and S. McGreevy-Nichols, 2010, *Exploring dance forms and styles: A guide to concert, world, social, and historical dance* (Champaign, IL: Human Kinetics).

Name: _____ Class: _____ Date: _____

STUDENT KNOWLEDGE QUEST WORKSHEET

Name of Dance:

1. Viewing: What did you see?
   Record your observations. Describe what you see. Be specific.

   _____

   _____

   _____

   _____

   _____

2. Connecting: What do you know?

   _____

   _____

   _____

   _____

   _____

3. Responding: What do you think? What do you wonder?

   _____

   _____

   _____

   _____

   _____

4. Performing: What can you do?

   _____

   _____

   _____

   _____

   _____

ANSWER SHEET FOR STUDENT KNOWLEDGE QUEST WORKSHEET

Name of Dance:

The following possible answers are based on general knowledge and characteristics of the dance. Exact answers depend on the specific video clips selected. Encourage students to view least two different clips, so they can see how the dance might vary.

1. **Viewing: What did you see?**
   Record your observations. Describe what you see. Be specific.

4-SQUARE LEVEL 1

How do the dancers use their bodies?	How do the dancers move?
Body parts most often in use torso (chest, hips) legs feet arms shoulders hands head	*Movement elements* with power with little power surprisingly continuously looking and moving in one direction looking and moving in more than one direction controlled uncontrolled
Shape of body angles curves straight twisted same on both sides different on both sides	
Moving one body part at a time	*Speed of movement* fast medium slow
Moving in place bending stretching twisting	*Are any movements accented or emphasized?* yes no
Movement that travels walk hop jump slide leap	*How long do the movements last?* long medium short
other (describe): _____	*Are there repeated rhythmic patterns?* yes no
	Types of movements include suspended shaking swinging percussive collapsing vibratory other: _____

From H. Scheff, M. Sprague, and S. McGreevy-Nichols, 2010, *Exploring dance forms and styles: A guide to concert, world, social, and historical dance* (Champaign, IL: Human Kinetics).

How do the dancers use the space around them?	What are the dancers' relationships to each other?
Size of movement 　　　large　　medium　　small *Body levels* 　　　low　　middle　　high *Movement done close to the body* *Movement done far from the body* *Dancers stand* 　　in circles　in squares　in lines 　　　scattered (spread out) *Foot patterns traced on the floor* 　　curved　　straight　　circular *Directions in which dancers travel* 　　　forward　　sideways 　　　backward　　diagonal	*Dancers dance* 　　　　alone　　in partners 　　in groups (trio, quartet, etc.) *Dancers relate to* 　　other dancer(s)　object　audience *Dancers' relationships to each other are mostly* 　　over　under　around　through 　　in front　behind　beside 　near each other　far from each other *Contact between and among dancers* 　　　touching　holding 　　supporting each other's weight 　　　lifting each other other: _____

4-SQUARE LEVEL 2

How do the dancers use their bodies?	How do the dancers move?
Body parts most often in use 　torso (chest, hips)　legs　feet 　arms　shoulders　hands　head *Shape of body* 　angles　curves　straight　twisted 　　symmetrical　asymmetrical *Isolations* *Nonlocomotor* 　*(axial):* 　bending　stretching　twisting 　*(peripheral):* 　　spoke　arc　carve *Locomotor* 　walk　hop　jump　slide　leap 　　sissonne (2 feet to 1 foot) 　　assemblé (1foot to 2 feet) other (describe): _____	*Movement elements (Laban efforts)* 　*Weight:*　with strength (powerfully) 　　　　with lightness (delicately) 　*Time:*　　suddenly (surprisingly) 　　　　sustained (continuously) 　*Space:*　　direct (one focus) 　　　　indirect (multifocal) 　*Flow:*　　bound (controlled) 　　　　free (uncontrolled) *Effort elements (Laban effort actions)* 　　dab　punch　float　glide 　　wring　press　flick　slash
	Time 　*Tempo:*　fast　medium　slow *Are movements organized into distinct phrases?* 　　　　yes　no *Are any movements accented or emphasized?* 　　　　yes　no *Duration of movements* 　　　long　medium　short *Are there repeated rhythmic patterns?* 　　　　yes　no *Movement qualities (force or energy)* 　suspended　shaking　swinging 　percussive　collapsing　vibratory other: _____

From H. Scheff, M. Sprague, and S. McGreevy-Nichols, 2010, *Exploring dance forms and styles: A guide to concert, world, social, and historical dance* (Champaign, IL: Human Kinetics).

DVD

How do the dancers use the space around them?	What are the dancers' relationships to each other?
Size of movement 　　　　large　　medium　　small *Levels* 　　　　low　　middle　　high *Near space (movement done close to the body)* *Far space (movement done far from the body)* *Formations* 　circles　　squares　　lines　　scattered *Pathways (floor patterns)* 　　　curved　　straight　　circular *Air patterns (trace patterns in the air left by dancers' movements, e.g., figure 8)* 　　　curved　　straight　　circular *Directions in which dancers travel* 　　　forward　　sideways 　　　backward　　diagona	*Dancers dance* 　　　　alone　　in partners 　　in groups (trio, quartet, etc.) *Dancers relate to* 　　other dancer(s)　　object　　audience *Dancers' relationships to each other are mostly* 　　over　　under　　around　　through 　　　in front　　behind　　beside 　　near each other　　far from each other *Contact between and among dancers* 　　　　touching　　holding 　　supporting each other's weight 　　　lifting each other other: _____

2. Connecting: What do you know?

Possible answers:

3. Responding: What do you think?

Note. At this level of thinking, there is seldom one right answer.

Possible answers:

Chart questions that students wonder about. Have them do more research on questions or solve problems through movement.

4. Performing: What can you do?

Re-create
When re-creating the dance, the students should do the following:

Create
Dance contains the following:

***If you need music and don't have it among your resources, use the video.**

From H. Scheff, M. Sprague, and S. McGreevy-Nichols, 2010, *Exploring dance forms and styles: A guide to concert, world, social, and historical dance* (Champaign, IL: Human Kinetics).

GLOSSARY

adapted—Aspects taken and changed to fit a new situation.

adopted—Aspects taken as a whole from the new culture.

aesthetic—Pertaining to a sense of the beautiful and a philosophical theory or idea of what is artistically valid at any given time.

aesthetic values—Knowing what *you* like and consider valuable and worth your attention and what you consider beautiful or pleasing.

arabesque—A back leg extension.

arcing—Drawing hemispheric patterns in the air.

assemblé—A jump step where you leave the floor from one foot (while the other is extended) and you land with both feet together at the same time.

ball change—A changing of the weight on the balls of the feet from one foot to the other; executed forward, to the side, or in place. Weight can be on one foot with the other coming down just on the ball. This would be like walking with one foot on a curb and the other in the street.

Bloom's taxonomy—A hierarchy of six levels of the complexity of human thinking.

Bollywood dance—A dance form used in modern Indian films that is a mixture of belly dancing, classical Indian styles such as Kathak and Indian folk dance, Western pop dance styles, and modern and jazz dance. It gets the name from the play on the word *Hollywood*; the B stands for *Bombay*.

bourreés—Tiny steps done on the balls of the feet or the tips of pointe shoes in ballet.

break—A different step that occurs repeatedly after sequences of steps; also refers to the same type of action in drum beats.

breech cloth—A form of apparel for Native American men. It starts with a rope tied around the waist and a panel of fabric that hangs from that in front and back to the mid-thigh.

call and response—One person moves and the other person's movement responds (answers the movement of the initial mover).

canon—A musical or dance structure in two or more parts. The main phrase is imitated by the successive musicians or dancers at successive intervals. Also known as a round.

carving—Drawing patterns in the air with hands or feet leading.

chassé—A gallop.

chance dance—A choreographic form that can be described as a series of dance phrases performed in a random order. Each time the dance is done, it is in a different order and therefore has a different appearance.

choreographic structures—Sometimes called choreographic forms. These are ways to organize choreography.

classical ballet—A style of ballet that evolved over the past 300 years, starting in France.

codified—Formalized or systematized course of study.

collapse—Giving in to gravity.

concert dance—Dance that appears on the stages of the world for the benefit, enjoyment, and education of the audience.

conflict—A struggle, trial of strength, or disagreement.

contemporary ballet—A concert form of ballet where the choreography uses movement from the modern dance vocabulary as well as the ballet vocabulary.

contract–release—This movement is based on exhalation and inhalation. Contraction is the act of flexing abdominal muscles so that the center of the body is in a curve and the shoulders remain over the hips.

controlled movement—Movement that is guided; also bound (Laban effort).

culture—The predominant attitude and behaviors that characterize a group of people, their patterns, their arts, their beliefs, and their institutions.

cultural blending—A mixing of aspects from different cultures.

Dabkee—A line dance that uses a grapevine step to move from place to place.

dance history—The study of dance from the beginning of time to the present.

dance historians—People who research historical dances and record the steps, when and where they were done, and why they were done.

dance sentence—A short movement phrase.

dance study—An explanation of an idea through the creation of a short dance.

dance terminology or dance vocabulary—The names of the steps and movements that go into making up the way dancers communicate verbally.

diversity—Variety. In dance this term can refer to ethnicity, culture, religion, form, or style.

divertissement—A section of a formal ballet, usually performed with some brilliant steps, making it a tour de force for dancers.

djembe—Large drum used by African drummers.

double time or duple meter—Doubling the basic beat.

dunun—A large drum used by African drummers.

emboité—A prance in dance with the knees lifted as the feet are exchanged.

en avant—To the front.

era—A period of time from one specific date to another.

essence—A basic movement associated with soft shoe and containing many and varied rhythmic patterns. It is also used in other tap dance styles and has a wide variety of moves such as single essence, back essence, Virginia essence, and double essence.

ethnic dance—A category of dance that represents the traditions, beliefs, and values of the people and the community that dance them. Also called *folk dance.*

etude—A music or dance study.

facings—The directions to which the dancers face to do their movements.

fall and recovery—An idea based on falling away from and returning to equilibrium.

floor pattern—Dancers' pathways on the floor as they move through space.

folk dance—A category of dance that represents the traditions, beliefs, and values of the people and the community that dance them. Also called *ethnic dance.*

form—Type of dance (e.g., Hula, ballet, modern).

formation—Where dancers stand in relation to other dancers.

fusion—Melting or blending together.

ghillies—Soft shoes that are worn by women in Irish dancing.

grand walkaraound—This term is associated with the Cakewalk; before the actual dance begins people walk alone or in pairs around the perimeter of the room.

graphic organizers—Worksheets that visually organize information.

habits of mind—Thinking skills or behaviors that that help us function in all types of learning situations.

Harry Fox—A Vaudeville actor who is known for inventing the Fox-trot.

historical dance—Sometimes referred to as *early dance.* It actually covers an expansive variety of dance forms and styles from the past.

historical dance clubs—Organizations that practice, preserve, and perform dances from the past.

Hmong—A hill tribe people from various countries in southeast Asia.

indigenous—Originating and living or occurring naturally in an area or environment. Native to the area.

Irish step dancing—A codified (formal) form of dance from Ireland. It is accented by heel work and series of small hops and jumps.

isolation—A dance move using only one part of the body.

Jack Cole—Known as the father of theatrical jazz dance.

jeté—A small leap from one foot to another (like leaping over a puddle from one foot to another).

kaftan—A mode of dress worn by women in several countries including India and Egypt. It is a loose-fitting garment that hangs from the shoulders to the ankles with elbow-length sleeves.

klezmer music—Music from Eastern European culture; used for Yiddish dance forms and borrowed by Slavic and surrouding areas. Instruments can be clarinet, violin, some percussion, and sometimes an accordion.

Laban effort actions—Combinations of three of the following effort elements:

  dab—Uses light weight, sudden time, and direct space.

  flick—Uses light weight, sudden time, and indirect space.

  float—Uses light weight, sustained time, and indirect space.

  glide—Uses light weight, sustained time, and direct space.

  press—Uses strong weight, sustained time, and direct space.

  punch—Uses strong weight, sudden time, and direct space.

  slash—Uses strong weight, sudden time, and indirect space.

  wring—Uses strong weight, sustained time, and indirect space.

Laban efforts—The attitude toward the energy that is exerted when doing a movement:

  flow—Attitude toward flow is bound (controlled) or free (uncontrolled).

  space—Attitude space is direct (movement has a single focus) or indirect (the movement has many foci).

  time—Attitude toward time is sudden (showing urgency or anxiety) or sustained (showing a relaxed, easygoing feeling).

  weight—Attitude toward weight is strong (expending much energy) or light (using a fine or delicate touch).

Labanotation—A system of writing dance movement using graphics in the form of shapes.

leggings—For Native American men and women, a form of trousers that are straight fitting but have room enough for the constant moving of the legs.

locomotor—Movement that transports the body away from a starting position.

maintained—Aspects kept as they originally were.

mariachi band—The traditional band for Mexican folkloric dance; includes guitars, vocals, and some small percussion. They walk or stand behind the dancers.

Maxixe—A Brazilian dance that comes from the Tango.

minstrel show—An American form of entertainment popular in the late 1800s and early 1900s.

movement elements—Actions through the use of space, time, and energy.

movement skills—Skills made up of locomotor and nonlocomotor movements.

musicality—The quality of being musical.

musical theater or musical comedy dance—Dances that are imbedded in the Broadway shows that include music and song. The dances are often used to move the story along.

nonlocomotor—Movement that comes without the transferring of weight in any direction (axial).

paddle turn—Could pertain to numerous movements associated with the soft shoe, Greek dances, Mexican folkloric dance, and others. It is usually done as a turn but can be done in place or traveling to the side. Starting with one foot flat on the ground and the other poised on the ball of the foot, push up on the ball of the foot and then come down on the flat foot.

pa ndau—story cloths from the Hmong culture.

Pavane—A court dance from the Renaissance.

pas—A step; used in ballet and court dances.

pas de basque—A triple step: step-toe-step, usually done in a side-to-side motion.

pas de deux—A dance for two.

percussive—Relating to sharp, striking sounds of percussion instruments, hand and body clapping, or foot stomping.

performance art—A form of theatrical art featuring the activity of the artist and works presented in a variety of media.

pick-up beat—The beat before a new measure of music, sometimes counted as "and" before the one.

pirouette—Any kind of a turn.

plattling—A hand clapping and slapping pattern done in many German dances.

pogrom—An organized, often officially encouraged massacre or persecution of a minority group, especially one conducted against Jews.

popular dance—According to most scholars, the non-folk social dances of the 20th century.

reel shoes—The shoes men and boys wear for Irish step dancing; made of black leather with a soft sole and a hard heel.

rhythm—The patterned recurring alternations of contrasting elements of sound.

ring shout—An ecstatic dance ritual, first practiced by African slaves in the West Indies and the United States; worshippers move in a circle while shuffling their feet and clapping their hands. Shouting aloud is not an essential part of the ritual and it usually would take place during or after a religous meeting.

ritual dances—Dances done about rites of passage.

Romantic ballet—Ballet from the Romantic era characterized by story line and light, flowing movement.

Sanskrit—An ancient language of Hinduism and the Vedas; it is the classical literary language of India.

shtetls—Villages in Eastern European Jewish settlements.

Scott Joplin—One of the best-known composers for ragtime music, which is the basis for many Cakewalk tunes.

set—A grouping of dance steps.

shaking—A vibratory movement.

social dance—The primary focus is interacting with others through dance.

socioeconomic—Involving both social and economic factors.

sociopolitical—Involving both social and political factors.

spoking—Shooting movements outward from the body into space.

star formation—A dance formation in world, social, and historical dance where the dancers reach into the square with one arm held high in close proximity to the other dancers, who are doing the same thing.

structure—Something made up of a number of parts that are held or put together in a particular way. Music and dance have structure.

style—Characteristic movement and expression of the choreographer or dancer.

suspension—A moment when the movement performed is lifted and held.

swing dance—A style of dance that developed concurrently with the swing style of jazz music in the 1920s, '30s, and '40s. Lindy Hop is a swing dance.

syncopation—A character of rhythm that occurs when accents occur in unexpected paces within an otherwise predictable or repetitive pattern.

tapestry—A woven wall hanging that depicts a scene.

technique—The tools and skills needed to produce a particular style.

theatrical dance—A dance created with the audience in mind.

time period—A specified amount of time, usually in regard to something of significance.

tour de force—A dance especially created to show the dancer's brilliance and high level of achievement in the execution of the difficult dance steps in the choreography.

universal themes—Subject matter that has an impact on a diverse population.

values and beliefs—Two significant elements of a culture.

Vaudeville—Stage entertainment consisting of a variety of acts; popular in the early 20th century.

vernacular—A social dance of a particular period; a popular style.

warm-up—A process of getting the body ready to move.

world beat—Any combination of folk and popular music, especially the fusion of Western popular music with indigenous music of another culture.

world dance—Dances that stem from within an ethnic culture and express the movement aesthetic of that culture.

REFERENCES & RESOURCES

Adshead-Landsdale, Janet and June Layson. 1974. Editors. *Dance history: An introduction.* London and NY: Routledge Press.

An American Ballroom Companion: Dance Instruction Manuals, ca. 1490-1920. *Baroque dance.* http://memory.loc.gov/ammem/dihtml/diessay4.html.

American Dance Legacy Institute. www.adli.us.

Anderson, Jack. 1974. *Dance.* New York: Newsweek Books.

Anderson, Lorin W. et al. 2001. *A taxonomy for learning, teaching, and assessing: A revision of Bloom's taxonomy of educational objectives.* http://projects.coe.uga.edu/epltt/index.php?title=Bloom%27s_Taxonomy.

Bagwell, Orlando. 1993. Producer and director. *Dancing: New worlds, New Forms.* NY, NY: Thirteen—WNET.

Balanchine, George and Francis Mason. 1954. *101 stories of the great ballets.* New York: Dolphin Books, Doubleday & Co. (ch. 5, p.137)

Casner-Lotto, Jill and Mary Wright Benner. 2006. *Are they really ready to work?: Employers perspectives on the basic knowledge and applied skills of new entrants to the 21st century U.S. workforce.* The Conference Board, Partnership for the 21st Century Skills, Corporate Voices for Working Families, and the Society for Human Resources Management. Annual Report. New York: The Conference Board.

Cass, Joan. 1993. *Dancing through history.* New Jersey: Prentice Hall.

Curry, James and John Samara. 1991. *Curriculum guide for the education of gifted high school students.* Austin, TX: Texas Association for the Gifted and Talented (TAGT).

The dance notebook. 1984. Philadelphia, PA: Running Press.

Franko, Mark. 2001. Writing dancing. In *Moving history/Dancing cultures,* ed. Ann Dils and Ann Cooper Albright, 191. Middletown, CT: Wesleyan University Press.

Gatlif, Tony. 1996. *Latcho Drom.* New Yorker Video. NY, NY: New Yorker Films Artwork.

Guide to Dance Etiquette. www.cdny.org/etiquette.html.

Hanna, Judith Lynne. 1987. *To dance is human: A theory of nonverbal communication.* Revised 1979 edition. Chicago: University of Chicago Press.

Hanna, Judith Lynne. 1999. *Partnering dance and education: Intelligent moves for changing times.* Champaign, IL: Human Kinetics. (p. 99)

Harvy, Stephanie and Anne Goudvis. 2000. *Strategies that work.* Portland, ME: Stenhouse Publishers.

Hetland, Lois, Ellen Winner, Shirley Veenema, and Kimberly M. Sheridan. 2007. *Studio thinking: The real benefits of visual arts education.* NY: Teachers College Press.

Jewison, Norman. 2001. *Fiddler on the roof.* Santa Monica, CA: MGM Home Entertainment.

Kassing, Gayle. 2007. *History of dance: An interactive arts approach.* Champaign, IL: Human Kinetics.

Kreigal, Luigi, Lorrain Kriegel, and Francis James Roach. 1997. *Luigi's jazz warm up: An introduction to jazz style and technique.* Pennington, NJ: Princeton Book Company.

Lavender, Larry. 1996. *Dancers talking dance: Critical evaluation in the choreography class.* Champaign, IL: Human Kinetics.

Lihs, Harriet R. 2002. *Appreciating dance: A guide to the world's liveliest art.* 3rd ed. Hightstown, NJ: Princeton Book Company.

Malnig, Julie. 2001. Two-stepping to glory. In *Moving history/Dancing cultures,* ed. Ann Dils and Ann Cooper Albright, 273. Middletown, CT: Wesleyan University Press.

Maryland's Voluntary State Curriculum Glossary, 9.1.04. http://mdk12.org/instruction/curriculum/arts/index.html.

McGhee, Diane B. and Pamela Sofras. 2003. *Volume II: Donald McKayle's Rainbow Repertory Etude Lesson.* In *Roots and branches: Exploring an evolving dance legacy.* A consortium project directed by the American Dance Legacy Institute with the Harlem Dance Foundation in collaboration with Brown University and The Southeast Center for Dance Education.

Mueller, Lorraine. 2001. Educational theory of David Perkins. *New Foundations*. www.newfoundations.com/GALLERY/Perkins.html.

The National Center on Education and the Economy (NCEE). 2007. *Tough choices for tough time: The report of the new commission on the skills of the American workforce*. Hoboken, NJ: Jossey-Bass.

Parsons, Michael J. 1987. *How we understand art: A cognitive developmental account of aesthetic experience*. New York: Cambridge University Press.

Penrod, James and Janice Gudde Plastino. 2005. *The dancer prepares: Modern dance for beginners*. 5th ed. NY: McGraw-Hill.

Shipley, Glenn. 1976. *Modern tap dance dictionary*. Los Angeles, CA: Action Marketing Group.

Sonny Watson's West Coast Swing Dance. www.streetswing.com/histclub.htm.

Sprague, Marty, Helene Scheff, and Susan McGreevy-Nichols. 2006. *Dance about anything*. Champaign, IL: Human Kinetics.

Strategies to Extend Student Thinking. www.bcps.org/offices/lis/office/inst/think.html.

U.S. Historical Archive. *An American ballroom companion, volume 2: Containing 45 historical dance manuals*. www.ushistoricalarchive.com/cds/dance2.html.

Wood, Melusine. 1982. *Historical dances (twelfth to nineteenth century): Their manner of performance and their place in the social life of the time*. London: Dance Books, Ltd.

Wright, Judy Patterson. 2003. *Social dance: Steps to success*. 2nd ed. Champaign, IL: Human Kinetics.

ABOUT THE AUTHORS

Helene Scheff, RDE, is a conference planner for the National Dance Education Organization. She has taught all forms and styles of dance for about 50 years in all sectors and venues, including K-12, higher education, and the private sector. She has coauthored several other dance books and conducted presentations at local, regional, national, and international conferences and seminars.

Ms. Scheff is a member of the American Alliance for Health, Physical Education, Recreation and Dance. In her leisure time she enjoys viewing dance and theater and spending time with her family, including her 10 grandchildren.

Helene Scheff

Marty Sprague, MA, teaches at the Providence Academy of International Studies in Providence, Rhode Island. She has taught and performed dance (concert, world, social, and historical) for more than 50 years, including various dance forms and styles at the elementary, middle, secondary, and university levels. A coauthor of several dance books, she has presented and consulted at the local, regional, national, and international levels.

Ms. Sprague has been a member of numerous dance companies and was artistic director of her own dance company. She codesigned graduate-level coursework in dance certification and has been a choreographer. In 2005, the National Dance Education Organization honored her with the K-12 Dance Educator of the Year award. In her leisure time, she enjoys taking dance classes, spending time with God and her family, and reading.

Marty Sprague

Susan McGreevy-Nichols, BS, is a national consultant in arts education programming and curriculum. She was the founder and director of a nationally known middle school dance program in Providence, Rhode Island, and taught in public schools for 28 years before moving on to higher education. She is also a guest teaching artist at the elementary level in the Los Angeles Unified School District.

Ms. McGreevy-Nichols, who was the National Dance Teacher of the Year in 1995, serves as president of the National Dance Education Organization. She is a past president of the National Dance Association and a senior partner at the Griffin Center for Inspired Instruction. Ms. McGreevy-Nichols is also the coauthor of many books, including *Building Dances*, *Building More Dances*, *Experiencing Dance*, and *Dance About Anything*. In her spare time, she likes to travel, read, and spend time with friends.

Susan McGreevy-Nichols

You'll find other outstanding
dance resources at
www.HumanKinetics.com

DVD-ROM USER INSTRUCTIONS

System Requirements

Windows

- IBM PC compatible with Pentium processor
- Windows 98/2000/XP/Vista
- DVD-ROM drive

Macintosh

- Power Mac recommended
- System 10.4 or higher
- DVD-ROM drive

User Instructions

The PDFs on this DVD-ROM can only be accessed using a DVD-ROM drive in a computer (not a DVD player on a television). To access the PDFs, follow these instructions:

Microsoft Windows

1. Place the *Exploring Dance Forms and Styles* DVD in the DVD-ROM drive of your computer.
2. Double-click on the "My Computer" icon from your desktop.
3. Right-click on the DVD-ROM drive and select the "Open" option from the pop-up menu.
4. Double-click on the "Documents and Resources" folder.
5. Select the PDF file that you want to view or print.

Macintosh

1. Place the *Exploring Dance Forms and Styles* DVD in the DVD-ROM drive of your computer.
2. Double-click the DVD icon on your desktop.
3. Double-click on the "Documents and Resources" folder.
4. Select the PDF file that you want to view or print.

Note: You must have Adobe Acrobat Reader to view the PDF files.

For customer support, contact Technical Support:

Phone: 217-351-5076 Monday through Friday (excluding holidays) between 7:00 a.m. and 7:00 p.m. (CST).

Fax: 217-351-2674

E-mail: support@hkusa.com